The Power of Ideas

The Power of Ideas

Words of Faith and Wisdom

Jonathan Sacks

First published in Great Britain in 2021 by Hodder & Stoughton
An Hachette UK company

1

All Scripture references are taken from the author's own translation.

A CIP catalogue record for this title is available from the British Library

Hardback ISBN 978 1 399 80001 3
Trade Paperback ISBN 978 1 399 80003 7
eBook ISBN 978 1 399 80004 4

Typeset in Sabon by Hewer Text UK Ltd, Edinburgh
Printed and bound in Great Britain by Clays Ltd, Elcograf S.p.A.

Hodder & Stoughton policy is to use papers that are natural, renewable and recyclable products and made from wood grown in sustainable forests. The logging and manufacturing processes are expected to conform to the environmental regulations of the country of origin.

Hodder & Stoughton Ltd
Carmelite House
50 Victoria Embankment
London EC4Y 0DZ

www.hodder.co.uk

Contents

CLARENCE HOUSE

Rabbi Lord Jonathan Sacks' voice was unmistakably one in the tradition of the greatest teachers among the Jewish people. With his incomparable store of learning and with his innate sense of the power of the story he defined, often with a stark urgency and conviction, the moral challenges and the choices our society faced. His voice spanned the sacred and the secular; bridging generations, transcending all barriers of culture and religion, and resonating far beyond the borders of our nation.

He and I were exact contemporaries, born in the year of the foundation of the State of Israel and, over many years, I had come to value his wise counsel immensely as a trusted guide, an inspired teacher and a true and steadfast friend. Many have been the occasions since his untimely and sad passing in November 2020 when I have wanted to seek his perspective, knowing he would have offered unfailing wisdom, profound sanity and moral insight which, in a confused and confusing world, are all too rare.

As an avid reader and follower of his work, I am therefore delighted to see the publication of these broadcasts, articles, speeches and lectures by Rabbi Sacks. Although this volume represents a mere fragment of his contributions during his lifetime, it demonstrates, once again, Rabbi Sacks' unique capacity for interpreting the present and predicting the future through a profound understanding of the past. Rich in learning and rooted in humility, this collection includes the lightness of touch, inclusive approach and elegant wit that Rabbi Sacks was so renowned for.

Yet it is also charged with an underlying passion and determination. As Rabbi Sacks once stated, "to bring the world that is a little closer to the world that ought to be." It is this constant striving for the common good that has ensured the timeless nature of his teachings and perspectives. That is why they remain important and relevant to the ongoing discussions about how we live our lives as individuals, as communities, as a nation and as a community of nations.

In 2013, as he completed his time as Chief Rabbi of the United Hebrew Congregations of the Commonwealth, I described Rabbi Sacks, deliberately misquoting Isaiah, as "a light unto this Nation." How true then; how more so now. In the years he was given to us, how brightly that light burned, how many lives were brightened, how many dark places illuminated. My sincere wish is that through his writings and the work of The Rabbi Sacks Legacy Trust, Rabbi Sacks' voice of wisdom and hope will continue to illuminate, inform and inspire our world for generations to come.

The untimely passing of Rabbi Lord Jonathan Sacks, of blessed memory, in November 2020 was mourned by people of all faiths and of none. [illegible]

[illegible]

Rabbi Sacks [illegible] the choice with which humankind is faced in every age is between the idea of power and the power of ideas. His was a life defined by ideas, his own and other [illegible]

Introduction
A Polymath of Our Age Who Guides Us Still

The untimely passing of Rabbi Lord Jonathan Sacks, of blessed memory, in November 2020 was mourned by people of all faiths and of none. The outpouring of shock and grief spoke volumes about the man he was, the impact he had, and the continued relevance of the legacy he leaves behind.

In bringing together some of Rabbi Sacks' many broadcasts, writings and speeches, this collection draws on part of that legacy and on the wisdom of a man who was considered, both within and beyond the Jewish community, in Britain and in many countries around the world, as a national treasure, a moral voice of reason, and one of the most relevant and important philosophers and commentators for our age.

I particularly want to thank HRH The Prince of Wales for providing such a heartfelt foreword to this collection, together with Ian Metcalfe, Chairman of Hodder Faith and Rabbi Sacks' publisher for many years, and Dan Sacker from The Rabbi Sacks Legacy Trust, who worked so professionally and diligently to compile this volume. I also want to acknowledge the support of Lady Sacks and the Sacks family for this project and the ongoing work of the Trust.

Rabbi Sacks once wrote that 'the choice with which humankind is faced in every age is between the idea of power and the power of ideas'.* His was a life defined by ideas, his own and other people's. Our physical time on Earth is finite, but ideas live on in the infinite space of time. Reading his writings several years

* Jonathan Sacks, *Judaism's Life-Changing Ideas: A Weekly Reading of the Hebrew Bible* (Jerusalem: Maggid, 2020), p. xxiii.

on from when they were originally published, one is struck not only by the clarity of thought, moral wisdom and eloquence they contain, but by the continued relevance of his ideas to our world today.

This goes to the heart of Rabbi Sacks' genius. He had a wonderful ability to extract the timeless from the timely, to see in current events enduring values and to challenge us and our age when these values slipped. His was a voice that caused us to pause, to stop for a moment and consider our actions as individuals and as a society. Taken together, this collection forms a commentary on our culture and society in recent decades and represents the inspiring and enduring idealism of an individual who spent much of his life in the public eye.

Part One of this collection contains a selection of transcripts from Rabbi Sacks' *Thought for the Day* broadcasts on BBC Radio 4. Delivered during *Today*, the most influential morning radio news programme in Britain, this slot of around two-and-a-half minutes is given to a person of faith to offer their reflections on something in the news. Despite its inclusion sometimes being questioned, in a *Thought for the Day* broadcast in March 2001[*], Rabbi Sacks explained that it remained an important space in the Radio 4 schedule because it offered public broadcasting opportunities for faith leaders to speak to audiences beyond the confines of their own religion. He wrote delivering *Thought for the Day* meant that 'I have to speak in a way that spans differences and communicates across boundaries,' which was 'a habit we all have to learn if we're going to be true to ourselves and yet make space for the people who aren't like us'.[†] Reading these broadcasts today, it is possible to see them in a renewed light and ways which continue to resonate.

* The full text of this particular *Thought for the Day* broadcast, together with a number of others, was published as part of a collection entitled *From Optimism to Hope* (London: Continuum, 2004).

† *Thought for the Day* broadcast by Rabbi Sacks on BBC Radio 4 on 26 March 2001.

Part Two is a selection of Rabbi Sacks' Credo columns, originally published in *The Times*. As one of the first four regular contributors to the Credo column, Rabbi Sacks wrote a column every month until he stepped down as Chief Rabbi in 2013. He valued Credo because, like *Thought for the Day*, it created a bespoke – one might say sacred – space for the religious voice within the day-to-day, fast-paced world of newspaper publishing. A number of his earlier Credo columns were re-worked and published in an earlier collection*; as such, the columns selected here are taken from 2000 onwards. Reading them today does not lessen their impact; on the contrary, they continue to provide powerful examples of how the wisdom of Judaism provides a prism for understanding our world today and the many challenges we face.

Part Three includes a selection of articles written for a variety of newspapers and publications. As a public intellectual and a religious leader, Rabbi Sacks was always careful not to insert himself into the political arena – with a very few exceptions – but rather to go beyond the news and offer a broader perspective in whatever he wrote. The news focused on today. But the great faiths, he believed, 'remind us both of yesterday and tomorrow'.† They were, he argued, 'our living dialogue with the past and the future; those two essential things called memory and hope'.‡ As such, his articles always constructed a bigger picture for the reader, placing current issues in a historical light and drawing from them lessons that could enhance their lives today, and improve the lives of generations not yet born.

Part Four features a selection of his speeches from the House of Lords. Rabbi Sacks took great pride in being a British citizen and was humbled to be raised to the peerage in October

* This collection was entitled *Celebrating Life: Finding Happiness in Unexpected Places*. First published by Fount in 2000, it was subsequently republished by Bloomsbury Continuum, most recently in 2017.

† *Thought for the Day* broadcast by Rabbi Sacks on BBC Radio 4 on 26 March 2001.

‡ Ibid.

2009. He chose his title as Baron Sacks of Aldgate in the City of London to reflect his love of the country and the city that was home to his mother and offered his father refuge as he fled persecution in Europe. Sitting as a member of the Crossbench – effectively an independent – he never once formally voted, passionately believing in the separation between religion and politics, a theme that appears prominently in many of his writings. Rabbi Sacks' contributions in the Chamber gave him a voice, not a vote. He wanted to share ideas in the hope they would inform, and perhaps at times influence, public debate, not because he wanted to exert any power.

His speeches focused on national topics such as the state of British society, the importance of education, the role of Britain's faith communities and the universal right to freedom of religion and belief, and, when required, specifically advocated for the needs or concerns of the Jewish community he represented on issues such as Israel, the religious slaughter of animals and rising levels of antisemitism, among others. Although his participation was limited due to the pressures of his role, his speeches always garnered the attention of fellow Peers. Members of both the House of Lords and the House of Commons would frequently refer to comments Rabbi Sacks made, demonstrating the impact his words had on the public conversation.

Part Five includes a small selection of his many and varied speeches and lectures. In every speech he delivered, Rabbi Sacks proved himself to be a master storyteller and communicator of ideas whose insight and passion for the breadth of subjects he spoke about was internationally renowned. Certain overarching themes are evident across many of his lectures: interfaith relations; the relationship between religion and the state; the nature of society; the meaning of the common good; and the loss of morality suffered during the course of the twentieth century and beyond, and how to recover it and our collective moral sense. He was, once again, accomplished at delivering a universal and particular message; speaking on behalf of, and to, all faiths (for example, when he greeted Pope Benedict XVI on his 2010 visit to the United Kingdom) and being an ambassador on behalf of the global Jewish people (for example, when he travelled to the European Parliament in 2016 to warn Europe's leaders of the growing dangers of antisemitism).

As a teacher of Torah, Rabbi Sacks dedicated his life to enlightening the world with his insights into the Hebrew Bible and the Jewish faith.* As a moral philosopher and public intellectual, Rabbi Sacks sought to offer his perspective on some of our world's biggest challenges, always acknowledging the role his religious beliefs played in the formulation of those views, but not being restricted in his thinking by them. In doing so he was able to demonstrate, in an inclusive rather than exclusive way, to both Jews and people of all faiths and of none, the role faith could contribute to the public square or to, as he described it, 'the conversation of humankind'.

Rabbi Sacks taught us to prioritise the collective over the individual, the 'Other' over the 'Self'. He emphasised that 'our common humanity precedes our religious differences', and that society was 'a conversation scored for many voices'. His voice was but one in this conversation, yet he found a way to balance the timely with the timeless, and to do so with a humility and a grace rarely seen. He was a giant of our age, a polymath, whose ideas continue to resonate and impact our world and inform the challenges we face. May the wisdom found in this collection and Rabbi Sacks' remarkable canon of work stand as a testament to

* Much of this work is contained in Rabbi Sacks' published series of essays on the Hebrew Bible called *Covenant & Conversation*, as well as in his commentaries to the Jewish prayer book and festival prayer books. This collection is focused more on his work as it addressed societal, cultural, economic and political issues at a national and international level. A full bibliography of Rabbi Sacks' published works is included at the end of this collection.

a life well lived, and as a source of inspiration that will continue to guide us long into the future.

By Henry Grunwald OBE QC,
Chair of The Rabbi Sacks Legacy Trust
London, August 2021

The Rabbi Sacks Legacy Trust exists to promote and perpetuate the teachings and ideas of Rabbi Sacks, of blessed memory. To access the digital archive containing much of Rabbi Sacks' writings, recordings and speeches, or to support the Trust's work, please visit www.rabbisacks.org. You can also follow The Rabbi Sacks Legacy Trust on social media. Find us on Facebook, Twitter, Instagram and YouTube (@RabbiSacks).

Part One

Thought for the Day

The following *Thought for the Day* reflections were first broadcast on BBC Radio 4's *Today* programme.

Religious Tolerance and Globalisation

4 April 2008

'Our love of God must lead us to a love of humanity.'

Last night Tony Blair gave a major lecture on faith and globalisation, and later this year he'll be teaching a course on the same subject in America, at Yale University. And it'll be interesting to compare the responses, because this is one area in which Britain and America are extraordinarily different. In Britain, as Prime Minister, Tony Blair never spoke in public about his religious beliefs despite the fact that he was, and is, a deeply religious man. Famously one of his aides said, 'We don't *do* God.'

In America, despite its principled separation of church and state, the situation is exactly the opposite. Every single American President has spoken about God in their Inaugural Address, from Washington's first in 1789 to today. So much so that Eisenhower was reputed to have said that an American President has to believe in God – and it doesn't matter which God he believes in.

Every nation has to find its own way to tolerance. Some find it by talking about God, others by not talking about God. That was the real difference between the French and American revolutions. As Alexis de Tocqueville said in the early nineteenth century: 'In France I saw religion and liberty marching in opposite directions. In America, I saw them walking hand in hand.'

There is no one way of charting the relationship between religion and public life; but equally there is no way of avoiding the fact that religion has an impact on public life, whether people talk about it or not.

The real question, which has echoed time and again through the corridors of history, is whether we can find ways of living together, despite the fact that we can't find ways of believing or worshipping together.

That is what the Bible teaches in its very first chapter, when it says that we are all, every one of us, in the image of God. Our love of God must lead us to a love of humanity.

I find it extraordinary that in an age in which globalisation is forcing us together, all too often, across the globe, faith is driving us apart. We should be fighting environmental destruction, political oppression, poverty and disease, not fighting one another, least of all in the name of God whose image we all bear.

That is why I believe the time has now come, even in Britain, to bring a message of religious tolerance into the public square. For if the voice of reconciliation does not speak, the voices of extremism will.

The Age of Greed

3 October 2008

'The real test of a society is not the absence of crises, but whether we come out of them cynical and disillusioned, or strengthened by our rededication to high ideals.'

Next week in the Jewish community we'll observe Yom Kippur, the Day of Atonement, the holiest day of the Jewish year. We'll spend the whole day in synagogue, fasting, confessing our sins, admitting what we did wrong, and praying for forgiveness.

Something like that seems to me essential to the health of a culture. Often, we see things go wrong. Yet rarely do we see someone stand up, take responsibility and say: 'I was wrong. I made a mistake. I admit it. I apologise. And now let us work to put it right.'

Instead, we do other things. We deny there's a problem in the first place. Or, if that's impossible, we blame someone else, or say, 'It's due to circumstances beyond our control.' The result is that we lose the habit of being honest with ourselves.

In America in 1863, in the midst of the civil war, Abraham Lincoln proclaimed a national day of fasting and prayer. It was an extraordinary thing to do. Lincoln, after all, was fighting for a noble cause, the abolition of slavery. What did he or those on his side have to atone for?

Yet America was being torn apart, so he asked the nation to set aside one day for reflection and prayer. 'It is the duty of nations as well as of men', the proclamation said, 'to confess their sins and transgressions, in humble sorrow, yet with assured hope that genuine repentance will lead to mercy and pardon.' It was America's Day of Atonement.

The result was that two years later Lincoln was able, in his Second Inaugural, to deliver one of the great healing speeches of all time, calling on Americans 'to bind up the nation's wounds', and care for those who had suffered during the war and were still suffering.

We're living through tough times globally, and we'll need all the inner strength we have to survive the turbulence, learn from the mistakes of the past, and begin again. The real test of a society is not the absence of crises, but whether we come out of them cynical and disillusioned, or strengthened by our rededication to high ideals.

The age of greed is over. Will the age of responsibility now begin? That will depend on whether we are capable of admitting our mistakes and renewing our commitment to the common good. Atonement, the capacity for honest self-criticism, is what allows us to weather the storm without losing our way.

Holocaust Memorial Day

30 January 2010

'Faith in God after the Holocaust may be hard; but faith in humanity is harder still, knowing the evil people do to one another, and the hate that lies dormant but never dead in the human heart.'

Today is National Holocaust Memorial Day, and this year the focus will be on one small group of people in the Warsaw Ghetto and the astonishing task they took on themselves for the sake of future generations.

The Warsaw Ghetto, into which hundreds of thousands of Jews were herded, was not some remote spot far from public gaze. It was near the centre of one of Europe's capital cities. There 100,000 Jews died of starvation and disease; 270,000 were taken in cattle trucks to Treblinka and other camps to be gassed, burned and turned to ash. Eventually in April 1943 the Nazis gave the order that everyone left should be killed and it was there that the ghetto inhabitants mounted an extraordinary act of resistance, keeping the German army at bay for five weeks until they were overcome.

But by then a quite different act of resistance had taken place, and it's this we're going to remember this year. It was the brainchild of a Jewish historian, Emanuel Ringelblum, who realised that the Nazis were unlike any previous group bent on conquest. All others had preserved a record of their victories for posterity. But the Germans were intent on obliterating or falsifying every trace of their mass exterminations of Roma, Sinti, homosexuals, the mentally and physically disabled and the Jews.

Ringelblum understood that they were preparing a systematic

denial of the Holocaust at the very time it was taking place. So in the ghetto he brought together a group of academics, teachers, journalists, religious leaders, artists and the young to gather testimonies from people in the ghetto, so that the world would one day know what happened. Unbelievably, they gathered 35,000 documents, stories, letters, poems and records. They hid them in tin boxes and milk churns, where they lay for years until the handful of survivors led the way to their location.

What an astonishing act of faith: that evil would ultimately be defeated, that the documents would be found and not destroyed, and that truth would win out in the end. Faith in God after the Holocaust may be hard; but faith in humanity is harder still, knowing the evil people do to one another, and the hate that lies dormant but never dead in the human heart.

Ringelblum and his friends had faith in humanity, and they left us a legacy of hope preserved intact in the very heart of darkness. In our still tense and troubled age, may we be worthy of that faith, that hope.

Interfaith Relations

19 November 2010

'. . . tolerance was born when people with strong beliefs recognised that others who disagreed with them also had strong beliefs and they too should have, as far as possible, the right to live by them.'

Starting this Sunday, the various religious communities in Britain will be coming together in a series of events to mark Interfaith Week, the latest chapter in the history of British tolerance. But it wasn't always so.

Britain was the first country to expel its Jews, in 1290. They weren't allowed back until 1656. And the Pilgrim Fathers who set sail from Britain to America in the early seventeenth century were Calvinists, fearing persecution here and seeking liberty there.

What changed Britain, leading it to become the birthplace of the doctrine of religious liberty, was one transformative insight. For years Catholics and Protestants had fought each other throughout Europe, each convinced that it had the truth, each seeking the power to impose it. The destructiveness of this was immense.

Eventually people realised that instead of saying, 'Religious convictions are important, therefore everyone should have the correct ones,' you could draw a different conclusion. 'Religious convictions are important; therefore, everyone should have the right to live according to his or her beliefs.'

That one move led John Locke to the idea of toleration that eventually inspired Thomas Jefferson in America and Jean-Jacques Rousseau in France.

In other words, tolerance was born when people with strong beliefs recognised that others who disagreed with them also had strong beliefs and they too should have, as far as possible, the right to live by them.

That was one of the transformative moments of the modern world. And it's important that we continue the story into the twenty-first century now that there is greater religious diversity in Britain than ever before.

Two years ago, we all marched together – Christians, Jews, Muslims, Hindus, Sikhs, Buddhists, Jains, Zoroastrians and Baha'i – to draw attention to global poverty. A few months later we travelled together to Auschwitz to remind ourselves where hate can lead. This summer we came together to commit our respective communities to strengthening civil society.

I don't know any other country in the world where the leaders of the faith communities have such strong personal friendships. And the idea of Interfaith Week is to take this to the grass roots, because that's where it counts. The good news about faith is that it builds communities. It takes a lot of 'Me's' and turns them into an 'Us'. The bad news is that it can divide communities, into a 'Them' and an 'Us'. So next week extend the hand of friendship to someone who is not of your faith. That really is a transformative act.

A Royal Wedding

29 April 2011

'Love, like faith, is the redemption of solitude, the slender bridge joining soul to soul, inspiring us to deeds of selflessness and sacrifice.'

Well, it's finally arrived, the Royal wedding that's captured the imagination not just of Britain but of much of the world. I've just come back from a week in America, and there wasn't a day without a blizzard of stories about Prince William and Catherine, almost as if 1776 and the Declaration of Independence hadn't happened at all. Somehow their joy has been contagious; their manner exactly right for our time, relaxed, informal, their acclaim lightly worn, as if it really didn't matter that 2 billion people will be watching, making it the most viewed ceremony in history.

That is Britain and royalty at its best, the glittering scene and elaborate ceremonial serving as the setting for something universal that transcends the boundaries of custom and culture: the simple moving sight of two people pledging themselves to one another in a bond of loyalty and love, setting out on a journey together to that undiscovered country called the future, knowing, in the words of the psalm, that 'I will fear no evil for you are with me' (Psalm 23:4).

Since the dawn of civilisation marriage has been more than the private agreement of two people. It's been a moment of collective and communal celebration, often invested with the solemnity of a religious ritual. And there are few ideas in the history of faith more beautiful than the prophetic insight that the love of husband and wife is as close as we will get to understanding the love of God for humanity.

'I will betroth you to me for ever,' said Hosea, 'I will betroth you in righteousness and justice, love and compassion. I will betroth you to me in faith, and you will know the Lord' (Hosea 2:21–22). 'Though the mountains be shaken,' said Isaiah, 'and the hills be removed, my love for you will not be shaken nor my covenant of peace be removed' (Isaiah 54:10). Those were the blessings I had in mind when I officiated at the weddings of my children as I wished them *mazal tov*. And they're the blessings we would surely wish Prince William and Catherine today.

For there is something sacred about the joy we feel at a wedding, as we sense the power of love to bathe human beings in its radiance and make gentle the life of this world. Love, like faith, is the redemption of solitude, the slender bridge joining soul to soul, inspiring us to deeds of selflessness and sacrifice. May God bless Prince William and Catherine, and may they be a blessing to one another and to us all.

The King James Bible

6 May 2011

'In the beginning was the word, and whether spread by printing or the internet, it still calls us to create the freedom that honours all equally as the image of God.'

This week sees the 400th anniversary of the book that changed the world, the King James Bible. Not exactly, you might think, a scoop to tweet about. But I want to suggest that that moment is extraordinarily similar to what's happening today throughout the Middle East.

What had happened, centuries ago, was the invention of a new form of information technology – printing, developed by Gutenberg in Germany and Caxton in England. This suddenly made books cheaper and opened up, to whole populations, knowledge that previously had been the prerogative of an elite.

Then came the Reformation and the democratising idea that it was each individual, not just the religious establishment, who had a personal relationship with God.

Putting these two developments together, people started translating the Bible into the vernacular so that everyone could read it. In England, this was done most famously by William Tyndale. The authorities tried to put a stop to this. Tyndale was arrested and put to death.

But it's hard to stop the tide of information once it starts flowing. English scholars fled to Geneva and produced their own version which sold in huge numbers until King James realised that what he couldn't stop he could at least control. So he assembled a team of scholars who produced their own version, a masterpiece of English prose that owed much to Tyndale.

But the turbulence continued, eventually becoming a full-scale revolution. James' son Charles I was executed, and it wasn't until the Restoration in the 1660s and the Bill of Rights in 1689 that the political storm subsided, the face of English politics permanently changed.

The similarities between that and the Arab Spring that's led to uprisings in Tunisia, Egypt, Libya, Syria, Bahrain and Yemen, are many. Again, the driver has been new information technology – the internet, smartphones and social networking software. There's been a religious revival and a challenge to the ruling elites, who find that they can no longer control the flow of information or the democratisation of power.

Right now, we're at the beginning of the process, and if the events of four centuries ago are any guide, we're in for a period of turbulence that may last for decades. The outcome is likely to be, as it was then, greater liberty and more effective limits to the use of power. In the beginning was the word, and whether spread by printing or the internet, it still calls us to create the freedom that honours all equally as the image of God.

The Council of Christians and Jews

18 November 2011

'Today we take interfaith activity for granted. We forget what a leap of imagination and courage it took in those early days.'

Seventy years ago, in the midst of one of humanity's darkest nights, Archbishop William Temple and Chief Rabbi Joseph Hertz came together to light a candle of hope. Jews were being massacred in vast numbers by the Nazis, and Temple believed that Christians had to take a stand. Hertz concurred, and thus was born the first national interfaith organisation in Britain, the Council of Christians and Jews.

Today we take interfaith activity for granted. We forget what a leap of imagination and courage it took in those early days. For the better part of 2,000 years the relationship between the church and the Jews had been marked by a hostility that added a whole series of words to the vocabulary of human suffering: disputation, forced conversion, inquisition, auto-da-fé, ghetto, expulsion, and pogrom.

For Jews and Christians to come together, both sides had to overcome deeply entrenched attitudes of suspicion and fear. Yet they did. Temple used the BBC World Service to make a broadcast to the Hungarians to rescue Jews wherever they could. He delivered an impassioned address in the House of Lords in 1943, saying that Christians stood before the bar of history, of humanity and God. This was religious leadership of a high order, and we still benefit from it today in the form of the hundreds of interfaith organisations that now exist throughout Britain, creating friendship across the boundaries of faith.

A simple example: A synagogue in Swansea was vandalised and its holiest objects, the Torah scrolls, were desecrated. As soon as people heard about it, a local Christian group came together to help the Jewish community repair the damage. When I officiated at the reconsecration, more than half of the congregation in the synagogue were members of local churches.

And of course the work has spread beyond Jews and Christians. The day after 9/11 one of our rabbis, the late Leonard Tann, went to the Imam of the largest mosque in Birmingham and said, 'These will be difficult days for Muslims, and I want you to know that the Jewish community will be standing with you.' Birmingham became a role model of how the leaders of all faiths worked together to promote good relations.

There are places in the world where religion is still a source of conflict. In Britain, not always but mostly, faiths estranged for centuries now meet as friends. We owe much of that to the pioneering work of the Council of Christians and Jews, whose example continues to inspire today.

Leadership

29 December 2011

'Not all of us have power. But we all have influence, whether we seek it or not.'

This programme has focused on leaders and leadership, and there's an insight in the Bible I find fascinating and it's still true today.

The Hebrew Bible tells the stories of two kinds of leader: prophets and kings. The kings were always fighting each other, waging war against external enemies or facing plots and threats from their enemies within. Kings had power, and people fight for power.

The prophets were leaders of a different kind altogether. They led almost against their will. When God summoned them, Isaiah said, 'I am a man of unclean lips.' Jeremiah said 'I can't speak; I'm just a child.' Jonah tried to run away. As for Moses at the burning bush, when God said 'Lead,' Moses kept saying 'No. Who am I? They won't believe in me. I'm not a man of words. Send someone else.'

Yet who do we remember all these centuries later? Most of the kings are long forgotten, yet the words of the prophets continue to inspire. Which is odd, since they had no power at all. They commanded no troops, headed no government, didn't even have legions of disciples. What they had was more enduring than power. They had influence. And as Kierkegaard once said: 'When a king dies, his power ends. When a prophet dies, his influence begins.'

I think of the heroes of my lifetime, leaders from Martin Luther King to Aung San Suu Kyi of Burma, who gave the hopeless hope;

people like Bill Gates and Warren Buffett, who taught us that the best thing you can do with money is give it away in a noble cause; and the unsung heroes of our hospitals, schools and local communities who daily remind us that happiness lies in what we give to the world, not what we take from it. Some of these had power, others didn't, but what made them great was influence, the way they inspired others and spoke to the better angels of their nature.

Not all of us have power. But we all have influence, whether we seek it or not. We make the people around us better or worse than they might otherwise have been. Worse if we infect them with our materialism or cynicism, better if we inspire them with what Wordsworth called 'the best portion' of a good life, our 'little, nameless, unremembered acts / of kindness and of love'. That quiet leadership of influence seeks no power, but it changes lives. In tough times like now we need it more than ever.

The Fragility of Nature

27 September 2012

'. . . as well as knowledge we need wisdom, and the better part of wisdom is knowing that we are guardians of a Universe we can easily endanger and which we still don't fully understand.'

For Jews the festival season is well and truly on us. We've just celebrated the New Year and the Day of Atonement, and next week we have Sukkot, known in English as Tabernacles. It's difficult to explain Sukkot in Britain, especially this year, because it's a festival of prayer for rain, whereas here we've had all too much of it, including the floods still doing damage in York, Liverpool and Wales. But in the Holy Land, where the Bible is set, rain was and still is the scarcest resource, and without it there's drought and famine.

So on Sukkot we take four kinds of things that need rain to grow: a palm branch, a citron and leaves from a willow and myrtle tree, and holding them we thank God for rain and pray for it in the Holy Land in the year to come – even if we happen to be living in the soggiest of climates. Sukkot is, if you like, a festival about the fragility of nature as a habitat hospitable to humankind.

The natural world is something science and religion both speak about in their very different ways. Science explains; religion celebrates. Science speaks, religion sings. Science is prose, religion is poetry, and we need them both.

Science continues to inspire us in the way it reveals the intricacy of nature and the power of the human mind. Rarely was this more so than earlier this year with the almost certain confirmation of the existence of the Higgs boson, which someone with a sense of humour called 'the God particle' on the grounds that it exists everywhere but it's so hard to find.

But science can sometimes make us think we're in control, which is why we need moments like Sukkot to restore our sense of humility. We're so small in a Universe so vast, and our very existence depends on an extraordinarily delicate balance between too much and too little, whose symbol is rain. Too much and we have floods. Too little and we have drought.

So, as well as knowledge we need wisdom, and the better part of wisdom is knowing that we are guardians of a Universe we can easily endanger and which we still don't fully understand. Perhaps it's not crazy, once a year, to lift our eyes towards heaven, the way we do when we're praying for rain, and remember how dependent we are on things beyond our control. The more scientific knowledge and power we have, the more humility we need.

Belief and Rituals

22 March 2013

'Rituals are how civilisations preserve their memory, keeping faith with those who came before us and handing on their legacy to the future.'

When people talk about religion in Britain, they tend to speak about beliefs. Which, for Jews, is very odd. Yes, belief is important, but for us religion is fundamentally about rituals, the things we do together as an expression of collective memory and shared ideals. Ritual is the poetry of deed, the choreography of faith, and nowhere is this clearer than on Passover, Pesach, the festival we begin celebrating this Monday night.

On it we tell the story of the framing event of Jewish history, the Exodus from Egypt and the long walk from slavery to freedom. We tell it around the dinner table, usually in extended families, and we don't just tell it: we taste it as well, eating *matzah* (unleavened bread) and *maror* (bitter herbs), to remind us of what it felt like to be oppressed, and we drink wine and sing songs to celebrate the fact that we're here to tell the tale.

What gives Passover its enduring power is that it's a way of handing on our memory and identity across the generations. It begins with a series of questions asked by the youngest child, and I can still remember when I asked them all those years ago when I was four or five in the company of my grandparents.

It's a bit of a shock to realise that now I'm the grandparent and the young people doing the asking are my grandchildren. But what continuity that represents, seeing in the course of my life five generations telling the same story, asking the same questions, singing the same songs, learning what freedom means and what losing it feels and tastes like.

That's the power of ritual, simple deeds that we do as children because it's fun, and as adults because we know that the battle for freedom and human dignity is never over and we must be prepared to fight for them in every age.

Rituals are how civilisations preserve their memory, keeping faith with those who came before us and handing on their legacy to the future. The most important thing my parents gave me, and the thing I most tried to give our children, was ideals to live by. Everything else was just gift-wrapping, briefly enjoyed then forgotten.

Beliefs inspire our children and eventually change the world when they're translated into the songs we sing, the stories we tell and the rituals we perform. The proof is Passover, the story that has given Jews hope for more than 3,000 years.

Margaret Thatcher

17 April 2013

'Sometimes leaders have to be strong at the cost of being divisive, because they see no other way of getting from here to there.'

As the funeral service for Margaret Thatcher takes place today, I will be thinking not of the public person but of the private one. I knew her when I was a child at school. She was my local MP, and when I had an essay to write about politics, I used to go and see her in her constituency office to hear what she had to say.

I remember once mentioning the words 'proportional representation' and she glared at me as if I had committed a cardinal sin. 'You're not a liberal, are you?' she said. And I had hurriedly to say that I wasn't advocating it, just writing an essay about it.

Even then, back in 1963, she was being described as a parliamentary Boadicea, brandishing Hansard in one hand and a handbag in the other. Yet she was always willing to help a fifteen-year-old schoolboy whose political affiliation she didn't know and who wouldn't even have a vote for another six years.

In public, her leadership style was more like Moses than Aaron, more conviction and confrontation than compromise and conciliation. But we need both. Aaron was more loved than Moses. The sages said that when Aaron died, everyone mourned, but when Moses died, not everyone did. But without Moses, there would not have been a Jewish people. Sometimes leaders have to be strong at the cost of being divisive, because they see no other way of getting from here to there.

Years later, in 1997, I wrote a book about politics* to challenge the statement attributed to her that there is no such thing as society. I thought she'd never speak to me again, but she read it, and commended it to her friends, and stayed as warm as ever.

Which says a lot. She read. She loved ideas. She was intensely considerate to those with whom she worked. And even most of her critics didn't doubt her integrity or courage, or the dignity she showed in her last difficult years. Such values matter in a free society, because politics *is* about conflict, and without civility it can quickly degenerate into abuse and the war of all against all.

Those who serve their country with dedication and distinction deserve respect in life. How much more so in death. And she did so serve, with all her heart. She loved Britain and fought for it. She loved responsibility and practised it. She loved freedom and lived for it. She was a fighter all her life. And now in death may her soul find peace.

* Jonathan Sacks, *The Politics of Hope* (London: Vintage, 1997).

The Danger of Power

5 July 2013

'Politics is about power and who wields it, but liberty is about the moral limits of power, about self-restraint in imposing our views on others.'

My thoughts today are with the people of Egypt as they wait to see the results of their second revolution in two years: first, the overthrow of President Mubarak, and now the overthrow of President Morsi, elected just a year ago by democratic vote.

What the future will bring we cannot know. But surely we have just witnessed an extraordinarily deep truth about the nature of politics.

We owe our way of talking about politics to the ancient Greeks, in particular to the citizens of Athens some twenty-six centuries ago. It was they who coined the word democracy, and they who, under Solon, created its first incarnation.

It meant, as Abraham Lincoln put it, 'government of the people, by the people, for the people'. Yet it was the citizens of Athens who, not many centuries later, saw it descend into tyranny. Along the way they sentenced one of their greatest thinkers, Socrates, to death for corrupting the young by teaching them to think for themselves. The road to freedom is long and hard and it always will be.

The danger of democracy, said John Stuart Mill, is that it can lead to the tyranny of the majority and hence the oppression of minorities. A democratic vote does not in and of itself create a free society. For that you need other things as well: respect for minorities, justice and the impartial rule of law, a collective commitment to the common good and a delicate balance of rights and responsibilities.

My own view, which I don't expect everyone to share, is that the single most important insight is the idea, contained in the first chapter of the Bible, and shared by all three Abrahamic monotheisms, that every human being, regardless of colour, culture, creed or class, is in the image of God. This means that one who is not in *my* image, whose faith or ethnicity are different from mine, is still in God's image, and therefore possessed of inalienable rights.

Judaism, Christianity and Islam may not always have lived up to that ideal, but it remains our guiding light as we strive for justice, human dignity and the good society. Politics is about power and who wields it, but liberty is about the moral limits of power, about self-restraint in imposing our views on others. So, while we pray for freedom for the people of Egypt, let's remember that freedom isn't won by protests or even democratic elections, but by making space for the people not like us.

Free Speech

9 August 2013

'Free speech does not mean speech that costs nothing. It means speech that respects the freedom and dignity of others. Forget this and free speech will prove to be very expensive indeed.'

One of the ongoing stories this summer has been the emergence of a worrying pattern of abuse through social networking sites. There was the intimidation of a Classics professor, and threats against women campaigning to have Jane Austen's portrait on banknotes. Most worrying by far has been the link made between one site, based in Latvia, and the suicides of four children, two in Britain, two in Ireland. The reason many feel this site is dangerous is that it allows people to post hurtful and hateful comments anonymously. More than 60 million young people use the site, posting 30 million messages a day, so some are going to be vicious, and some recipients are going to be vulnerable.

All in all, it's a new chapter in the world's oldest story, the use of words as weapons by people seeking to inflict pain. New – because in the past most communications were face to face and set in some kind of social context, in which parents, teachers or friends were aware of what was going on and could intervene. There were the occasional anonymous letter writers; but at least the pain they caused was private, not public the way social networking messages often are. By allowing people facelessly to make threats or be offensive or spread false rumours, the new sites are offering the demons of our nature the maximum of temptation combined with the maximum of opportunity.

Greek myth told the story of Gyges' ring which made whoever wore it invisible so he or she could get away with anything. The internet comes pretty close to being Gyges' ring, allowing people to hide behind a mask of invisibility, and even the service providers can usually escape by relocating beyond the reach of regulation.

The technology is new, but the moral challenge is old. Judaism's sages were eloquent on the dangers of what they called evil speech, by which they meant derogatory, demeaning or offensive words. They called this a cardinal sin and said that it destroys three people, the one who says it, the one he says it against and the one who listens in. Words injure; they hurt; they wound. And every new technology that allows us to share words more widely calls for a renewed insistence on the ethics of communication. Free speech does not mean speech that costs nothing. It means speech that respects the freedom and dignity of others. Forget this and free speech will prove to be very expensive indeed.

Faith

30 August 2013

'You don't need to be religious to be moral, but it makes a huge difference to be part of a community dedicated to being a blessing to others.'

This is the last *Thought for the Day* I'll be giving in my role as Chief Rabbi. On Sunday I induct my successor, Rabbi Ephraim Mirvis, and before then I wanted to say thank you for the privilege of serving as a religious leader in a society where there's genuine respect for other people's religious beliefs or lack of them; that understands what I call the dignity of difference. And if you were to ask me what I have cherished most these past twenty-two years, it's been the chance to see the difference faith makes to people's lives.

I've seen it do its work in Jewish communities throughout the Commonwealth, moving people to visit the sick, give hospitality to the lonely and help to those in need. You don't need to be religious to be moral, but it makes a huge difference to be part of a community dedicated to being a blessing to others.

I've seen faith help Holocaust survivors to survive and not be traumatised by their memories. I saw it help my late father survive four difficult operations in his eighties so that he, who had come to this country as a refugee, could be there to see his son inducted as a Chief Rabbi. It was the faith I learned from him that kept me going through some of the worst crises of my life.

Faith brought our people into being almost forty centuries ago when Abraham and Sarah heard God's call to leave home and begin a journey that is not yet complete and won't be, until we learn to make peace with one another, recognising that not just us but even our enemies are in the image of God.

Faith isn't science. It's not about *how* the world came into being but about *why*. I believe that God created the Universe and us in love and forgiveness, asking us to love and forgive others. And though that's often very hard, I believe it still makes it more likely than if we think that the Universe just happened, that humanity is a mere accident of biology and that nothing is sacred.

And yes, sometimes it seems as if we have just enough religion to make us hate one another and not enough to make us love one another. But the answer to that is more faith, not less: faith in God who asks us to love others as He loves us. That's faith's destination, and there's still a way to go.

Birdsong

11 March 2014

'I think we miss something essential when we take Darwinian selection to be more than a law about biology and turn it into a metaphor for life itself.'

Amid the doom and gloom of yesterday's news, one stray item caught my eye. It was headed: 'Darwin wrong about birds and bees', and it was about birdsong.

A century and a half ago Darwin argued that birdsong was all about sexual selection. It was males who did the singing, hoping to make female birds swoon at hearing the ornithological equivalent of Justin Bieber, giving the most tuneful males a better chance of handing on their genes to the next generation.

Well, it turns out to be not quite like that after all, because scientists have now discovered that female birds do almost as much singing as the males, and it has less to do with sexual selection than with simply saying: 'I'm here.'

The reason the story caught my eye was that after stepping down as Chief Rabbi last summer I've gone back to my first love, which is teaching. I've just spent six weeks doing that in New York. Which meant that I missed the British rain, and instead found myself deep in the snow of the coldest New York winter in living memory.

Rarely has coming back felt more magical, to be greeted by the first auguries of spring: crocuses in the grass, blossoms on the trees, and, best of all, hearing the dawn chorus from my bedroom window. That was when I realised that what I'd missed was the birdsong, something you don't hear in downtown New

York above the hooting taxis, speeding cars and the sheer pace and pressure of life. And suddenly it felt like an epiphany, like all those psalms that speak of creation singing a song to the creator, and the wonderful closing line of the last psalm of all: 'Let everything that breathes praise the Lord' (Psalm 150:6).

I think we miss something essential when we take Darwinian selection to be more than a law about biology and turn it into a metaphor for life itself, as if all that matters is conflict and the struggle to survive, so that love and beauty and even birdsong are robbed of their innocence and reduced to genetic instincts and drives.

Wordsworth was surely right when he spoke about the power of nature's beauty so to lift us 'that neither evil tongues, / rash judgments, nor the sneers of selfish men . . . shall e'er prevail against us, or disturb / our cheerful faith, that all which we behold / is full of blessings'. Not all is wrong in a world where birds sing for the joy of being alive.

Shame and Guilt Cultures

4 November 2014

'We need to make it easier for people to be honest and apologise, which means that we too must learn how to forgive.'

Yesterday the General Medical Council and the Nursing and Midwifery Council issued guidelines telling doctors and nurses to be honest with patients and apologise when mistakes are made. It's the first time such guidance has been given.

What's extraordinary is that such guidelines have to be given at all. Doctors and nurses are among the most caring, dedicated and altruistic people there are. And yes, we've become a very litigious society, but has it really got to the stage when even the best have to be told to be honest, and when in the wrong, to apologise?

Something significant but almost invisible has happened to the West this past half century and to understand it we have to turn to a great anthropologist: Ruth Benedict. It was she who taught the distinction between shame cultures like ancient Greece, and guilt cultures like Judaism and Christianity.

They both teach people how they ought to behave, but they have very different approaches to wrongdoing. In shame cultures what matters is what other people think of you: the embarrassment, the ignominy, the loss of face. Whereas in guilt cultures it's what the inner voice of conscience tells you. In shame cultures, we're actors playing our part on the public stage. In guilt cultures, we're engaged in inner conversation with the better angels of our nature.

The biggest difference is that in shame cultures, if we're caught doing wrong, there's a stain on our character that only time can erase. But guilt cultures make a sharp distinction between the doer and the deed, the sinner and the sin. That's why guilt cultures focus on atonement and repentance, apology and forgiveness. The act was wrong, but on our character there's no indelible stain.

In shame cultures, if you've done wrong, the first rule is, don't be found out. If you are, then bluff your way through. Only admit when every other alternative has failed, because you'll be disgraced for a very long time indeed.

Shame has a place in any moral system, but when it dominates all else, when all we have is trial by public exposure, then the more reluctant people will be to be honest, and the more suspicious we'll become of people in public life, not just in medicine but in politics, the media, financial institutions, corporations, and let's be honest, in religious organisations too.

We need to make it easier for people to be honest and apologise, which means that we too must learn how to forgive.

Taking Democracy for Granted

23 April 2015

'Democracy is one of the great achievements of humankind and we should never take it for granted.'

Coming back to these shores having spent some weeks in America, it's been fascinating to compare the general election campaign here with the presidential campaign just launched there.

There are some striking differences. For instance, in America one of the first things presidential candidates have been boasting about is how much money they've raised. Somehow, I can't imagine candidates doing the same here, where we still feel, I think, that votes shouldn't be something money can buy.

Then again, much of the talk in America is about the various segments of the electorate. Can candidate X win the Hispanic vote, or the evangelical vote, or the African American vote? Whereas here, it seems to me, we still think of voters as individuals who have views independent of their ethnicity or religion or lack of it. And those are attitudes worth valuing and protecting.

But despite the differences I find myself thinking more and more about what a difficult achievement democracy is and how much history had to be worked through and how pain endured before Britain and America arrived at it.

Just a quarter of a century ago, as the Berlin Wall fell, the Soviet Union imploded and the Cold War came to an end, people spoke as if democracy had won its final battle and would now spread throughout the world. Then almost immediately, we were faced with bloody ethnic war in the former Yugoslavia.

Just four years ago, with the Arab Spring, again it seemed as if democracy was about to spread throughout the Middle East. And instead, again there has been bloodshed and civil war.

There is nothing natural about democracy. It's the legacy of two great ancient civilisations: Greece, that gave us the word 'democracy' itself, and the Judeo-Christian heritage, that said that we are all equally in the image and likeness of God and should therefore have an equal say in deciding our collective future.

Its first stirrings came in the seventeenth century after Europe had been ravaged by religious war. That was when Milton, Hobbes, Spinoza and Locke turned to the Hebrew Bible and there found the idea of the wrongness of ruling over others against their will. Full democracy still took time, but that's where it began.

So, when people speak of an election campaign being boring, I say: three cheers for boredom, once you consider what the alternatives really are. Democracy is one of the great achievements of humankind and we should never take it for granted.

Religion's Two Faces

23 November 2015

'Terror committed in the name of God is a self-inflicted injury at the heart of faith itself.'

Yesterday I found myself deep in cognitive dissonance.

With memories of Paris and Mali still fresh in the mind, and with Brussels in lockdown fearing another terrorist outrage, we heard the Archbishop of Canterbury confess that even he had doubts about where God was. 'Why is this happening?' he found himself asking, 'Where are You in all this?'

Yet at the same time, yesterday, one of the great moments of blessedness between faiths was taking place, here in Britain and in nineteen other countries across the world. It's called Mitzvah Day, *mitzvah* being the Jewish word for a good deed, a gracious act. It began seven years ago in the Jewish community. The idea was that on one day a year we should all do an act of kindness to someone beyond our faith, that we should reach out in love across the boundaries that divide us.

It was such a beautiful idea that first the Hindu community, and then Christians and Muslims, and eventually all the faiths, joined in, bringing food to the needy, clothes and shelter to the homeless, company to the elderly and those living alone and toys for children in hospitals. Churches, synagogues and mosques all took part, showing that goodness can be contagious, and that faith can bring us together if we let it move us to heal some of the fractures of our much-injured world.

How do you reconcile these two faces of religion? There is, I think, a profound message here. God as He is in heaven is beyond change. But God as He is on Earth – what we call in Judaism the *Shekhinah*, the Divine presence – depends on what we do in His name.

If we serve God in love and acts of kindness, especially to strangers, especially when it's hard, then God's name is sanctified and we feel His presence among us, opening our hearts to one another, lifting us on the wings of grace. But if we use God's name to justify violence against the innocent, murdering those God Himself has endowed with His image, then His name is desecrated, and His presence exiled from the world. When that happens, even the most religious find themselves asking: 'Where is God in all this?'

Terror committed in the name of God is a self-inflicted injury at the heart of faith itself. Only when the world's faiths declare this and act on it will we bring the Divine presence back into the shared spaces of our interconnected lives.

The Good Society

19 February 2016

'. . . the good society is one where we all have the chance to flourish because we are all equally children of God.'

Tomorrow is the United Nations World Day of Social Justice, which is interesting, because one of the great thinkers of the twentieth century, Friedrich Hayek, thought there was no such thing as social justice. He called it a mirage, a will-o'-the-wisp, a vacuous concept, a hollow incantation, a mark of sloppy thinking and intellectual dishonesty. He thought there was justice for individuals, the kind you get from laws and courts, but for society as a whole, no.

The Hebrew Bible, though, argues otherwise. It has two words for justice, *tzedek* and *mishpat*. *Mishpat* means individual justice. But *tzedek* means social justice, and I think that's one of the great contributions of the Bible to the world. What it means is that we are all equal in the sight of God. We all bear His image. We are all created in His likeness. And society should in some way reflect this, not necessarily in terms of wealth or power, but at least in dignity and opportunity. It was perhaps the first attempt in history to break away from the social hierarchies that appeared with the birth of cities and civilisations, and it's been an inspiration to the West for many centuries.

So, are we getting there? Not yet. There was an item in yesterday's news that people from poorer backgrounds are still not getting to the best universities in anything like proportionate numbers. In recent years several leading American thinkers have argued, with compelling evidence, that social mobility in the

United States is declining to the point where the American story is no longer true: that anyone can make it if they work hard enough. The American dream, they say, is broken.

And it's going to get worse, because we are still just at the start of the information revolution. Already artificial intelligence has reached the point where my phone is smarter than I am. And it's going to go much further. Many things people are currently employed to do will be done in future by machines. Either there will be more unemployment, or we will have to find ways of sharing work and increasing leisure. Inequalities are growing throughout the world. How far will we let this go?

We're going to have to decide whether we really believe in social justice or not. Perhaps life is just a Darwinian struggle in which the strong survive. But I believe the Bible tells us otherwise: that the good society is one where we all have the chance to flourish because we are all equally children of God.

The Impact of Social Media

4 November 2016

'Whether it's building pyramids or digital devices, we sometimes forget that technology is made to serve us. We were not made to serve technology.'

'Streaming instead of dreaming', went the headline that caught my eye this week. Using phones or tablets before bedtime, it said, is stopping kids from sleeping. A series of research exercises suggests that young people who use electronic devices around bedtime are twice as likely to have inadequate sleep and three times more likely to feel drowsy the next day. Even having one in the room and not using it is, they say, bad for sleep.

There have been quite a few similar news items in recent weeks. One spoke about the harmful effects of sleep deprivation on health. Another discovered that seven in ten children and nine in ten teenagers have electronic devices in their bedrooms. A third, surveying thirteen countries around the world, showed that we British are the worst sleepers in the world.

Let me say immediately that's not been my experience. In fact, whenever I start speaking, people around me show signs of drowsiness, leading me belatedly to the conclusion that rabbis and anaesthetists are in the same line of occupation.

I mention all this because of a recent conversation I had with a woman from the west coast of America where much of this technology comes from. She was a huge fan of smartphones and social media, as I am, but, she said, too much was having a bad effect on her children. It wasn't just spoiling their sleep. It was robbing them of social skills, shortening their attention spans and disrupting family meals.

So she and her family made a radical decision. Once a week they would have a screen-free day. No phones, no tablets, no laptops, no TVs. Just family and friends, talking together, eating together, celebrating life without the distraction of being 24/7 online. It's been tough but terrific, she said. What enthralled me was the name she gave it. Some call it a digital detox, she said. We call it our screen Sabbath.

Wow. Well done, Moses, I thought. Some 3,000 years ago you gave us the Sabbath to free us from slavery to Pharaoh, and now we've rediscovered it to give us freedom from smartphones.

Yet maybe the principle's the same. Whether it's building pyramids or digital devices, we sometimes forget that technology is made to serve us. We were not made to serve technology.

So, whether it's an hour a day or a day a week, let's switch off our screens, enjoy one another face-to-face, and rediscover the magic of dreaming, not streaming.

Handling Change

28 June 2017

'Change is threatening. It's one of the reasons that species, cultures, even civilisations become extinct. And seldom has the world changed faster and more relentlessly than it's doing now.'

I've just come back from the trip of a lifetime, from the Galapagos Islands, where the young Charles Darwin had his first intuition of natural selection and the origin of species, and Machu Picchu, the almost perfectly preserved ruins of an Inca citadel set high in the Peruvian mountains. And it was strange to hear from so far away of the political turmoil happening in Britain these past few weeks. Was there, I wondered, some insight to be gained from that kind of distance?

As I was asking myself that question, I caught sight of a sentence attributed to Darwin, inscribed on the inside wall of the boat in which we were travelling. 'It is not the strongest or most intelligent who will survive, but those who can best manage change.' And that, it suddenly occurred to me, was at the heart of the turbulence that's recently affected so much of the world, including Britain.

We are living through some of the most rapid and dramatic changes the world has ever seen, and this has divided whole societies between those who welcome change and those who feel threatened by it and all its economic, social and cultural repercussions. Change is threatening. It's one of the reasons that species, cultures, even civilisations become extinct. And seldom has the world changed faster and more relentlessly than it's doing now.

And then I thought back to the history of my own faith and I wondered: what was it about Judaism that allowed my ancestors to keep going through centuries of uncertainty, never knowing when the next expulsion or persecution would happen, or whether the friends of today would become the enemies of tomorrow? What is it about a faith that gives a people the courage to manage change?

Three things. First, we never lost our sense of identity, of who we were and why. In all our festivals we remembered our ancestors' journey through the wilderness in search of freedom. Second, we never lost our sense of hope, that God was with us on the way however distant He sometimes seemed. And third, we never forgot the destination: a world of justice, compassion and peace, not yet reached but glimpsed, as it were, from afar. If you remember where you come from, where you are going to, and why, you can handle change because you have a map of values that don't change.

Perhaps we all need a little faith right now to help us through a turbulent world without fear.

Disagreement and Debate

10 November 2017

'. . . truth emerges from disagreement and debate.'

Coming in to Broadcasting House this morning I saw for the first time the statue unveiled this week, of George Orwell, with its inscription on the wall behind, 'If liberty means anything at all, it means the right to tell people what they do not want to hear.' How badly we need that truth today.

I've been deeply troubled by what seems to me to be the assault on free speech taking place in British universities in the name of 'safe space', 'trigger warnings', and 'microaggressions', meaning any remark that someone might find offensive even if no offence is meant. So far has this gone that a month ago, students at an Oxford College banned the presence of a representative of the Christian Union on the grounds that some might find their presence alienating and offensive. Luckily the protest that followed led to the ban being swiftly overturned. But still . . .

I'm sure this entire movement has been undertaken for the highest of motives, to protect the feelings of the vulnerable, which I applaud, but you don't achieve that by silencing dissenting views. A safe space is the exact opposite: a place where you give a respectful hearing to views opposed to your own, knowing that your views too will be listened to respectfully. That's academic freedom and it's essential to a free society.

And it's what I learned at university. My doctoral supervisor, the late Sir Bernard Williams, was an atheist. I was a passionate religious believer. But he always listened respectfully to my views, which gave me the confidence to face those who disagree with everything I stand for. That's safety in an unsafe world.

And it's at the very heart of my faith, because Judaism is a tradition all of whose canonical texts are anthologies of arguments. In the Bible, Abraham, Moses, Jeremiah and Job argue with God. The rabbinic literature is an almost endless series of Rabbi X says this and Rabbi Y says that, and when one rabbi had the chance of asking God who was right, God replied: 'They're both right.' 'How can they both be right?' asked the rabbi, to which God's apocryphal reply was: 'You're also right.' The rabbis called this 'argument for the sake of heaven'.

Why does it matter? Because truth emerges from disagreement and debate. Because tolerance means making space for difference. Because justice involves *Audi alteram partem*, listening to the other side. And because, in Orwell's words, liberty means 'the right to tell people what they do not want to hear'.

Antisemitism

20 April 2018

'. . . difference is what makes us human. And a society that has no room for difference has no room for humanity.'

I've been doing *Thought for the Day* for thirty years, but I never thought that in 2018 I would still have to speak about antisemitism. I was part of that generation, born after the Holocaust, who believed the nations of the world when they said: 'Never again.'

But this week, there was an unprecedented debate about antisemitism in Parliament. Several MPs spoke emotionally about the abuse they'd received because they were Jews, or more scarily, because they'd fought antisemitism. According to the Community Security Trust, antisemitic incidents in Britain have risen to their highest level since record keeping began in 1984, at an average of four a day. This is not the Britain I know and love.

In Paris, a month ago, just before Passover, an eighty-five-year-old Holocaust survivor was murdered because she was a Jew, the most harrowing in a whole series of such attacks in Europe in recent years. There is today almost no European country where Jews feel safe, and this within living memory of the Holocaust, in which 1.5 million children were murdered simply because their grandparents were Jews.

It's happened because of the rise of political extremism on the right and left, and because of populist politics that plays on people's fears, seeking scapegoats to blame for social ills. For a thousand years Jews have been targeted as scapegoats because they were a minority and because they were different. But difference is what makes us human. And a society that has no room for difference has no room for humanity.

The appearance of antisemitism is always an early warning sign of a dangerous dysfunction within a culture, because the hate that begins with Jews never ends with Jews.

At the end of his life, Moses told the Israelites: 'Don't hate an Egyptian because you were strangers in his land.' It's an odd sentence. The Egyptians had oppressed and enslaved the Israelites. So why did Moses say, 'Don't hate'? Because if the people continued to hate, Moses would have taken the Israelites out of Egypt, but failed to take Egypt out of the Israelites. They would still be slaves, not physically but mentally. Moses knew that to be free you have to let go of hate. Wherever there is hate, freedom dies, which is why each of us, especially we leaders, have to take a stand against the corrosive power of hate.

All it takes for evil to flourish is for good people to do nothing. Today I see too many good people doing nothing, and I am ashamed.

Loving Life

20 June 2019

'The Book of Psalms speaks of those who love life. I think that's the common factor between great religious leaders, great artists and scientists and the great communicators.'

There was a fascinating diary piece in the press this week about Sir David Attenborough and his fellow naturalist Desmond Morris, both of whom are in their nineties and still going strong. They were comparing notes about health. Morris asked Sir David, 'Have you ever done any exercise?' To which the answer was 'no'. 'Ever gone to a gym?' 'No.' 'Ever been on a diet?' 'No' again. 'Neither have I,' said Morris. 'Maybe that's the secret.'

It probably isn't, but it's interesting to ask why. The reason, I think, is that we are not only physical beings but intellectual, spiritual and moral ones as well. We have not only bodies but also minds and what we used to call souls. They too have their own form of diet and exercise: researching, exploring, investigating, thinking and communicating. That's what keeps those who do these things young.

David Galenson, a research social scientist, published a book, *Old Masters and Young Geniuses,** about why some people in the arts – like the director Orson Welles or the composer Felix Mendelssohn – do their best work when they're young, while others, like Cézanne, Monet and Verdi, do their best work in old age.

* David Galenson, *Old Masters and Young Geniuses: The Two Life Cycles of Artistic Creativity* (Princeton: Princeton University Press, 2008).

His view was that the young geniuses came with a fully formed vision that they translated into their work. It was there pretty much from the beginning which is why their early work had such impact. The old masters, by contrast, just kept learning and experimenting and getting better. That was their equivalent of working out in the gym.

The Bible says of Moses that at the age of 120, 'his eye was undimmed and his natural energy unabated' (Deuteronomy 34:7). I used to think that these were just two descriptions, but I eventually realised that the first was the explanation of the second. His energy was unabated because his eye was undimmed, because he never lost the ideals of his youth or his passion for justice. He stayed young because, despite his many setbacks, he never gave way to disillusion or despair.

The Book of Psalms speaks of those who love life. I think that's the common factor between great religious leaders, great artists and scientists and the great communicators like Desmond Morris and Sir David Attenborough. They love life and enhance the lives of others. And sometimes that can be as good as a diet or a workout as a way of staying young.

Confronting Racism

28 November 2019

'We still have to fight for the truth that every group should feel safe; and that our differences, not just our similarities, are what make us human.'

A few days ago, two Jewish children were sitting with their parents in a train on the London Underground when a man came up to them and for almost twenty minutes harangued them with antisemitic abuse. Someone intervened but was threatened with violence. Then a young woman confronted the man and calmly told him what he was doing was wrong. This distracted him and saved the day. It was a heroic act. The hero was a young Muslim woman wearing a hijab. Her name was Asma Shuweikh.

She herself has known what it's like to be abused. Muslims suffer from this as much as Jews. But instead of allowing that to intimidate her, she used it to identify with the Jewish family. That is what the Book of Exodus means when it says, 'Do not oppress a stranger for you know what it feels like to be a stranger' (Exodus 23:9). Use your pain to sensitise you to the pain of others.

That we in Britain should still be talking about antisemitism, Islamophobia, or racism at all is deeply shocking. But it reminds us of the distance between public utterances of politicians and the reality, and it's been like that for a very long time. Thomas Jefferson, who drafted the line in the American Declaration of Independence, 'We hold these truths to be self-evident, that all men are created equal', was a slave owner. A century after the French revolution, with its commitment to liberty, equality and fraternity, France at the time of the Dreyfus trial had become a world leader in antisemitism. The Germany of Goethe, Schiller, Beethoven and Kant, that gave us some of the finest expressions of universal humanity, later became the birthplace of the most murderous racism Europe has ever known. Racism has returned to Europe and to Britain – are we, and the politicians who represent us, doing enough to stop it?

We still have to fight for the truth that every group should feel safe; and that our differences, not just our similarities, are what make us human. The Bible taught this in its opening chapter by saying that every human being is in the image and likeness of God. Meaning that one who is not in my image – whose colour, culture or creed is not mine – is nonetheless in God's image.

Asma Shuweikh, the lady in the train, who later said, 'I wouldn't hesitate to do it again,' chose not to be a bystander but to confront racism head on. Her quiet courage should be a model for us all.

Love

14 February 2020

'Tending it daily keeps the flame of love alive.'

Today is Valentine's Day, traditionally associated with expressions of love. I wouldn't normally speak about it because it's not a Jewish day. Its history goes back to the early Christian martyrs, then the age of chivalry, and through Chaucer to Shakespeare's Ophelia. It's a lovely day, just not ours.

But this year I've been unusually conscious of the joy that comes through love. It's just over fifty years since I met, fell in love with and proposed to Elaine, and this year we'll celebrate our golden wedding. Recently we took our children and grandchildren away for a weekend and on Sunday morning we took a walk together along the Thames.

Then I realised that Elaine and I used to take just this walk when we were first married, and we hadn't done so since, and I suddenly had an intense experience of being taken back across the years to then, when we were young. At that time, we had no idea where the path was taking us. Then I looked up and came back to the present and saw the figures ahead of us on the path: our children and grandchildren, our joy.

I wondered what had kept us on that path, and instinctively I knew. First, we thanked God for every good thing that happened to us. Social scientists tell us that bad events have four or five times as much impact as good ones. So, it's important to equal the score by celebrating the good.

Second, we find something to praise in each other – something the other one has done – every single day. We learned this from a speech therapist who taught us that daily praise within a family gives everyone the confidence to change and grow.

And third, forgive. Most of us have much that needs to be forgiven, and how can that happen unless we ourselves are prepared to forgive?

These things became daily rituals. As the American writer David Brooks puts it, commitment is falling in love with someone or something and then building a structure of behaviour around it for the moment when love falters. Tending it daily keeps the flame of love alive.

We have a tradition in Judaism that every weekday Jewish men recite the lovely words of the prophet Hosea, 'I will betroth you to me for ever' (Hosea 2:21). That is our daily valentine, between us and God, between us and those we love. And it's love that guides our feet along the path to joy.

The Coronavirus Pandemic

15 May 2020

'When war or disease affects all of us, you learn to care for all of us.'

When the worst of the pandemic is over, what kind of future will we seek? Will we try as far as possible to go back to the way things were? Or will we try to create a more just and caring society? What impact does collective tragedy have on the human imagination?

The philosopher Hegel said that the one thing we learn from history is that we learn nothing from history. But the great prophets of the Bible who experienced tragedy, like Isaiah and Jeremiah, said in effect, we must learn from history if we are to avoid repeating it. We have to use the pain we've been through to sensitise ourselves to the pain of others, the poor, the weak and the vulnerable – the widow, the orphan and the stranger. Collective suffering can move us from 'I' to 'We', from the pursuit of self-interest to care for the common good. Which will it be for us?

It's worth looking at the last two great tragedies in Western history, World War I and the Spanish Flu pandemic of 1918, and World War II. After 1918, nothing much changed. It was an age of individualism and inequality, of the Roaring Twenties and *The Great Gatsby*, wild dances and even wilder parties, as if people were trying to forget and put the past behind them.

It was fun, but it led to the General Strike of 1926 and the Great Crash of 1929, the recession of the 1930s and the rise in mainland Europe of nationalism and fascism. And a mere twenty-one years after the war to end all wars, the world was at war again. On that occasion, Hegel was right. People learned nothing from history.

The reaction to World War II was quite different. There was the 1944 Education Act that extended secondary education to everyone. There was the National Health Service and the birth of the welfare state. America produced the Marshall Plan that helped a ravaged Europe to rebuild itself. The result was seventy-five years of peace. People knew they had to build something more inclusive. When war or disease affects all of us, you learn to care for all of us.

I hope that's what happens now, that we build a fairer society, where human values count as much as economic ones. We've been through too much simply to go back to where we were. We have to rescue some blessing from the curse, some hope from the pain.

Part Two
Credo

The following articles were first published in the Credo column in *The Times*.

Charity

26 February 2000

'Active citizenship begins with the insight that we are worth what we are willing to share with others.'

Sir Moses Montefiore was one of the great figures of Victorian Britain. In the course of a long life he became Sheriff of the City of London, President of the Board of Deputies of British Jews, and an international spokesman in defence of human rights. His philanthropy extended to Jews and non-Jews alike, and on his ninety-ninth and hundredth birthdays, *The Times* devoted editorials to his praise. He had shown, said *The Times*, 'that fervent Judaism and patriotic citizenship are absolutely consistent with one another'.

One story in particular made a deep impression on me. Someone once asked him: 'Sir Moses, what are you worth?' He thought for a while and named a figure. 'But surely', said his questioner, 'your wealth must be much more than that.'

With a smile, Sir Moses replied: 'You didn't ask me how much I own. You asked me how much I am worth. So, I calculated how much I have given to charity thus far this year – because we are worth what we are willing to share with others.'

I was reminded of this story by the speech recently given to the National Council of Voluntary Organisations by Gordon Brown. The Chancellor spoke with rare eloquence about the need to enhance the voluntary sector of British society and about the importance of giving, both in terms of money and time. He called for a new 'civic patriotism' to break through the twin dangers of a culture of contentment and a culture of despair.

He was right to do so. For too long, politics in this country has veered between two poles: the individual and the state. The market represents the private choices of individuals. Government action represents the collective response of the state. For over fifty years the question has been framed thus: either we leave a problem to the workings of the market, or we confront it by Government intervention.

But this is an impoverished way of looking at things, because it omits a third alternative: the voluntary sector, the work done every day by hundreds of thousands of groups and individuals to bring help to those in need and comfort to people struggling alone.

The voluntary sector differs from the state and the market in one vital respect. The state is about the production and distribution of power. The market is about the production and distribution of wealth. But power and wealth are, at any given moment, zero-sum games. If I have total power and then I share it with nine others I am left with only a tenth of what I had. If I have a thousand pounds and then share it with nine others, again I have only a tenth of the amount with which I began. Politics and economics are about competition – they are arenas of mediated conflict.

But there are other goods – among them love, friendship, trust – which are different. The more I share them, the more I have. Indeed, they only exist in virtue of being shared. That is why communities, neighbourhood groups and voluntary organisations are vital to the health of society. They are not arenas of conflict, but rather the seedbeds of co-operation.

Not everything can be solved by voluntary action. We will always need the market and the state. But so too we will always need acts and organisations built on altruism. Active citizenship begins with the insight that we are worth what we are willing to share with others.

Marriage

10 June 2000

'. . . looking back, I know that whatever I have done I could not have done alone, and I try to say so as often as I can.'

Elaine and I were married young. She was 21, I was 22. At that time, we had no idea what life would bring. As the Yiddish saying has it: 'The one thing that makes God laugh is to see our plans for the future.'

I had gone to university to study economics. I then changed to philosophy. For a while I toyed with the prospect of becoming a barrister. After a short encounter, though, I concluded that the legal profession was meant for more exalted minds than mine. It took several years before I heeded the inner voice calling me to the rabbinate. During those years, Elaine – a radiographer – was the breadwinner, and I the (not very good) housekeeper.

Our life has had its twists and turns, its unexpected blessings and crises. But looking back, I know that whatever I have done I could not have done alone, and I try to say so as often as I can.

I don't think we were unusual. For most of us life just is a long journey into the unknown. Rarely do we know in advance what the next bend will bring. The only certainty we had was that we would be there for one another, and it was enough, more than enough. We knew – and surely that knowledge is what marriage means – that we would find strength in the unspoken presence of love, come what may.

That made the hardest moments bearable. Looking back, you realise the power of that slender bond by which two people pledge themselves to one another, turning love into loyalty and a source of new life.

We have paid a heavy price for misunderstanding one of the key words of the Hebrew Bible, *emunah*, usually translated as 'faith'. Because the Bible entered Western civilisation through the medium of Greek, and because to the Greeks the highest vocation was the pursuit of knowledge, we have for centuries thought of faith as a kind of knowledge: intuitive, visionary perhaps, but cognitive. On this view, to have faith is to know, or believe, certain facts about the world.

That is not the Jewish view at all. *Emunah* is about relationship. It is that bond by which two persons, each respecting the freedom and integrity of the other, pledge themselves by an oath of loyalty to stay together, to do what neither can do alone. It means, not 'faith' but 'faithfulness', the commitment to be there for one another, especially in hard times. In human terms, the best example is marriage. In religious terms, it is what we call a covenant, of which the classic instance is the pledge between God and an ancient people, Israel, on Mount Sinai thirty-three centuries ago.

Faith is a marriage. Marriage is an act of faith. So, at any rate, the prophets of Israel believed. To this day, Jewish men, as they bind the strap of their phylacteries round their finger like a wedding ring, recite the lovely words of God quoted by the prophet Hosea: 'I will betroth you to me in faithfulness and you shall know God' (Hosea 2:22).

I find it hard to say how sad it is that marriage is in decline. It was and is the single greatest source of beauty in ordinary lives – moral beauty, a song scored for two voices in complex harmony. Marriage is the supreme example of a religious concept translated into simple human terms. Faith is the redemption of human loneliness through the sacred bond of love.

Listening

14 December 2002

'There are times when friendship calls simply for a human presence, a listening ear and an understanding heart, so that soul can unburden itself to soul.'

Viktor Frankl survived three years in the concentration camps of Dachau and Auschwitz. On the basis of his experiences there, he went on to found a new school of psychotherapy, Logotherapy, based on finding meaning in suffering.

He once told the following story. A woman phoned him in the middle of the night and calmly told him that she was about to commit suicide. Frankl kept her on the telephone and talked her through her depression, giving her reason after reason to carry on living. Eventually she promised him she would not take her life, and she kept her word.

When they met later, Frankl asked her which of his reasons she had found convincing. 'None,' she replied. What then persuaded her to go on living? Her answer was simple. Frankl had been willing to listen to her in the middle of the night. A world in which someone was prepared to listen to another's distress seemed to her one in which it was worthwhile to live.

What an underrated art listening is. Sometimes it is the greatest gift we can give to a troubled soul. It is an act of focused attention. It means being genuinely open to another person, prepared to enter their world, their perspective, their pain. It does not mean that we have a solution to their problem. There are some problems that cannot be solved. They can only be lived through, so that time itself heals the rupture or loss. When we listen, we share the burden so that its weight can be borne. There are times when friendship calls simply for a human presence, a listening ear and an understanding heart, so that soul can unburden itself to soul.

There is no book in the Bible as haunting as the story of Job. Job loses everything: his family, his property, his health. For chapter after chapter, he gives voice to his complaints, rejecting the false comforts of his friends. Finally, out of the whirlwind, God appears to him. Instead of giving him answers to his questions, however, God asks him four chapters of unanswerable questions of His own. After this, Job finds the strength to carry on.

After reading this strange book many times it eventually occurred to me that it is a meditation on listening itself. Job did not seek to be vindicated. He merely demanded a hearing. Unlike his comforters, he did not believe that every instance of human suffering has an explanation we can understand. That always will be beyond the scope of the human imagination. What Job wanted was something else: confirmation that his plight was known, and his words heard. That is what he discovered in the heart of the whirlwind. God listens. The Universe is not deaf to our cry. God, the personal presence at the core of being, enters the broken heart and makes it whole again. To be listened to is to be affirmed.

That is what God does in the Bible. He listens to those who otherwise go unheard – to Ishmael, driven from home; to Leah, unloved; to Rachel and Hannah, longing for a child; to the Israelites as they groan under the burden of slavery; to David as he pours out his emotions in the Book of Psalms. God listens, and in listening gives us the strength to live.

Not accidentally are the most famous words of Jewish prayer *Shema Yisrael*. I used to translate this as 'Hear, O Israel'. I now know that it means, 'Listen, O Israel'. Listening is where pain is healed by being shared.

Religious Fundamentalism

3 August 2004

'. . . what is wrong with the word 'fundamentalism' is its assumption that the fundamentals of faith are dangerous. On the contrary, religions become dangerous when we forget their fundamentals.'

In our abrasive culture, where it sometimes seems that to get ahead you need postgraduate qualifications in rudeness, the worst thing you can call someone is a fundamentalist. You believe? You must be crazy. You pray? You must be a fanatic. You keep religious laws? You must be dangerous. No wonder a well-known press officer is reported to have once said: 'We don't do God.'

Lurking beneath the surface of these put-downs is fear of fundamentalism. Those who believe in the fundamentals of faith are, we seem to assume, living in the past, hostile to the present, incapable of tolerance, vehement in their condemnation of non-believers, and capable of violence. This is a terribly jaundiced view and will do us, in the long run, great harm.

To be sure, every faith has episodes in its past of which it ought to be ashamed. That was the message of the prophets. Every sacred scripture has passages which, if wrongly interpreted, can lead to hate. That is why Jews, and not only Jews, believe that sacred texts need commentaries. Any system of belief can go wrong. That applies to secular, no less than to religious, ideologies. The twentieth century's two great secular substitutes for faith, Nazism and Communism, began in dreams of Utopia and ended in nightmares of Hell. The difference is that religions contain what secular alternatives rarely do: the concept of repentance, a willingness to admit we got it wrong. That is why secular ideologies die but religious faith survives.

No, what is wrong with the word 'fundamentalism' is its assumption that the fundamentals of faith are dangerous. On the contrary, religions become dangerous when we forget their fundamentals. The God of Abraham is a God of love, not war; forgiveness, not revenge; humility, not arrogance; hospitality, not hostility. Abraham fights and prays for the people of his generation even though their faith was not his own. He welcomes strangers into his tent and makes a peace treaty with his neighbours. That is the ancestor Jews, Christians and Muslims take as their own. Those are the fundamentals to which we are called.

There is a powerful version of liberalism which holds that the only way to create a free society is through doubt. Because we are not certain, we do not impose our certainties on others. Because we might be wrong, we give people the space to disagree. Isaiah Berlin ended one of his most influential essays with a quote from Joseph Schumpeter: 'To realise the relative validity of one's convictions and yet stand for them unflinchingly is what distinguishes a civilised man from a barbarian.'

I am moved by this idea. It is genuinely noble. But in the end, it fails. If our convictions are only relatively valid, why stand for them unflinchingly? If kindness is only relatively good, why oppose cruelty which is only relatively bad? If all we have is doubt, we will quickly find ourselves in the situation memorably described by W. B. Yeats where 'the best lack all conviction, while the worst are full of passionate intensity'. Relativism is no defence of liberty.

Another Oxford philosopher, John Plamenatz, was much closer to the truth when he pointed out that the modern doctrine of freedom was born in the seventeenth century in an age of strong and conflicting religious beliefs. 'Liberty of conscience', he wrote, 'was born, not of indifference, not of scepticism, not of mere open-mindedness, but of faith.'

How so? Because people who cared deeply about their own religious convictions eventually came to realise that others who had quite different convictions cared no less deeply about theirs. If I claim the right to practise my faith in freedom, can I deny you yours? That is how European liberalism was born, not through relativism but in the religious belief that God does not want us to impose our faith on others by force.

The only defence against dangerous fundamentalism is counter-fundamentalism: belief, rooted in our sacred texts, in the sanctity of life and the dignity of the human person, the imperative of peace and the need for justice tempered by compassion. We are not blind concatenations of genes endlessly seeking to replicate themselves with no purpose other than survival. We are here because we were created in love, and we fulfil our purpose by creating in love.

These are beliefs most Jews, Christians and Muslims share, as do those of other faiths or none. They are the real fundamentals. What matters now is that they, not their denials, prevail.

Terrorism

9 July 2005

'Terror fails and will always fail because it arouses in us a profound instinct for life.'

As if mocking the scenes of jubilation at London's successful Olympic bid, Thursday's terrorist explosions left devastation in their wake. Today in all our synagogues we will be joining our prayers with those of others, grieving for the dead, praying for the injured and sharing our tears with those of the bereaved.

Terror has become the scourge of our age, and it will take all our inner strength to cope with it. I have met far too many victims of terror: survivors of the Istanbul synagogue bombing in 2003; of the 1994 terrorist attack on the Jewish community centre in Buenos Aires; in Israel, where almost everyone knows someone who has been affected; as well as survivors of the massacres in Cambodia, Bosnia, Rwanda and Kosovo. Like others I have wept for the broken families and shattered lives and the injuries, physical and psychological, that may never heal.

But I have wept also at the courage of the victims. Each year a group of us go to perform concerts for people who have suffered terrorist attacks. One we met was an eleven-year-old boy who had lost his mother, father and three other members of his family in a suicide bombing. He himself had lost his sight. In the hospital ward, he sang with the choir a hauntingly beautiful religious song. We had gone to give him strength. Instead, he gave us strength.

Terror fails and will always fail because it arouses in us a profound instinct for life. Will we ever forget the heroism of the New York firemen on 9/11, or the courage of the passengers on

Flight 93, or the kindness of strangers who brought comfort to the traumatised survivors?

Terror makes us vigilant in defence of what we otherwise take for granted: the sanctity of life, the importance of freedom and the countless natural restraints that allow us to live together in safety and trust.

Free societies are always stronger than their enemies take them to be. Enemies of the West mistake its openness for vulnerability, its tolerance for decadence, its respect for difference for a lack of moral conviction. Britain has exceptionally strong links of friendship between its different faith and ethnic communities. That is a vital source of stability when nerves are frayed and fears aroused. London itself has a long history of courage. That too was evident in the calm that prevailed on Thursday.

The best response to terror is not anger but the quiet strength to carry on, not giving way to fear. I think of Judea Pearl, father of the murdered American journalist Daniel Pearl, who has become a campaigner for deeper understanding between Islam and the West. When I asked him what motivated him, he replied: 'Hate killed my son, and you cannot defeat hate by hate.'

I think of one of the most promising young men our community has produced, Yoni Jesner, who was killed at 19 in a suicide bombing in Tel Aviv. His family, out of deep religious conviction, donated his organs to save life – among them a seven-year-old Palestinian girl who had waited two years for a kidney transplant.

Michael Walzer has written: 'Terrorists are like killers on a rampage, except that their rampage is not just expressive of rage or madness; the rage is purposeful and programmatic.'

Its victims, deliberately, are the innocent and uninvolved: workers in an office, passengers on a train, passers-by on a pavement. Its aim is fear. It advances no interest. It has no conceivable claim to justice. It dishonours any cause it claims to represent.

The real answer to terror was enacted in London and elsewhere five days before. Millions of people took to the streets and parks to demonstrate their solidarity with the victims of poverty in Africa.

Their methods were peaceful, their weapons, song and celebration, and their greatest strength was the justice of their cause.

The people with whom they were identifying – the hundreds of millions of children who lack food, shelter, clean water and medical facilities, sustenance and hope – have never resorted to terror to bring their plight to the attention of the world, nor did they need to.

The choice humanity faces was set out long ago by Moses: 'I have set before you life and death, the blessing and the curse. Therefore choose life, so that you and your children may live' (Deuteronomy 30:19). The strongest answer to the forces of death is a renewed commitment to the sanctity of life.

Natural Disasters

15 October 2005

'The paradox of the human condition is that selfish genes produce remarkably unselfish persons.'

First there was the tsunami. Then Hurricane Katrina. Now the earthquake in Kashmir has claimed tens of thousands of lives. Our prayers go out to the affected and afflicted, the injured and bereaved, to all those whose world has been shaken and destroyed.

In each case the response has shown us the true face of human care. We have discovered that we are still moved by the sight of suffering, however far away. Funds, food, medical teams and shelters have been rushed to the scenes of catastrophe. There has been little evidence of 'compassion fatigue'. We weep. We act. We do what we can to stretch out the hand of help. The paradox of the human condition is that selfish genes produce remarkably unselfish persons. That, in troubled times, is no small consolation. But does a succession of tragedies coming so soon after one another signal something more?

Earlier ages believed so. In *Julius Caesar*, Shakespeare has Casca speak of times when 'these prodigies do so conjointly meet' that they are 'portentous things unto the climate that they point upon'.

A succession of unnatural events was seen as an omen, a sign, a warning. The elements were restless. The gods were in a rage. The prophets of ancient Israel were unlike the oracles of ancient Greece, yet they too saw meaning in history. Disaster was a call from Heaven, a summons to repent. Is that way of thinking available to us today?

The idea that natural catastrophe is divine punishment is, for me, morally unacceptable. We are not prophets. We have no privileged access to the mind of God. We know that the victims of these disasters include children, the innocent, the old and frail, the poor. They were not the evil, the cruel or the corrupt.

These past few years I have heard far too many religious leaders, from all the Abrahamic faiths, confidently proclaiming that this or that event was divine retribution for one or other sin. These are the Job's comforters of our time. They forget that the task of the prophet is to comfort the afflicted, not to add to their affliction by saying that they deserved their fate.

However, I am moved by the story of Elijah, who encountered God, not in the whirlwind or the earthquake or the fire, but in the still, small voice that followed. It is not in the event itself but in its aftermath that we hear God's word. So, it seems to me now. When all the work of rescue and rebuilding is done, a quiet call will remain.

These terrifying events have shown us how small we are in the scheme of things. We have discovered that despite our differences – cultural, political, religious – there is much we share. We all need food, clothing, shelter, safety. An earthquake, a tidal wave, a hurricane, make no distinctions between rich and poor, believer and unbeliever, righteous and not-yet-righteous. The language of tears is universal. It needs no translator. That is precisely what makes us feel implicated in someone else's tragedy. Beneath our varied cultural clothing, we are a single family bound by a covenant of human solidarity.

Why then do we expend so much energy on ethnic conflict, war and terror? Why do we so unthinkingly deplete the Earth's resources, pollute its atmosphere, threaten its biodiversity? Why have we allowed some to grow rich beyond imagining while millions starve and die? All these things come from a world of narrow horizons, where what matters is me, here, now. If natural catastrophe has one blessing, it is its ability to make us forget, for a moment, our personal comfort zones and enter into the plight of others – so different, so far away, yet so like us.

There are times when it seems as if our moral-spiritual state has regressed to the age of tribal wars in the name of God, dishonourable then, inexcusable now. If this terrible sequence of disasters recalls us to our senses, reminding us of our vulnerability in the face of nature, our smallness when set against the Universe, our solidarity in the midst of suffering and our share in the collective fate of humankind, we may still rescue a blessing from the curse. In the silence after the tremors that have shaken our world, we may yet hear the still, small voice of hope.

Religion and Politics

10 December 2005

'Politics turns into virtue what religions often see as a vice – the fact that we do not all think alike, that we have conflicting interests, that we see the world through different eyes.'

The election of David Cameron as leader of the Conservative Party has quickened the pulse of British politics, and though I believe profoundly that religion and politics should never mix, there are times when it is important to say something religious about the political process itself.

In 1996, when one party had been in power for almost a generation, I asked a civil servant in an unguarded moment which he thought more dangerous for a nation: the coming into office of a party most of whose members had no experience of government, or the lack of a credible opposition. Without hesitation he chose the second. Politics lives, he said, on the existence of alternatives, the clash of opinions, the cut and thrust of debate. Without that, democracy dies.

In a flash I realised that he had clarified for me the profound difference between religion and politics and why neither must ever invade the territory of the other.

Democratic politics – the worst system ever invented apart from all the others – is more than the rule of the majority. That, as Alexis de Tocqueville rightly said, can lead to the tyranny of the majority and the loss of rights on the part of minorities. Its virtues are that it allows for the non-violent resolution of conflict. It makes possible a change in government without revolution or civil war. Most importantly, it safeguards the free expression of dissent.

Politics turns into virtue what religions often see as a vice – the fact that we do not all think alike, that we have conflicting interests, that we see the world through different eyes. Politics knows what religion sometimes forgets, that the imposition of truth by force and the suppression of dissent by power is the end of freedom and a denial of human dignity. When religion enters the political arena, we should repeat daily Bunyan's famous words: 'Then I saw that there was a way to Hell, even from the gates of Heaven.'

This is easily said, but behind liberal democracy lies a long and bloody past. Twice in the history of the West, religion discovered its inadequacy as a means of conflict resolution. The first occurred in the first century CE, when Jews began their disastrous rebellion against Rome. It failed because of internecine rivalry between Jews themselves. The result was the destruction of the Second Temple and an exile that lasted almost 2,000 years. It was Jewry's worst self-inflicted tragedy.

The second took place in Christian Europe between the Reformation in 1517 and the Treaty of Westphalia in 1648. For more than a century Europe was convulsed by religious war, Christian fighting Christian as Jew had once fought Jew. Out of these experiences, first Jews, then Christians, eventually learnt to separate religion from politics, influence from power, the noble dream from the willingness to compromise that alone allows us to live graciously with those with whom we disagree.

It may seem odd to say that the most important feature of liberal democracy is its modesty. Humility is a virtue not always associated with politicians. Yet it is built into the system. The secular democratic state has no ambitions to proclaim the truth, fulfil the metaphysical longings of the soul, or pass judgment on the great questions of ethics. It is there to help us get along with one another, making our several contributions to the common good. It is the best way yet discovered of allowing us all to feel heard, our views considered if not always accepted, and of constructing a society we see as tolerable if not ideal.

There is something noble about this self-limitation. Liberal democracy does what few great religions have ever achieved. It makes space for difference. It honours the person regardless of his or her beliefs. It allows societies to negotiate change without catastrophe. It teaches us the difficult arts of listening to our opponents and – in Isaiah's phrase – 'reason together' (Isaiah 1:18). These are modest virtues but necessary ones.

We are living in an age in which, not just in Britain but throughout the world, many people are disillusioned with secular politics, and are turning to religion instead. In itself that is a blessing. Religious faith is our noblest effort to understand ourselves and our place in the Universe. The expansive air of the spirit redeems the narrowness of the material world. But to expect it to solve political problems is to invite disaster. Religion becomes political at its peril, and ours.

Volunteering

15 June 2005

'The paradox of volunteering is that the more we give, the more we are given.'

Last week was Week of the Volunteer in Britain. Next week we in the Jewish community celebrate the festival of Shavuot (Pentecost). Seeking a connection between the two – the timely and the timeless – I found it in the text we read on the festival: the Book of Ruth.

The story of Ruth has a simple beauty that never fades. It is about two women, an Israelite, Naomi, and her Moabite daughter-in-law Ruth, and the human bond between them. Naomi's husband and sons have died. Both women are now childless widows. Naomi tells Ruth that they must part and rebuild their separate lives. Ruth refuses. She accompanies Naomi back to Israel and eventually marries another member of the family, Boaz. From that marriage, three generations later, David, was born, Israel's greatest king.

One Hebrew word epitomises the book: *chessed*, usually translated as 'loving kindness'. It is what links the book's main characters. In fact, it added a word to the English language. In Middle English 'ruth' meant kindness. Today only its negation remains: the word 'ruthless'. But the story has immense power. Childless widows were the most vulnerable, defenceless members of ancient societies. In addition, Ruth and Naomi were divided by ethnicity. The Israelites and Moabites were long-standing enemies. They had nothing in common but mutual distrust. Whenever I read the book, the words that come to mind are the famous phrase of

Tennessee Williams: 'the kindness of strangers'. Ruth is about the simple gestures that transcend differences, the universal language of help to those in need.

Its message still stands. Shavuot is when we celebrate the giving of the law at Mount Sinai. The fact that we read Ruth's story at this time tells us that society cannot be made by laws alone. It needs something more – the unforced, unlegislated kindness that makes us reach out to the lonely and vulnerable, even if we are lonely and vulnerable ourselves. Then and now, society needs the kindness of strangers.

That is what volunteering is – and it is part of the unsung greatness of Britain today. We are a ruthful, not a ruthless, nation; 26 million of us are engaged in some form of voluntary work. Another 11 million describe themselves as 'waiting to be asked'. The numbers continue to rise, especially among the young.

We saw this in the outpouring of generosity that followed the tsunami tragedy last year. It is evident again in the Make Poverty History campaign. We care. We want to give. We seek to help. We are not just concatenations of selfish genes. Like Ruth and Boaz, we find ourselves stretching out a hand to the stranger. Kindness, compassion, *chessed*, lie at the core of our humanity. They represent the strange, unexpected truth that by sharing our vulnerabilities, we discover strength.

The paradox of volunteering is that the more we give, the more we are given. I lose count of the number of times I have thanked people for their voluntary work, only to be told: 'It is I who want to give thanks for the chance to serve.' Lifting others, we ourselves are lifted. Happiness – the sense of a life well lived – is born in the blessings we bestow on others. Bringing hope to someone else's life brings meaning to our own.

I find it moving that the Bible dedicates a book to the story of David's great-grandmother Ruth, as if to say that her life was no less significant than his. She was a stranger, an outsider, someone with nothing but her own force of character, her refusal to walk away from another person's troubles. David was a military hero, a master politician, a king. There is a form of greatness, suggests the Bible, that has nothing to do with power, fame or renown. It exists in simple deeds of kindness and friendship, generosity and grace. Rarely do they make the news. But they change lives, redeeming some of the pain of the human situation.

Britain's volunteers are our Ruths. Each is writing their own sequel to her story. Volunteering is rarely glamorous and never easy, especially for those with many other pressures on their time. But few things count more when it comes to looking back on a life than being able to say, 'I made a difference.' Beneath the clamour of self-interest, a quieter voice within us whispers the deeper truth, that the greatest gift is to be able to give.

Prayer

7 January 2006

'Starve a body of food and it dies. Starve a soul of prayer and it atrophies and withers.'

A classic Jewish story: a learned rabbi and a taxi driver depart this world at the same time and arrive together at the gates of Heaven. The angel at the gate signals to the taxi driver to enter, then turns to the rabbi and sadly shakes his head. 'What is this?' asks the rabbi. 'I am a learned rabbi, and he is only a taxi driver who, not to put too fine a point on it, drove like a lunatic.' 'Exactly so,' replies the angel. 'When you spoke, people slept. But when they got into his taxi, believe me, they prayed!'

That's a way of reminding us that prayer isn't always predictable. We never know in advance when we will feel the need to turn to God. Why, then, the discipline of daily prayer?

Preparing a new edition of the Jewish prayer book has made me yet more vividly aware of how powerful prayer really is. It is, said the eleventh-century poet Judah Halevi, to the soul what food is to the body. Starve a body of food and it dies. Starve a soul of prayer and it atrophies and withers. And sometimes prayer is all the more powerful for being said in words not our own, words that come to us from our people's past, hallowed by time, resonant with the tears and hopes of earlier generations, words that gave them strength and which they handed on to us to use and cherish.

I remember visiting Auschwitz, walking through the gates with their chilling inscription, 'Work makes you free', and feeling the chill winds of Hell. It was a numbing experience. There were no words you could say. It was not until I entered one of the blocks where there was nothing but an old recording of the Jewish memorial prayer for the dead that I broke down and cried. It was then that I realised that prayer makes grief articulate. It gives us the words when there are no words. It gives sacred space to the tears that otherwise would have nowhere to go.

I think back to my father, a Jew of simple faith. In his eighties he had to go through five difficult operations, each of which made him progressively weaker. The most important things he took with him to hospital were his *tefillin* (the leather boxes with straps worn by Jewish men during weekday morning prayer), his prayer book and a Book of Psalms. I used to watch him reciting psalms and see him growing stronger as he did so. He was safe in the arms of God: that was all he knew and all he needed to know. It was only when he said to us, his sons, 'Pray for me' that we knew the end was near. For him, prayer was life, and life a form of prayer.

Prayer changes the world because it changes us. It opens our eyes to the sheer wonder of existence. Is there anything in the scientific literature to match Psalm 104 as a hymn of praise to the ordered complexity of the Universe? There is something in the human spirit that, however intricately it understands the laws of physics and biochemistry, wants not merely to explain but also to celebrate; not just to understand but also to sing.

Prayer teaches us to thank, to rejoice in what we have rather than be eternally driven by what we don't yet have. Prayer is an ongoing seminar in what Daniel Goleman calls emotional intelligence. It sensitises us to the world beyond the self: the real world, not the one defined by our devices and desires.

Daily prayer works on us in ways not immediately apparent. As the sea smooths the stone, as the repeated hammer blows of the sculptor shape the marble, so prayer – repeated, cyclical, tracking the rhythms of time itself – gradually wears away the jagged edges of our character, turning it into a work of devotional art, aligning it with the moral energies of the Universe.

Prayer is not magic. It does not bend the world to our will; if anything it does the opposite. It helps us to notice the things we otherwise take for granted. It redeems our solitude. It gives us a language of aspiration, a vocabulary of ideals. And seeing things differently, we begin to act differently. The world we build tomorrow is born in the prayers we say today.

Armistice Day

11 November 2006

'A nation is not merely a place where we happen to be. It is also a narrative of which we are a part.'

Each year I find myself profoundly moved by the Remembrance Sunday ceremony at the Cenotaph. Though it mainly commemorates events that happened before most of us were born, it speaks eloquently of the qualities we will need if we are to build a decent future.

Originally known as Armistice Day, it was instituted to mark the moment when the guns fell silent at the end of World War I in 1918, on the eleventh hour of the eleventh day of the eleventh month. The poppies are reminders of those that grew in the fields of Flanders, where some of the most prolonged and bloody battles were fought. It was called 'the war to end all wars', but twenty-one years later the world again became a battlefield. Peace and liberty are hard to win, but they are harder still to sustain.

What is it about the ceremony that makes it so potent? First – and foremost – it is a national event, an act of collective identity and belonging. Gathered around the Cenotaph are the Queen and other members of the Royal Family, Prime Ministers past and present, representatives of Parliament and Commonwealth governments, heads of the Armed Forces, religious leaders and, above all, the large contingent of ex-servicemen and women who fought for the freedom we now enjoy. If we seek a living symbol of social cohesion – a nation united in dedication to an ideal – it is there.

Secondly, the Remembrance Sunday ceremony reminds us of the debt we owe to those who came before us. It is an act of thanksgiving by the present to the past – perhaps the only gift the living can give the dead.

Society, said Edmund Burke, is a contract between the dead, the living and those not yet born; and without that sense of intergenerational loyalty, we would never make the sacrifices necessary to a future we may not live to see. We must make space, by way of public silence, to hear the call across the years of those who died: 'When you go home, tell them of us and say / for your tomorrow, we gave our today.'

Thirdly, the ceremony tells us that there can be no identity without a sense of history. To be British, whether by birth or adoption, is to be part of a story, honoured and enacted in rituals, symbols and ceremonies of remembrance.

A nation is not merely a place where we happen to be. It is also a narrative of which we are a part. A society is more than an aggregation of people in a given space. It has a dimension of time as well. It is woven out of the gossamer strands of collective memory: learnt at school, embodied in institutions, reflected in a country's art and literature, poetry and music. Lose these and a nation will suffer the collective equivalent of Alzheimer's disease.

Today we face new battles, radically different from those in the past. There is the fight against terror and the preachers of hate. There is the ongoing struggle to bring stability to parts of the world riven by ethnic and religious rivalries. There is the fight against preventable disease that daily claims the lives of 30,000 of the world's children. There is the campaign against environmental destruction that threatens the very future of life on Earth. The challenges change but the virtues need to stay the same: vision, courage, collective purpose, a willingness to sacrifice for the sake of the future – and above all a sense of history.

Freedom, said Moses at the end of his life, needs the active cultivation of memory. 'Remember the days of old; consider the generations long past. Ask your father and he will tell you, your elders, and they will explain to you' (Deuteronomy 32:7).

If we forget how painfully freedom is won, we will lose it. If we take it for granted, it will not survive. To be guardians of our children's future, we must keep faith with our ancestors' past.

John McCrae, a doctor serving with the Canadian Armed Forces in 1915, saw the devastation of war and scribbled in his pocket book a short poem, *In Flanders Fields*, that gave immortal voice to the charge of the dead to us:

> To you from failing hands we throw
> The torch; be yours to hold it high.
> If ye break faith with us who die
> We shall not sleep, though poppies grow
> In Flanders fields.

Failure

24 February 2007

'Failure is the supreme learning experience and the best people, the true heroes, are those most willing to fail.'

'Tell me,' the young man asked the guru, 'which is the path to success?' The guru said nothing but pointed to a path nearby. The young man almost ran in his enthusiasm to follow the wise one's instructions. Minutes later came a loud 'splat'.

The young man reappeared, bedraggled and covered in mud. Convinced that he must have misunderstood the guru's advice, he asked the wise one again: 'Which is the path to success?' Again the guru pointed in the same direction. A second time the young man set out, and again there was a loud 'splat'.

This time he reappeared before the guru shaking with rage. 'Twice you have pointed to a path, and twice I fell into a muddy pit. This time, no more gestures. Speak. Tell me the path to success.'

The guru looked at the young man and said: 'Success is that way.' Then he added: 'Just a little past splat.'

So write Jerry Porras, Stewart Emery and Mark Thompson in their engaging new book, *Success Built to Last*,* and they are quite right. Success does not mean a life without failure. To the contrary, almost all the great figures in any field – arts, the sciences, business, and certainly the religious life – had more than

* Jerry Porras, Stewart Emery and Mark Thompson, *Success Built to Last: Creating a Life That Matters* (London: Financial Times/Prentice Hall, 2006).

their share of disasters. What marked them out was, first, their willingness to take risks, to experiment, and secondly, their ability to learn from failure rather than be defeated by it.

In my own pear-shaped moments, I think of George Bernard Shaw, who wrote five novels, each of which was turned down by every publisher. Or Van Gogh who, in his lifetime, sold only one of his 1,700 paintings, even though his brother Theo was an art dealer. Or David Hume, who said about his *A Treatise of Human Nature*,* one of the enduring classics of philosophy, that it 'fell stillborn from the press'. And so on.

One of my favourite stories is about Thomas Watson, the legendary head of IBM in the early years of computing. One of IBM's employees had made a bad decision which cost the company $12 million. Eventually he was summoned to see the boss. 'You are right to fire me, Mr Watson. I made a mistake, and it was a bad one.' 'Fire you?' said Watson, 'We've just spent $12 million educating you!'

That is one of the deepest lessons of the spirit. Read the Bible and you will discover that Moses, Elijah, Jeremiah, Jonah and Job all reached a point in their lives when they prayed to die. They felt they had failed. Yet their lives inspire us still, centuries later. They were among the great leaders of all time.

Failure is the supreme learning experience and the best people, the true heroes, are those most willing to fail. Whenever a young rabbi comes to seek advice after making a mistake, I tell him about professional photographers. They take dozens of exposures in the hope that one will be presentable. A success ratio of one in several dozen sounds like failure. But it is that willingness to endure failure in pursuit of an ideal that marks the true professional.

In fact, that is not a bad definition of faith. One of the most empowering truths of Judaism and Christianity is that God forgives our failures so long as we acknowledge them as failures.

* David Hume, *A Treatise of Human Nature* (London: Penguin Classics, 1985).

He does not expect us to be perfect. As Ecclesiastes says: 'No one on Earth is so righteous as to do only right and never to sin' (Ecclesiastes 7:20).

God lifts us when we fall, gives us hope when we despair, and believes in us more than we believe in ourselves. In truth, the great religious leaders did not believe in themselves at all. 'I am not a man of words,' said Moses when asked to lead the Israelites. 'I cannot speak, I am only a child,' said Jeremiah, when told to preach God's word.

'The credit belongs,' said Theodore Roosevelt, to one 'who strives valiantly' and errs often, 'because there is no effort without error or shortcoming.' Even if such a person fails, he 'fails while daring greatly, so his place shall never be with those cold and timid souls who know neither victory nor defeat.'

Even more than the strength to win, we need the courage to try, the willingness to fail, the readiness to learn and the faith to persist.

Resolutions

5 January 2008

'The great religions are our richest treasuries of wisdom when it comes to the question of how best to live a life.'

Have you made your new year resolutions? If not, try the following. Each is potentially life changing.

1. Give thanks. Once a day, take quiet time to feel gratitude for what you have, not impatience for what you don't have. This alone will bring you halfway to happiness. We already have most of the ingredients of a happy life. It's just that we tend to take these for granted and focus on unmet wants, unfulfilled desires. Giving thanks is better than shopping – and cheaper too.
2. Praise. Catch someone doing something right and say so. Most people, most of the time, are unappreciated. Being recognised, thanked and congratulated by someone else is one of the most empowering things that can happen to us. So don't wait for someone to do it for you: do it for someone else. You will make their day, and that will help to make yours.
3. Spend time with your family. Make sure that there is at least one time a week when you sit down to have a meal together with no distractions – no television, no phone, no email, just being together and celebrating one another's company. Happy marriages and healthy families need dedicated time.
4. Discover meaning. Take time out, once in a while, to ask: 'Why am I here? What do I hope to achieve? How best can I

use my gifts? What would I wish to be said about me when I am no longer here?' Finding meaning is essential to a fulfilled life – and how can you find it if you never look? If you don't know where you want to be, you will never get there, however fast you run.

5. Live your values. Most of us believe in high ideals, but we act on them only sporadically. The best thing to do is to establish habits that get us to enact those ideals daily. This is called ritual, and it is what religions remember but ethicists often forget.
6. Forgive. This is the emotional equivalent of losing excess weight. Life is too short to bear a grudge or seek revenge. Forgiving someone is good for them but even better for you. The bad has happened. It won't be made better by your dwelling on it. Let it go. Move on.
7. Keep learning. I learnt this from Florence in Newcastle, whom I last met the day she celebrated her 105th birthday. She was still full of energy and fun. 'What's the secret?' I asked her. 'Never be afraid to learn something new,' she said. Then I realised that if you are willing to learn, you can be 105 and still young. If you are not, you can be twenty-five and already old.
8. Learn to listen. Often in conversation we spend half our time thinking of what we want to say next instead of paying attention to what the other person is saying. Listening is one of the greatest gifts we can give to someone else. It means that we are open to them, that we take them seriously and that we accept graciously their gift of words.
9. Create moments of silence in the soul. Liberate yourself, if only five minutes daily, from the tyranny of technology, the mobile phone, the laptop and all the other electronic intruders, and just inhale the heady air of existence, the joy of being.
10. Transform suffering. When bad things happen, use them to sensitise you to the pain of others. The greatest people I know

> – people who survived tragedy and became stronger as a result – did not ask 'Who did this to me?' Instead, they asked 'What does this allow me to do that I could not have done before?' They refused to become victims of circumstance. They became, instead, agents of hope.

Most of these are, of course, integral elements of a religious life, which may be why so many surveys have shown that those who practise a religious faith tend to live longer, have lower levels of stress and report higher degrees of well-being than others. This is not accidental. The great religions are our richest treasuries of wisdom when it comes to the question of how best to live a life.

Life is too full of blessings to waste time and attention on artificial substitutes. Live, give, forgive, celebrate and praise: these are still the best ways of making a blessing over life, thereby turning life into a blessing.

Climate Change

5 April 2008

'Genesis 1 is best understood not as pseudo-science, still less as myth, but as jurisprudence; that is to say, as the foundation of the moral law.'

If we understood the first chapter of Genesis, we might put an end to some of the needless arguments between scientists and religious believers.

The first thing to note is its sheer brevity. It takes a mere thirty-four verses. The Hebrew Bible takes some fifteen times as long to describe the Israelites' creation of the sanctuary in the wilderness. It is astonishing that the world's greatest and most influential account of the origins of the Universe is so short.

Next is its numerical structure. We know the significance of the number seven. The Universe is made in seven days. Seven times the word 'good' is used. But the pattern goes deeper than that. The first verse of Genesis contains seven Hebrew words, the second, fourteen. The account of the seventh day contains thirty-five. The word 'God' appears thirty-five times; the word 'Earth' twenty-one. The entire passage contains 469 (7 x 67) words. By these hints, something is being intimated. The Universe has a structure, and it is mathematical.

Then there is the structure itself. On the first three days God creates domains: light and dark, upper and lower waters, sea and dry land. On the next three days He populates these domains one by one: first the sun, moon and stars, then birds and fish, then land animals and human beings. The seventh day is holy. So, six (the days of creation) symbolises the natural order, seven the supernatural.

As if by way of unintended confirmation, Sir Martin Rees, the Astronomer Royal, wrote a book, *Just Six Numbers*,* in which he showed that the entire structure of the physical Universe is determined by six mathematical constants.

Beyond these structural features is a sharp polemic. Most readers of the Bible are only dimly aware of the degree to which it is shaped by a polemic against myth. In the case of Genesis 1 this is obvious. What is missing is the element of struggle between rival gods that dominates all mythical accounts of creation. In the biblical account there is no opposition, no conflict. God speaks and the world comes into being. Max Weber called this the 'disenchantment', the demythologising, of the world. He believed it to be the foundation of Western rationalism.

There are times when the polemic is more subtle. Read the account of the second day, when the waters are divided, and you will see that it alone of the six days lacks the word 'good'. Instead, 'good' appears twice on the third day. This is an allusion to one of the most common features of myth: the primal battle against the goddess of the sea, symbol of the forces of chaos. The Bible dismisses this in a single oblique reference, that imposing order on the primal waters took one and a half days instead of one. The creation account is anti-myth.

So Genesis 1 is not a proto-scientific account of the birth of the Universe and the Big Bang. Its purpose is clear. The Universe is good: hence world-denying nihilism is ruled out. It is the result of a single creative will, so myth is eliminated. The Universe is a place of structure and order, so the text is an invitation to science, by implying that the world is not irrational and ruled by capricious powers.

Why, then, is Genesis 1 there? We are puzzled by that question because we forget that the Hebrew Bible is called, in Judaism, Torah, meaning teaching, guidance or more specifically, law.

* Martin Rees, *Just Six Numbers: The Deep Forces That Shape the Universe* (London: Weidenfeld & Nicolson, 1999).

Genesis 1 is best understood not as pseudo-science, still less as myth, but as jurisprudence; that is to say, as the foundation of the moral law. God created the world; therefore, God owns the world. We are His guests – strangers and temporary residents, as the Bible puts it. God has the right to specify the conditions of our tenancy on Earth. The radical message of Genesis 1 is that Divine sovereignty is constitutional. God rules not by might, but by right, and so must we.

So Genesis 1 can be restated in terms with which even the most avowed secularist might agree. The world does not belong to us. We hold it as trustees on behalf of those who will come after us.

Renouncing our ownership of the Earth is all we need to ground what is surely the fundamental point of the story itself: that we are here to protect, not destroy or endanger, the Earth and all it contains.

Contracts and Covenants

23 January 2009

'Covenantal politics is less about governments than about "we, the people" and our responsibilities to one another.'

Watching Barack Obama deliver his Inaugural Address on Tuesday, we knew we were seeing history being made. All the ingredients were there: the first African American president in history, the sense of crisis to which he referred four times, the almost two million people present, stretching from the Capitol all the way to the Washington Monument, the hundreds of millions watching throughout the world.

But how many fully understood precisely what he was doing? He was doing something almost unintelligible in terms of British political culture, yet central to that of the United States. He was, and knew he was, renewing the covenant. From time to time British politicians use the word 'covenant'. But in the United States it is more than a word: it is its defining purpose as 'one nation under God'. In a sense deeper than we can readily imagine, America sees itself as a covenanted nation.

There is a fundamental difference between contracts and covenants. In a contract, two or more individuals, each pursuing their own interest, come together to make an exchange for mutual benefit. When we pay someone to do something for us, implicitly or explicitly we make a contract.

A covenant is something different. In a covenant, two or more individuals, each respecting the dignity and integrity of the other, come together in a bond of mutual responsibility to do together what neither can achieve alone. It is not about interests but about loyalty, fidelity, holding together when events seem to be driving you apart. A covenant is less like a deal than like a marriage: it is a moral bond.

In the seventeenth and eighteenth centuries, after more than a century of religious wars, European thinkers reflected deeply about what holds a nation together despite its differences. Out of this emerged a key idea shared by Hobbes, Locke and Rousseau: the social contract that creates a state.

The Founding Fathers of America thought in terms of a different idea. They derived it from the Bible: the moment at Mount Sinai when the Israelites bound themselves by sacred covenant to become one nation under God, a phrase that became part of the American pledge of allegiance. They thought not of the social contract that creates a state, but of the social covenant that creates a society.

A social contract is about power; a social covenant is about collective responsibility. A social contract is about governments and laws. A social covenant is about the shared ideals of its citizens, to which Barack Obama referred when he spoke about 'the God-given promise that all are equal, all are free and all deserve a chance to pursue their full measure of happiness'.

Virtually every American president since Washington in 1789 has renewed the covenant in his Inaugural Address, often in biblical terms. Obama's was a textbook example. There was the reference to the Exodus, a journey through the wilderness that involved crossing a sea: 'They packed up their few worldly possessions and travelled across oceans.' There was the covenant itself: 'Our Founding Fathers . . . drafted a charter to assure the rule of law and the rights of man.'

There was the key covenantal virtue, faithfulness: 'We the people have remained faithful to the ideals of our forebears and true to our founding documents.' There was the idea, central to covenant, of a commitment handed on by parents to children: 'that noble idea, passed on from generation to generation'. There was the principle that nations flourish not by the power of the state but by the duty and dedication of their citizens: 'It is ultimately the faith and determination of the American people upon which this nation relies.'

Obama's ending was little less than biblical: 'Let it be said by our children's children . . . that we did not turn back, nor did we falter; and with eyes fixed on the horizon and God's grace upon us, we carried forth that great gift of freedom and delivered it safely to future generations.'

Covenantal politics is less about governments than about 'we, the people' and our responsibilities to one another. It measures the strength of a nation not by the size of its army or its economy, but by the willingness of its citizens to rise to the call of our 'duties to ourselves, our nation, and the world'.

What Barack Obama has understood is that covenant creates the politics of hope. Never has the future of freedom needed it more.

The Probability of Faith

27 February 2009

'You don't have to be religious to have a sense of awe at the sheer improbability of things.'

We owe a debt to the British Humanist Association for its advert on buses: 'There's probably no God.' It is thought-provoking in a helpful way, because it invites us to reflect not only on God but also on probability.

One of the discoveries of modern science is the sheer improbability of the Universe. It is shaped by six fundamental forces which, had they varied by an infinitesimal amount, the Universe would have expanded or imploded in such a way as to preclude the formation of stars. Unless we assume the existence of a million or trillion other universes (itself a large leap of faith), the fact that there is a Universe at all is massively improbable.

So is the existence of life. Among the hundred billion galaxies, each with billions of stars, only one planet known to us, Earth, seems finely tuned for the emergence of life. And by what intermediate stages did non-life become life?

It's a puzzle so improbable that Francis Crick was forced to argue that life was born somewhere else, Mars perhaps, and came here via meteorite, so making the mystery yet more mysterious.

How did life become sentient? And how did sentience grow to become self-consciousness, that strange gift known only to *Homo sapiens*? So many improbabilities, Stephen J. Gould concluded, that if the process of evolution were run again from the beginning it is doubtful whether *Homo sapiens* would ever have been born.

You don't have to be religious to have a sense of awe at the sheer improbability of things. A few weeks ago, James Le Fanu published a book, *Why Us?*[*] In it he argues that we are about to undergo a paradigm shift in scientific understanding. The complexities of the genome, the emergence of the first multicellular life forms, the origins of *Homo sapiens* and our prodigiously enlarged brain: all these and more are too subtle to be accounted for on reductive, materialist, Darwinian science.

A week later Michael Brooks brought out *13 Things That Don't Make Sense*,[†] the most important being human free will. The more science we learn, the more we understand how little we understand. The improbabilities keep multiplying, as does our cause for wonder.

And that's just at the level of science. What about history? How probable is it that one man who performed no miracles and wielded no power, Abraham, would become the most influential figure who ever lived, with more than half of the six billion people alive today tracing their spiritual descent to him?

How probable is it that a tiny people, the children of Israel, known today as Jews, numbering less than a fifth of a per cent of the population of the world, would outlive every empire that sought its destruction? Or that a small, persecuted sect known as the Christians would one day become the largest movement of any kind in the world?

How probable is it that slavery would be abolished, that tyrannies would fall, that Apartheid would end and that an African American would be elected President of the United States? Everything interesting in life, the Universe and the whole shebang is improbable, as Nicholas Taleb reminds us in *The Black Swan*, subtitled 'The Impact of the Highly Improbable'.[‡] The book's

* James Le Fanu, *Why Us?: How Science Rediscovered the Mystery of Ourselves* (London: HarperPress, 2010).

† Michael Brooks, *13 Things That Don't Make Sense: the Most Baffling Scientific Mysteries of Our Time* (New York: Doubleday, 2008).

‡ Nicholas Taleb, *Black Swan: The Impact of the Highly Improbable* (New York: Random House, 2007).

title is drawn from the fact that people were convinced that, since no one had ever seen a black swan, they did not exist – until someone discovered Australia.

One interesting improbability is that the man who invented probability theory, a brilliant young mathematician called Blaise Pascal, decided at the age of thirty to give up mathematics and science and devote the rest of his life to the exploration of religious faith.

Faith is the defeat of probability by the power of possibility. The prophets dreamt the improbable and by doing so helped to bring it about. All the great human achievements, in art and science as well as the life of the spirit, came through people who ignored the probable and had faith in the possible.

So the bus advertisement would be improved by a small amendment. Instead of saying 'There's probably no God', it should read: 'Improbably, there is a God'.

Crisis

29 May 2009

'Somehow, within every crisis lies the glorious possibility of rebirth.'

You find yourself in the midst of crisis. You lose your job or miss the promotion you were expecting. You find yourself with a medical condition that requires a radical change of lifestyle. You make a bad investment that costs you dearly. You find an important relationship in your life under stress. Any of these, or the thousand other shocks that flesh is heir to, can plunge you, without warning, into crisis. What then do you do? How do you survive the trauma and the pain?

I have found one biblical passage deeply helpful. It is not an obvious one. It does not come from the Book of Psalms, that lexicon of the soul, or from Isaiah, the poet laureate of hope. Instead, it comes from the famous, enigmatic passage in Genesis 32 in which Jacob, far from home, wrestles with an unknown, unnamed adversary from night until the break of day.

The context is important: twenty-two years earlier Jacob had left home, fearing that his brother Esau, whose blessing he had taken, would kill him. Now he is returning when he hears that Esau is on his way to meet him with a force of 400 men. Jacob, says the Bible, was 'very afraid and distressed' (Genesis 32:8), an unusually emphatic phrase in a book that often tells us little about people's emotions.

Jacob becomes a whirl of activity. He dispatches emissaries with gifts of flocks and herds, hoping to propitiate his brother. He prays to God for protection. He divides his camp into two, so that if one is destroyed the other may survive. Jacob's hyperactivity is not only pragmatic, covering all the options. It is also a measure of the stress he is under. He knows he is facing the defining crisis of his life.

It is then that the famous scene enacts itself: 'Jacob was left alone, and a man wrestled with him till daybreak' (Genesis 32:25).

Who was the man? The text does not say. The prophet Hosea said that Jacob wrestled with an angel. Jacob himself believed he was wrestling with God. He called the place Peniel, 'the face of God', saying: 'It is because I saw God face to face, and my life was spared' (Genesis 32:31).

Jacob's struggle tells us three things. First, the wrestling match takes place after Jacob has made all his preparations. The real crisis, the inner crisis, catches us unaware and unprepared. However much we plan in advance, factor in all the contingencies, rehearse every scenario, there are events that take us by surprise. That is the human condition. We live with constitutive uncertainty. Those who fear risk fear life itself. 'One thing', goes the old Jewish saying, 'makes God laugh: seeing our plans for the future.' Freedom means the courage to live with the unknowable-in-advance. That is why freedom is ultimately impossible without faith.

The second is that the real battle that decides our future lies within the self, the soul. If Jacob can successfully wrestle with God, then he can face his brother Esau without fear. If we can win the struggle 'in here', we can also win it 'out there'. That is what Roosevelt meant when he said in 1933, in the midst of the Great Depression, that 'the only thing we have to fear is fear itself'.

It is the third point, though, that has made all the difference to me. Jacob says to the stranger/angel/God, 'I will not let you go until you bless me' (Genesis 32:27).

Somehow, within every crisis lies the glorious possibility of rebirth. I have found, and so surely have many others, that the events that at the time were the most painful were also those that in retrospect most caused us to grow. They helped us to make difficult but necessary decisions. They forced us to ask: 'Who am I, and what really matters to me?' They moved us from the surface to the depths, where we discovered strengths we did not know we had, and a clarity of purpose we had hitherto lacked. I have learnt to say to every crisis: 'I will not let you go until you bless me' (Genesis 32:27).

The struggle is not easy. Though Jacob was undefeated, after it he 'limped' (Genesis 32:32). Battles leave scars. Yet God is with us even when He seems to be against us. For if we refuse to let go of Him, He refuses to let go of us, giving us the strength to survive and emerge stronger, wiser, blessed.

Religion and Science

29 August 2009

'Judaism recognises two distinct sources of knowledge, wisdom and Torah, the products respectively of reason and revelation.'

In 1993 I received an honorary doctorate from Cambridge University, with James Watson, co-discoverer with Francis Crick of DNA. The meeting gave me the opportunity to say the blessing, coined by the sages 2,000 years ago and still to be found in all Jewish prayer books, thanking God for bestowing his wisdom on human beings.

Essentially it is a blessing to be said on seeing a great scientist, although the word 'scientist' was not coined until 1833. What a difference between the first century and now, when there seems so often to be at worst hostility, at best estrangement, between religion and science. It should not be like that.

The rabbis had every reason to fear science. It was done, in their day, by the Greeks, and there was a profound difference between the two cultures, so much so that Jews had fought a war – essentially a war of culture – against Hellenism. The name Epicurus, the Greek thinker who more than anyone presaged atomic science, was synonymous for Jews with heretic.

Yet the rabbis knew wisdom when they saw it, and they valued it even though they dissented from some of its conclusions. They did so for three reasons. First, it was evidence of the fact that God had indeed created humankind 'in His image, after His likeness' (Genesis 1:27), meaning, according to Jewish tradition, 'with the capacity to understand and discern'. Intellect, insight, the ability to frame and test hypotheses: these are God-given and a reason to give thanks.

Second, scientific method can apply to religion as well. The Talmud tells the story of a Rabbi Shimon Ha'amsoni who had spent a lifetime applying certain exegetical principles to biblical texts. On one occasion he encountered a verse which, if interpreted by his rules, would yield an unacceptable conclusion. He then and there declared his principles unsound, in effect abandoning his entire life's work. His students were aghast. They asked him: 'Are you really willing to give up everything you have taught because of one counter example?' He smiled and said, 'Just as I received a [Divine] reward for the exposition, so I will receive a reward for the retraction.' This is in effect an anticipation, many centuries earlier, of Karl Popper's account of scientific method. Religion may not be science, but it can use the same rules of logic.

Third, science, regardless of the conclusions drawn from it, provides stunning testimony to the law-governed orderliness of the Universe and the beauty and intricacy of creation. That was evident to the sages long ago, and it has become all the more pronounced today. I lose count of the number of times I have had reason to say, reading about some new scientific discovery, 'How many are your works, O Lord: You have created them all in wisdom' (Psalm 104:24).

The rabbis felt so strongly about this that they said of those who could study astronomy but failed to do so that they were the people about whom the prophet Isaiah was speaking when he said, 'they have no regard for the deeds of the Lord, no respect for the work of His hands' (Isaiah 5:12).

One passage in the Talmud is indicative of the rabbinical approach. The topic under discussion is the question, 'Where does the sun go at night?' The sages give their account. Next, they give the Greek account, that of Ptolemy. They then conclude that the Greek explanation is more plausible than the Jewish one. End of discussion. They got it right; we got it wrong. That to me is a model of intellectual integrity.

I mentioned that the Jewish blessing on seeing a great scientist uses the word 'wisdom', and that is the key concept. Judaism recognises two distinct sources of knowledge, wisdom and Torah, the products respectively of reason and revelation. Entire books of the Bible, notably Proverbs, Ecclesiastes and Job, are dedicated to wisdom. Unlike revelation, wisdom is universal. Anyone can achieve it, regardless of religious belief, and traces of it are to be found in all the world's cultures.

There are tensions between reason and revelation, and that is particularly evident in Ecclesiastes and Job, two of the most dissident books ever to be included in a canon of sacred scriptures. Yet they too are part of the religious life.

So, let's continue to thank God for great scientists. Religion is about open hearts, not closed minds.

What Religions Teach Us

31 October 2009

'The best identities speak to the better angels of our nature, especially when they include saintly role models, high ideals and the imperative to love the stranger.'

Atheists tend to think that religion is about God. Of course, it is. But if that is all it is, it would hardly explain religion's tenacity and power, its hold on the human imagination and its strange capacity both to unite and divide.

Religion is also about identity. It is an answer to a set of questions that science cannot answer, perhaps cannot even understand. Who am I? Why am I here? Where do I belong? Of what story am I a part? How am I connected to those who came before me? How then shall I live?

The great religions answer these questions against the broadest possible background and in the richest possible way. They celebrate identity in stories, rituals, celebrations, prayers and holy days. They speak of the Universe, creation, revelation and redemption. They show us role models of sages and saints, heroes and heroines, exemplary lives. They tell us who we are and what we are called on to be.

Religions are not the only source of identity. Some find theirs in nationhood, others in their work, especially if they see it as a calling. Some find it in a cause. Yet others find it in ethnicity. Some even find it in the football team they support (remember Bill Shankly's 'Some people believe football is a matter of life and death, but I can assure you it's much, much more important than that'?).

Should we even have identities? There have been people who said 'no'. There were universalists such as Socrates, who said: 'I am not an Athenian or a Greek, but a citizen of the world.' There are cosmopolitans whose identity, like my grandmother's recipe for chicken soup, is 'a little bit of this, a little bit of that'. There are people who change lifestyles the way that other people change their clothes. There are even postmodernists who deny identity altogether. Life for them, as with advertising on television, is simply a series of episodes with no connecting thread.

One thing is clear: identity has become problematic in the modern world. The sociologist Peter Berger defined modernity as a state of permanent identity crisis. Many of the secular alternatives to religious identity proved terrifying in their consequences. National identity led to nationalism and two world wars. Ethnicity led to racism and the Holocaust. The 'cause' led, among other things, to Communism and Stalinist Russia. Even football, more harmless than most, can lead to violence. As for those who deny identity, it's quite hard to be everyone in general without being anyone in particular. Even cosmopolitans tend to be comfortable in the company of other cosmopolitans, and feel threatened in the presence of other, stronger identities.

This is one reason why religion has returned, centre stage, in the twenty-first century, because of the waning of secular alternatives. Most of us need identity as our way of being at home in the world. It helps to be able to say: 'This is my story; this is who I am.' It's within our particular identities that we learn to live, love, create communities and cultivate responsibilities. The best identities speak to the better angels of our nature, especially when they include saintly role models, high ideals and the imperative to love the stranger.

But there is a great danger, and those of us who are religious must be honest about it. Far too often in the past religious identities have been a source of strife. Identity can lead us to divide the world into two, 'Us' and 'Them', the children of light against the children of darkness. The history of the great monotheisms has been written in the tears caused by clashing identities. The great unsolved problem facing these religions is: can we make space for one another?

I think we can. The paradox of identity is that it is precisely when we speak from within our particularity that we strike a chord with others of different particularity. You don't have to be French to love Flaubert, Russian to admire Tolstoy or Japanese to enjoy a haiku. Affirming our identity need not involve negating anyone else's. I can say this is who I am, without saying or implying that this is the only way to be. If Jews, Christians and Muslims can rise to this generosity of spirit, then we can celebrate the fact that we each have our particular way of being at home within the glorious diversity of humankind.

Faith Schools

27 March 2010

'Communities last longer than any individual, so they preserve a respect for the past and responsibility toward the future.'

Faith schools – so their opponents argue – are divisive, retrograde, narrow, insular, hostile to science and the critical mind, unable to teach their pupils tolerance and fundamentally opposed to the values of a free society. These claims are not made lightly, nor should they be lightly dismissed.

But if they are true, there is an obvious question. Why do so many parents want to send their children to such schools? Do they passionately want their children to be narrow and insular? Is their deepest ambition to raise offspring who will have no truck with tolerance? Do they secretly long for the next generation to lead society boldly back to the Middle Ages? Maybe there are such people, but I haven't met one yet.

Here is the paradox. We are living in what is possibly the most secular age since *Homo sapiens* first set foot on Earth, and Europe is its most secular continent. Yet faith schools are the growth industry of our time. More and more people want them and are prepared to go to great lengths to get their children admitted. This applies to parents who are not themselves religious. What is going on?

The simple answer is that faith schools tend to have academic success above the average: so, at any rate, the league tables suggest. But why should this be so, if faith inhibits critical thought and discourages independence of mind? This is a question worth serious reflection.

My tentative suggestion is that faith schools tend to have a strong ethos that emphasises respect for authority, the virtues of hard work, discipline and a sense of duty, a commitment to high ideals, a willingness to learn, a sense of social responsibility, a preference for earned self-respect rather than unearned self-esteem and the idea of an objective moral order that transcends subjective personal preference.

The parents I meet worry about the breakdown of discipline in many schools. They read about violence and drugs, promiscuity and teenage pregnancy, dysfunctional families and feral teenagers. They are concerned about the sheer numbers of children who leave school without the most basic skills of numeracy and literacy. They recall the 2007 UNICEF report that found that British children were the most unhappy in the developed world. They sense that something is going wrong and they don't want to expose their children to that kind of risk.

These phenomena are not the fault of schools. To the contrary, they are the result of our culture as a whole, to which children are exposed through television, video games, the internet and the sheer materialism and shallowness of contemporary society. The parents may not be religious themselves – often they aren't – but they sense that faith schools preserve values, disciplines and habits of the heart that are elsewhere being lost.

I say this tentatively. I may be wrong. Of one thing I am convinced, that all schools and teachers are trying their hardest, but they often feel desperately unsupported by parents, the local community and the media. How can they mend what they did not break in the first place? Too often we expect schools to do the impossible. Teachers deserve our highest respect. They are the guardians of our civilisation, the trustees of our collective future.

But just as – in the words of the African saying – it takes a village to raise a child, so it takes a community to sustain a school, and communities are hard to find these days. A community is held together by shared beliefs, traditions, rituals, stories, conventions and codes: the regular enactments of a sense of shared belonging.

Communities last longer than any individual, so they preserve a respect for the past and responsibility toward the future. Nowadays it's hard to find a genuine community outside the world of faith. Lifestyle enclaves, fan clubs and virtual networks linked by Twitter and Facebook, yes; face-to-face *communitas*, no.

So, it may not be the faith in faith schools that makes them different, so much as the communities that build, support and sustain them. But this fact too should give us pause for thought. For is this not one of the great functions of faith, that it preserves values and institutions that would otherwise be swept away by the tide of time? One way or another, the critics should reflect on this simple question: If faith schools are so bad, why do thoughtful, often secular, parents think they are so good?

Books

24 September 2011

'Descartes said, "I think, therefore I am." Jews said, "I learn, therefore I am."'

One year, when David Blunkett was Secretary of State for Education, he mentioned that he was dedicating the coming school year to a campaign for literacy. Did I have, he asked, a Jewish saying about literacy? I replied that the start of the academic year almost always coincides with the Jewish High Holy Days, the New Year and the Day of Atonement. For the whole of that time we pray to God to 'write us in the Book of Life'. When Jews think of life, I said, they think of a book. For us, to read is to live.

So I was struck by Caitlin Moran's powerful plea in August for local libraries to be spared in the programme of government cuts. Libraries, she said, are 'cathedrals of the mind; hospitals of the soul; theme parks of the imagination. On a cold, rainy island, they are the only sheltered public spaces where you are not a consumer, but a citizen instead. A human with a brain and a heart and a desire to be uplifted, rather than a customer with a credit card.'

How true and beautifully said. It is impossible to exaggerate the extent to which Jews are – the phrase comes from the Koran – a 'People of the Book'. I have argued that Judaism took the form it did because of one of the great revolutions in information technology, the invention of the alphabet as opposed to the sign-based systems of Mesopotamian cuneiform and Egyptian hieroglyphics.

To understand those systems, you had to memorise hundreds of symbols, which meant that only a minority could do so. The result was literate elites and hierarchical societies. The first alphabet, Proto-Semitic, which appeared in the Sinai desert some thirty-eight centuries ago, had little more than twenty symbols. For the first time the possibility was born of a society of universal literacy. That is what Isaiah meant when he said, 'All your children will be learned of the Lord and great will be the peace of your children' (Isaiah 54:13).

From the beginning, Judaism became a religion in which education was the fundamental act. 'Teach your children,' says Moses time and again. 'Teach them', says our holiest prayer, the *Shema*, 'when you are sitting at home or travelling on a journey, when you lie down and when you rise up' (Deuteronomy 6:7). The Talmud holds study as a religious act higher even than prayer.

The holiest object in Judaism is a book, the Scroll of the Law. The reverence we pay it is astonishing. We stand in its presence as if it were a king, dance with it as if it were a bride, and if, God forbid, it is desecrated or ruined beyond repair we bury it as if it were a relative who had died.

Somehow that reverence transferred itself to books in general. Descartes said, 'I think, therefore I am.' Jews said, 'I learn, therefore I am.' That reverence for study stayed with Jews, however estranged from religion they became. Sergey Brin, co-founder of Google, once said about himself that he came 'from one of those Russian Jewish families where they expected even the plumber to have a PhD'.

So I resonated to Caitlin Moran's description of books as gateways – 'each book-lid opened was as exciting as Alice putting her gold key in the door'. A great book is a life-enlarging journey of the mind. That is an idea we must never lose. Libraries are an essential element of a good society. They democratise knowledge, giving us all equal access to the heritage of humankind. There are many kinds of poverty we should try to eliminate, but I wonder whether intellectual impoverishment may not be the deepest and most debilitating of all.

John Donne wrote that 'All mankind is of one author, and is one volume.' He related this to death: 'When one man dies, one chapter is not torn out of the book, but translated into a better language.' In Judaism, we prefer to think about life. We are each a letter in God's book. Like a letter, we have no meaning on our own, but joined to others in families, communities and nations we form sentences and paragraphs and become part of God's story.

Isaac Bashevis Singer once said: 'God is a writer, and we are His co-authors.' So, at this holy time of the year, we pray to be written into God's Book of Life. May we never lose our love of books or of life.

Jewish Advice

31 December 2011

'When business is bad, invest in the spirit. If the economy stops growing, your happiness can still increase.'

An old Jewish story: Mendel meets David. He says, 'Tell me, friend, how is life? I haven't got much time, so tell me in one word.' David says, 'In one word? Good.' Mendel says, 'Give me a bit more detail. In two words, how is life?' David replies: 'In two words? Not good.'

That was 2011. It may be true for 2012. As a nation, we're wealthier and healthier, but the economic outlook is uncertain and much of the world is troubled, if not in turmoil.

What would be some Jewish advice for the coming year? First, thank God. Jews call this *Barukh Hashem*, 'Blessed be the Lord.' In the shtetls, where Jews were poor and persecuted but deeply religious, if you asked: 'How is business?' the answer would come back: '*Barukh Hashem*.' 'How is the family?' '*Barukh Hashem*.' 'Your health?' '*Barukh Hashem*.'

You might be ill, your children rebellious, your business terrible, but you thanked God. Jews knew how to rejoice in the midst of hardship. They laughed, they celebrated, they had the gift of *simcha*, the Jewish word for joy. They were not fools. They knew their fate was wretched. But they felt close to God. After all, he prayed in the same synagogue that they did.

Second, love. Love your spouse and you will have a happy marriage. Love your children and you will have a happy family. Love your work and you will have a happy career. Love life and you will be blessed. 'If only' is the opposite of love. If only I was more attractive, my children more appreciative, my colleagues more friendly, if only I earned more, achieved more. 'If only' is toxic to happiness. It focuses on what we don't have instead of what we do. The consumer culture invites us to an existence of 'if only'. It's the worst investment in life.

True faith is all about love. Love God with all your heart, your soul, your might. Love your neighbour as yourself. Love the stranger because to others you are a stranger. You don't have to be religious to love, but you have to love to be religious. Love is the space we make for that which is not me. By opening ourselves to something bigger than ourselves, we grow.

Third, pray. Prayer is our dialogue with the infinite Other. It's also hard, which is why we have prayer books. The finest collection of prayers is the Book of Psalms. It embraces the spectrum of feeling from despair to jubilation. Prayer is to the soul what exercise is to the body, and without it we become emotionally flabby.

Some people don't pray because they try it and it does not work. They forget that prayer is done best in the company of others, in a holy place, in song, the language of the soul as it reaches out toward the unsayable. The most life-transforming prayers are choral not solo.

Iris Murdoch has a lovely analogy for what prayer can achieve. She describes looking out of a window in an anxious and resentful state of mind, oblivious of her surroundings, brooding on some resentment, feeling sorry for herself. Then, suddenly, she sees a hovering kestrel. 'In a moment', she says, 'everything is altered. The brooding self . . . has disappeared. There is nothing now but kestrel. And when I return to thinking of the other matter it seems less important.' She calls this 'unselfing', and that is what prayer achieves at its best. It opens our eyes to the wonder of the world.

Three suggestions: more next month. But the principle is simple. When business is bad, invest in the spirit. If the economy stops growing, your happiness can still increase.

Achieving Happiness

28 January 2012

'... happiness is not something we find but something we make.'

Last month I made some suggestions for finding happiness in hard times. Here are some more for 2012.

First, thank. Don't just thank God: thank people. There is almost nothing you can do to bring warmth into someone else's life than simple, honest recognition for something they have done, especially if it's the kind of thing most people take for granted. Do it for your children's teachers, your work colleagues, the person at the checkout counter, anyone who does the kind of work we often call 'thankless'.

If you have a spare moment – you're waiting in a queue somewhere – think back to someone who, many years ago, made a positive difference to your life and whom you didn't thank at the time: a teacher who inspired you, perhaps, or a friend who gave you good advice or lifted you when you were low. Write to them and tell them so. This one act can transform a life, and giving a satisfaction to others is the best way of finding it yourself. Remember Paul McCartney's words in *Abbey Road*: 'The love you take is equal to the love you make.' Ditto for happiness.

Second, resolve to be active not passive. Be a doer, not a complainer. Light a candle, don't curse the darkness. Don't criticise leaders: lead. Don't wait for something to happen: help bring it about. Life is too short to be a spectator rather than a player. So, sit less, exercise more. Drive less, walk more. Neuroscientists have made the heartening discovery that physical exertion renews our brain cells. It actually keeps us mentally as well as physically young. It also produces the endorphins that fight depression and produce exhilaration. Moses Maimonides, the twelfth-century rabbi who was also one of the leading physicians of his day, held that keeping fit was a religious duty. God gave us life and we honour Him by using it to the full.

Third, be part of a community. There is something transformative about being part of a group who pray, celebrate, remember and hope together. If it takes a village to raise a child, then it takes a community to reach a full flowering of happiness. Virtual communities linked by smartphones are no substitute for real face-to-face encounter. Community is where our grief is halved and our joy doubled by being shared with others.

Fourth, make a thorough clear-out of negative emotions. Apologise to those you've wronged and forgive those who have wronged you. Emotional energy is too precious to waste it on guilt on the one hand, resentment on the other.

We find it hard to apologise because we are our own best counsel for the defence. We rationalise, justify, make excuses, and are generally willing to blame anyone but ourselves. It wasn't me, or if it was, I couldn't help it, or I didn't mean it. Yet although we think we can persuade the jury, deep down we know we can't convince ourselves. Self-deception always carries too high a price.

One of the odd things about the Hebrew Bible is its devastating honesty. The Israelites blame no one but themselves. 'We sinned,' they said. 'We drifted, worshipped strange gods, we were ungrateful, disloyal, we dishonoured God.' The prophets never blamed other nations, other people or God. They were the polar opposite of the culture of victimhood that has become so popular in recent years. They absorbed all the guilt and turned it into the positive energy of repentance and renewal.

They were able to be honest because they knew that God forgives. In a wholly secular culture, forgiveness is either absent or, at best, some vague indifference to morality altogether. Forgiveness is not indifference. Apologising is not making excuses. The power of simply being able to say, 'I was wrong, I hurt you, I am truly sorry, forgive me,' is that it allows honesty to purge our lives of self-righteousness, the most toxic of all emotions.

All these are ways of saying that happiness is not something we find but something we make. You can tell the people who know this. They radiate positive energy. They give you a sense of worth and acceptance. When you speak, they listen. When you make an effort, they notice. In their presence you feel enlarged.

When love of God leads you to a love of life and a life of love, you will find happiness even in hard times.

A Life Worth Living

5 January 2013

'The great lives are ones where people heard a call, had a sense of vocation.'

I spend a lot of time with young people – pupils about to leave school, students at university and graduates about to start a career. Often they ask me for advice as they begin their journey into the future. Here are some of the ideas worth thinking about as we begin our journey into a new calendar year.

The first idea is to dream. Seemingly the least practical activity turns out to be the most practical, and most often left undone. I know people who spend months planning a holiday but very little time planning a life. Imagine setting out on a journey without deciding where you are going to. However fast you travel, you will never reach your destination because you never decided where you want to be. In fact, the faster you travel, the more lost you will become.

Dreams are where we visit the many lands and landscapes of human possibility and discover the one where we feel at home. The great religious leaders were all dreamers.

Within my own tradition there was Moses, who dreamed of a land flowing with milk and honey, and Isaiah, who dreamed of a world at peace. One of the greatest speeches of the twentieth century was Martin Luther King's 'I have a dream.' If I were to design a curriculum for happiness, dreaming would be a compulsory course.

The second idea is, follow your passion. Nothing – not wealth, success, accolades or fame – justifies spending a lifetime doing things you don't enjoy. I have seen too many people enter careers to earn money to give their partners and children everything they want, only to lose their partners and become estranged from their children because they never had time for them. People who follow their passion tend to lead blessed lives. Happy in what they do, they tend to spread happiness to those whose lives they touch. That is a life worth living.

The third idea I learnt from the psychotherapist who survived Auschwitz, Viktor Frankl, whose *Man's Search for Meaning** is one of the most widely read books of our time. Frankl used to say: 'Don't ask what you want from life. Ask what life wants from you.' The great lives are ones where people heard a call, had a sense of vocation. That is what set Abraham, grandfather of monotheism, on his journey and eventually it changed the world. Moses might have lived a life of ease as a prince of Egypt, but he heard the cry of his people as they suffered under slavery, and God's call to him to lead them into freedom.

There is a well-known story about three men who spent their lives quarrying rocks. When asked what they were doing, one replied, 'breaking rocks'. The second said, 'earning a living'. The third said, 'building a cathedral'. We don't need to ask which of the three had the most job satisfaction. The late Steve Jobs spent his life making technology people-friendly. The creators of Google sought to make the world of information available to all. An overarching sense of the 'Why' preceded the 'How'. Where what we want to do meets what is crying out to be done, that is where we should be.

The fourth idea is: make space in your life for the things that matter, for family and friends, love and generosity, fun and joy. Without this, you will burn out in mid-career and wonder where your life went. In Judaism we have the Sabbath, a dedicated day of stillness each week, where we make space for all the things that

* Viktor Frankl, *Man's Search for Meaning; The Classic Tribute to Hope from the Holocaust* (London: Rider, 2011).

are important but not urgent. Not every culture has a Sabbath, but life without dedicated time for renewal, like a life without exercise or music or a sense of humour, is a lesser life.

The fifth idea is work hard, the way an athlete or concert pianist or cutting-edge scientist works hard. The American psychologist, Mihaly Csikszentmihalyi, calls this the principle of 'flow'. By this he means the peak experience you have when you are working so hard at a task that you are unaware of the passing of time. No great achiever – even those who made it seem easy – ever succeeded without hard work. The Jewish word for serving God, *avodah*, also means hard work.

There are many other ideas, but these are some of the most important. Try them and you will be surprised by joy.

Parenthood

27 July 2013

'Every child conceived in love is testimony to a profound and moving faith in the future, in human renewal, and in life itself as the supreme blessing.'

Congratulations to the Duke and Duchess of Cambridge on the birth of their first child. In the words of the most ancient of blessings: May God bless him and protect him. May He make His face shine on him and be gracious to him. May God turn His face towards him and grant him peace.

There is something profoundly spiritual about the birth of a child. Stephen Hawking wrote at the end of *A Brief History of Time** that if we could only discover a unified field theory we would 'know the mind of God'. The truth, I suspect, is quite different. You don't need theoretical physics to come as close as humans ever will to understanding the mind of God. All you need is to become a parent. As one American Jewish mother put it: 'Since I have had a child, I find I can relate to God much better. Now I know what it feels like to create something you can't control.'

Some of the most joyous scenes in the Bible depict mothers on the birth of their first child. Sarah, Abraham's wife, said when Isaac was born, 'God has brought me laughter, and everyone who hears about this will laugh with me' (Genesis 21:6). On the birth of her child Samuel, Hannah sang, 'My heart rejoices in the Lord' (I Samuel 2:1). When Ruth had a child, people gathered

* Stephen Hawking, *A Brief History of Time and Other Essays* (New York: Bantam, 1998).

around Naomi, her mother-in-law, who had suffered much grief, and said: 'May the Lord be praised because he has not left you without a guardian today' (Ruth 4:14). Her new grandchild, they said, would be for her a 'restorer of life' (Ruth 4:15). The birth of a child, then as now, was more than just a private joy. It was a communal celebration. John Donne said: 'Any man's death diminishes me, because I am involved in mankind.' The corollary is we are all enlarged by the birth of a child, for every newborn baby is testimony to the love that brings new life to the world. That is where human love comes closest to the love of God that brought us and the Universe into being.

By describing God as a parent, the Hebrew Bible gave parenthood itself unprecedented dignity. In fact, the only verse in the entire Bible that explains why God chose Abraham to be the founder of a new covenant says, 'I have chosen him, so that he will direct his children and his household after him to keep the way of the Lord by doing what is right and just' (Genesis 18:19). Abraham and Sarah were chosen precisely for their gifts and dedication as parents, because God had faith that they would serve as role models for future generations in teaching their descendants to live by the high ideals of righteousness and justice.

Moses, too, spoke often of the duty of parents to educate their children, 'when you sit at home and when you travel along the way, when you lie down and when you rise up' (Deuteronomy 6:7). Isaiah envisaged a time when 'All your children will be taught by the Lord, and great will be the peace of your children' (Isaiah 54:13). He spoke of God's promise that 'My words that I have put in your mouth will always be on your lips, on the lips of your children and on the lips of their children from this time on and for ever' (Isaiah 59:21). Parents are the supreme educators, and they teach children less by what they say than by what they do and what they are. As Wordsworth put it in *The Prelude*: 'What we have loved / others will love, and we will teach them how.'

Parenthood is demanding. As the Yiddish saying has it: 'Without children, what would we do for aggravation?' Yet there is no more sacred task, nor any more rewarding. Every child conceived in love is testimony to a profound and moving faith in the future, in human renewal and in life itself as the supreme blessing. And every parent in his or her heart knows that the real privilege lies less in being loved than in being given the chance to love. Children, says Psalm 127, are 'a gift from the Lord' (Psalm 127:3), placed by Him into our safekeeping. They are, this side of heaven, our greatest intimation of immortality.

So may God be with the new Royal and his parents, protecting them from harm and bringing them blessing, joy and the unfolding of the many tender dimensions of love.

Faith

31 August 2013

'If faith in God means anything, it means humility toward oneself and love of neighbour and the stranger.'

Credo means 'I believe' in Latin. In Hebrew we say *ani ma'amin*. Since this is the last Credo I will write as Chief Rabbi, I thought I would use it simply to say what I believe.

I believe faith is part of what makes us human. It is a basic attitude of trust that always goes beyond the available evidence, but without which we would do nothing great. Without faith in one another we could not risk the vulnerability of love. Without faith in the future, we would not choose to have a child. Without faith in the intelligibility of the Universe we would not do science. Without faith in our fellow citizens, we would not have a free society.

Undergirding them all, in the West, is faith in God who created the Universe in love, who made every human being regardless of colour, creed or class, in His image, who lifts us when we fall, forgives us when we fail and asks us to place love at the centre of our moral world: love of neighbour, love of stranger, love of God.

One who asks for proof before he or she is willing to have faith does not understand that faith always involves risk. It is always possible to live without it, but such a life is, in Macbeth's words, 'cabined, cribbed, confined, bound . . . [by] doubts and fears'. Without faith in people, I become a cynic. Without faith in financial institutions, we stop investing and economies founder. Without faith in our fellow citizens, democratic freedoms die.

Without faith in God, the Universe slowly becomes meaningless. Life ceases to have an objective purpose. Human life is no longer sacred, nor are our promises, duties and responsibilities. Cultures that lose their religious faith eventually become individualistic and relativist. People become self-seeking and self-sustaining. At first this is experienced as a great liberation, but ultimately it leads to a breakdown of trust, and without trust, societies suffer entropy: a loss of energy and order, leading to decline and decay.

Greece, whose greatness in the fifth and fourth centuries of the pre-Christian era was unsurpassed, became in the third century BCE a society of cynics, sceptics, Stoics and Epicureans whose glory faded with frightening speed. The Europe of the Enlightenment, placing its faith in the power of science, eventually fell to the twin idolatries of nation and race, fighting two world wars and leaving tens of millions dead. Soviet Communism, the greatest ever attempt to build a society on scientific principle and social engineering, crushed human freedom until it collapsed under its own dead weight.

If faith in God means anything, it means humility toward oneself and love of neighbour and the stranger. Sadly, faith has not always led to these things. It can sometimes lead to self-righteousness and hatred of the stranger. The history of religion has often enough been written in the blood shed in the name of God, and this is not a consecration but a desecration.

Today in many parts of the world I see religion confused with the pursuit of power, as if that whole tragic history has been forgotten. The Hebrew Bible tells us that power belongs to God, who uses it to liberate the powerless. Religion has nothing to do with power and everything to do with the holy and the good and the pursuit of justice and compassion. When religion and politics become confused the result is disastrous for both.

Today's angry atheists, far from being profound, are like humourless individuals wondering why people laugh at a joke. Their attitudes have nothing to do with science and everything to do with a failure of imagination. We need science to tell us how the world is and religion to tell us how the world ought to be.

Both are necessary. Each properly understood can enhance our respect for the other.

Faith is understood in the living and proved in the doing. We encounter the Divine presence in prayer and ritual, story and song. These lift us beyond ourselves toward the infinite Thou at the heart of being, who teaches us to see His trace in the face of the human other, leading us to acts of loving kindness that make gentle the life of this world. Faith is the bond of loyalty and listening that binds us to God and through Him to humanity. Faith is life lived in the light of love.

Part Three
Articles

Reflections: One Year On

Published in The Jewish Chronicle *on 7 July 2006 to mark the one-year anniversary of the 2005 terrorist attacks in London, killing fifty-two people and injuring hundreds more.*

A year after 7/7, the day suicidal terror came to London, our first thoughts must be with the victims and their families. We grieve for those whose lives were cut brutally short. We pray for the injured and bereaved. They have suffered wounds, physical and psychological, that may never heal. Experts estimate that at least a thousand people affected by the blasts could today be suffering from full post-traumatic stress disorder.

Ours is an age of short attention spans. Events like 7/7 capture the eyes and ears of the world. Then something else happens, somewhere else. The news moves on. But the human pain remains. For the past three years, with the Shabbaton Choir, Elaine and I have been on missions to bring music to terror victims in Israel. We have been moved beyond words by their courage. Yet we have wept for the sheer mindless barbarity of the acts that left these scars that will never fully heal.

A year on, where are we? The first thing to remember is how calm the public remained. Politicians and the police knew that a terror attack on London was inevitable after the tragedies of 9/11, Bali, Istanbul, Beslan and Madrid. What they feared was not only the event itself – the deaths, the injuries, the undermining of confidence in the security of everyday life – but also its repercussions. There was genuine fear that a wave of anger might sweep over Britain, leading to retaliatory violence in cities where ethnic and religious tensions were already high and combustible.

It didn't happen. Britain grieved with quiet dignity. The multi-ethnic crowd that gathered in Trafalgar Square to remember the victims was united in grief. There was no anger. Crisis tests the underlying health of an organism. London was tested and found strong. This was Britain at its best.

The devastating discovery, however, was that the suicide bombers were not outsiders to Britain. They were born and educated here. Three of the four had grown up in Leeds. The fourth had spent his teenage years in Huddersfield. Mohammad Sidique Kahn, the leader of the group, was a primary school teacher, liked and trusted by his colleagues.

In his recent book, *Man in the Shadows*,* ex-head of Mossad Efraim Halevy argues that this makes the London bombings potentially the most serious of all the terrorist attacks since 9/11. Terror does not necessarily come to a society from outside. The virus can be incubated from within. Nor does it come from the unemployed, the disaffected, people with a reason to feel resentful. We now know, as a result of many research studies, that there is no specific sociological background or psychological profile that would allow us to identify in advance a potential suicide bomber. Terror gives no warning before it strikes.

What guidance do Judaism and Jewish history give in such circumstances? The first is that there is and can be no religious justification for terror. The Torah states this in the most dramatic possible way, near to the beginning of its story of the birth of civilisation. In the days of Noah, God saw a world 'filled with violence' (Genesis 6:5). In words of still-reverberating power it says that God 'regretted that He had created man on Earth and His heart was filled with grief' (Genesis 6:6).

This surely is self-evident. Yet Professor P. A. J. Waddington of Reading University has pointed out that the London bombings were followed by a series of evasions: denial of responsibility

* Efraim Halevy, *Man in the Shadows: Inside the Middle East Crisis with a Man Who Led the Mossad* (New York: St Martin's Press, 2006).

(the bombers were victims of alienation), blaming the victim (Londoners were collectively guilty for the war in Iraq) and denial of injury (the number killed on 7/7 were a handful in comparison to those who have died in Afghanistan and Iraq).

This is relativism run wild, a wilful obfuscation of the principles of moral responsibility. Free societies are not defeated by terror, but they begin to die when they lose their moral sense. As long as excuses are made for terror, freedom itself will remain at risk.

The second issue, of real consequence for the future of European societies, is the way domestic institutions – campuses, professional groups, charities and NGOs – are being hijacked for highly sectarian political ends. One after another, they are being turned into pressure groups designed to influence governments' foreign policy through a combination of threat, intimidation, boycotts and the creation of an atmosphere of fear.

In this regard, 7/7 was the extreme end of a spectrum of activities that are undermining the very fabric of one European society after another. We have now reached a situation in which conflicts far away have been imported into Britain, poisoning the atmosphere of trust and civility on which a liberal democracy depends.

In this, the 350th anniversary of British Jewry, we have had reason to reflect on the wisdom of Jeremiah's advice twenty-six centuries ago: 'Seek the peace of the city to which you are exiled and pray to God on its behalf, for if it prospers, you too will prosper' (Jeremiah 29:7). Every minority has a duty to honour the interests of the wider society of which it is a part, for its freedom and security are the guarantors of ours.

All Faiths Must Stand Together Against Hatred

Published in The Times *on 29 January 2009 to mark Holocaust Memorial Day and reflect on a visit of Britain's faith leaders to Auschwitz in November 2008.*

When the Archbishop of Canterbury and I led a mission of leaders of all the faiths in Britain to Auschwitz in November, we did so in the belief that the time has come to strengthen our sense of human solidarity. For the Holocaust was not just a Jewish tragedy but a human one. Nor did it happen in some remote corner of the globe. It happened in the heart of Europe, in the culture that had given the world Goethe and Beethoven, Kant and Hegel. And it can happen again. Not in the same place, not in the same way, but hate still stalks our world.

Nine years ago, when a National Holocaust Memorial Day was first mooted, Tony Blair asked me for my views. I said that I felt the Jewish community did not need such a day. We have our own day, Yom HaShoah, which is, for us, a grief observed. All of us, literally or metaphorically, lost family in the great destruction. All of us are, in some sense, survivors. To be a Jew is to carry the burden of memory without letting it rob us of hope and faith in the possibility of a world at peace.

But such a day might be valuable to all of us, Jew and non-Jew alike, were two conditions satisfied. The first was that, without diminishing the uniqueness of the Holocaust, we might use it to highlight other tragedies: Bosnia, Cambodia, Rwanda and now Darfur. The second was that the day was taken into schools. For it is our children and grandchildren who must carry the fight for tolerance into the future, and we must make sure that they recognise the first steps along the path to Hell.

It was the Holocaust survivors who taught me this. I cannot imagine what they went through. Yet trauma did not turn them inward. They, more than anyone, empathised with victims of subsequent tragedies, and went into schools, teaching children to cherish freedom and be prepared to fight for it. They remain my role models in turning personal pain into sensitivity to the pain of others.

About one Holocaust Memorial Day, in 2004, I was initially apprehensive. The organisers rightly chose to focus on the massacre in Rwanda ten years before. How, I wondered, would eighty-year-old Central Europeans relate to young survivors from Africa? My concerns turned out to be utterly misplaced. One survivor instinctively recognises another across the barriers of colour, culture, age and creed.

Six months later Mary Kayitesi Blewitt, the remarkable woman who has led the work with the survivors in Rwanda, came round to see me, bubbling with excitement. For years, she said, she had been working in obscurity, aided mainly by the Jewish community. Now, because of the prominence given to her work by Holocaust Memorial Day, she had been voted an international woman of the year. The Queen had invited her to Buckingham Palace and the British Government had given a large grant to build Aids clinics in Kigali.

Hence our decision to go to Auschwitz with leading British Christians, Jews, Muslims, Hindus, Sikhs, Buddhists, Jains, Zoroastrians and Baha'i. Grief has the power to unite. Of the 6,000 languages spoken throughout the world today, only one is truly universal: the language of tears. And now, when the tectonic plates on which humanity stands are shifting, leading to violence, conflict and terror throughout the world, we must take a stand against hate – the theme of this year's commemoration.

Never in my lifetime have we needed that message more. All the danger signs are flashing: financial meltdown, recession and a sense that 'things fall apart; the centre cannot hold; / mere anarchy is loosed upon the world'.* Antisemitism is only a small part of the problem. Instantaneous global communication ensures that conflicts anywhere can light fuses everywhere. The internet is the most powerful spreader of hate and paranoia invented.

The world has become more unstable and confusing. At such times people search for certainties. They rally round scapegoats and slogans that simplify. They resolve complex issues into polarities: 'Us' and 'Them', the children of light versus the children of darkness, friends and enemies, the saved and the damned. People lose faith in the long, slow process of conflict resolution. They lose the very precondition of justice: the ability to hear both sides. They see themselves as victims and identify someone else to blame.

Academics, who should be guardians of objectivity, become partisan and instigate boycotts. That is what happened in Germany in the 1930s. The greatest philosopher of his time, Martin Heidegger, was a Nazi. Doctors and scientists administered the Final Solution. Carl Schmitt, an antisemite, a Nazi, and the leading political thinker of his day, held that liberalism is too weak to sustain passion and conviction at times of crisis. For him, real politics is about identifying an enemy and a cause you are willing to die for. That is how it is in parts of the world today. It must not become the way it is in Britain.

We, the religious leaders and faith communities of Britain, must work hard at our friendship and stand together in this turbulent age. Our visit to Auschwitz-Birkenau was organised by the Holocaust Educational Trust. As we stood together that chill November night, lighting candles and saying prayers where 1.25 million people were gassed, burnt and turned to ash, we knew to the core of our being where hate, unchecked, can lead. We cannot change the past. We can, and must, change the future. For the sake of the victims, for the sake of our children, and for the sake of God, whose image we bear.

* W. B. Yeats, 'The Second Coming' in *The Collected Poems of W. B. Yeats* (1989).

Reversing the Decay of London Undone

Published in The Wall Street Journal *on 20 August 2011 to reflect on the London riots when thousands of people rioted in cities and towns across England, which saw looting, arson, as well as mass deployment of police and the deaths of five people.*

It was the same city, but it might have been a different planet. At the end of April the eyes of the world were on London as a dashing prince and a radiant princess, William and Kate, rode in a horse-drawn carriage through streets lined with cheering crowds sharing a mood of joyous celebration. Less than four months later the world was watching London again as hooded youths ran riot down high streets, smashing windows, looting shops, setting fire to cars, attacking passers-by and throwing rocks at the police.

It looked like a scene from Cairo, Tunis or Tripoli earlier in the year. But this was no political uprising. People were breaking into shops and making off with clothes, shoes, electronic gadgets and flat screen televisions. It was, as someone later called it, shopping with violence, consumerism run rampage, an explosion of lawlessness made possible by mobile phones as gangs discovered that by text messaging they could bring crowds onto the streets where they became, for a while, impossible to control.

Let us be clear. The numbers involved were relatively small. The lawkeepers vastly outnumbered the lawbreakers. People stepped in to rescue those attacked. Crowds appeared each morning to clear up the wreckage of the night before. Britain remains a decent, good and gracious society.

But the damage was real. Businesses were destroyed. People lost their homes. A sixty-eight-year-old man, attacked by a mob while trying to put out a fire, died. Three young men in Birmingham were killed in a hit-and-run attack. While it lasted, it was very frightening.

Politicians quickly saw that this was no minor incident. One by one they cancelled their holidays, rushed back home and reconvened Parliament. There was tough talk, especially from Prime Minister David Cameron, who said that Britain had experienced a moral collapse.

Courts sat without a break, working round the clock to try the almost 3,000 people arrested. A raft of measures was announced: stronger police powers, tougher punishments, support for troubled families, a new form of national service. There was talk of 'broken Britain'. The nation had caught sight of itself in the mirror and did not like what it saw.

It took everyone by surprise. It should not have done. Britain is the latest country to pay the price for what happened half a century ago in one of the most radical transformations in the history of the West. In virtually every Western society in the 1960s there was a moral revolution, an abandonment of its entire traditional ethic of self-restraint. 'All you need', sang the Beatles, 'is love.' The Judeo-Christian moral code was jettisoned. In its place came, whatever works for you. The Ten Commandments were rewritten as the Ten Creative Suggestions. Or as Allan Bloom put it in *The Closing of the American Mind*:* 'I am the Lord Your God: Relax!'

You do not have to be a Victorian sentimentalist to realise that something has gone badly wrong since. In Britain today more than 40 per cent of children are born outside marriage. Britain has the highest percentage of single-parent families and teenage mothers in the world. This has led to new forms of child poverty that serious government spending has failed to cure. In 2007 a UNICEF report found that Britain's children are

* Allan Bloom, *The Closing of the American Mind: How Higher Education Has Failed Democracy and Impoverished the Souls of Today's Students* (New York: Simon & Schuster, 2021).

the unhappiest in the world. The 2011 riots are one result. But there are others.

Whole communities are growing up without fathers or male role models. Bringing up a family in the best of circumstances is not easy. To try to do it by placing the entire burden on women – 91 per cent of single-parent families in Britain are headed by the mother – is practically absurd and morally indefensible. By the time boys are in their early teens they are physically stronger than their mothers. Having no fathers, they are socialised in gangs. No one can control them: not parents, teachers or even the local police. There are areas in Britain's major cities that have been no-go areas for years. Crime is rampant. So are drugs. It is a recipe for violence and despair.

That is the problem. At first it seemed as if the riots were almost random with no basis in class or race. As the perpetrators have come to court, a different picture has emerged. Some 60 per cent of those charged had a previous criminal record and 25 per cent belonged to gangs.

Part of the shock is that 40 per cent were previously law-abiding. But what is clear is that this was the bursting of a dam of potential trouble that has been building for years. The collapse of families and communities leaves in its wake unsocialised young people, deprived of parental care, who on average – and yes, there are exceptions – do worse than their peers at school, are more susceptible to drug and alcohol abuse, less likely to find stable employment and more likely to land up in jail.

The truth is, it is not their fault. They are the victims of the tsunami of wishful thinking that washed across the West saying that you can have sex without the responsibility of marriage, children without the responsibility of parenthood, social order without the responsibility of citizenship, liberty without the responsibility of morality and self-esteem without the responsibility of work and earned achievement.

What has happened morally in the West is what has happened financially also. Good and otherwise sensible people were persuaded that you could spend more than you earn, incur debt at unprecedented levels and consume the world's resources without thinking about who will pay the bill and when. It has been the culture of the free lunch in a world where there are no free lunches.

We have been spending our moral capital with the same reckless abandon that we have been spending our financial capital. Freud was right. The precondition of civilisation is the ability to defer the gratification of instinct. And even Freud, who disliked religion and called it the 'obsessional neurosis' of humankind, realised that it was the Judaeo-Christian ethic that trained people to control their appetites and practise the necessary ethic of self-restraint.

There are large parts of Britain, Europe, even the United States, where religion is a thing of the past and there is no counter-voice to the culture of buy it, spend it, wear it, flaunt it, because you're worth it. The message is that morality is passé, conscience is for wimps, and the single overriding command is 'Thou shalt not be found out.'

Has this happened before, and is there a way back? The answer to both is in the affirmative. In the 1820s, in Britain and America, a similar phenomenon occurred. People were moving from villages to cities. Families were disrupted. Young people were separated from their parents and no longer under their control. Alcohol consumption rose dramatically. So did violence. In the 1820s it was unsafe to walk the streets of London because of pickpockets by day and 'unruly ruffians' by night.

What happened over the next thirty years was a massive shift in public opinion. There was an unprecedented growth in charities, friendly societies, working men's institutes, temperance groups, church and synagogue associations, Sunday schools, YMCA buildings and moral campaigns of every shape and size, fighting slavery or child labour or inhumane working conditions. The common factor was their focus on the building of moral character, self-discipline, willpower and personal responsibility. It worked. Within a single generation, crime rates came down and social order was restored. What was achieved was nothing less than the re-moralisation of society – much of it driven by religion.

It was this that the young French aristocrat Alexis de Tocqueville saw on his visit to America in 1831. It astonished him. He had seen what it takes to make democratic freedom work, and he described it in phrases that have not lost their power since. He called it the 'art of association' that forms the 'habits of the heart' that constitute the 'apprenticeship of liberty'.

Tocqueville was expecting to see, in the land that had enacted the constitutional separation of church and state, a secular society. To his amazement he found something completely different: a secular state, to be sure, but also a society in which religion was, he said, the first of its political (we would now say 'civil') institutions. It did three things he saw as essential. It strengthened the family. It taught morality. And it encouraged active citizenship.

One hundred and eighty years later, the Tocqueville of our time, Harvard sociologist Robert Putnam, made the same discovery. Putnam is famous for his diagnosis of the breakdown of social capital he called 'bowling alone'. More people were going ten-pin bowling but fewer were joining teams. It was a symbol of the loss of community in an age of rampant individualism. That was the bad news.

A decade later, at the end of 2010, he published the good news. Social capital, he wrote in *American Grace*,* has not disappeared. It is alive and well and can be found in churches, synagogues and other places of worship. Religious people, he discovered, make better neighbours and citizens. They are more likely to give to charity, volunteer, assist a homeless person, donate blood, spend time with someone feeling depressed, offer a seat to a stranger, help someone find a job and take part in local civic life. Affiliation to a religious community is the best predictor of altruism and empathy: better than education, age, income, gender or race.

* Robert Putnam and David Campbell, *American Grace: How Religion Divides and Unites Us* (New York: Simon & Schuster, 2010).

Much can and must be done by governments, but they cannot of themselves change lives. Governments cannot make marriages or turn feckless individuals into responsible citizens. That needs another kind of change agent. Alexis de Tocqueville saw it then; Robert Putnam is saying it now. It needs religion: not as doctrine but as a shaper of behaviour, a tutor in morality, an ongoing seminar in self-restraint and pursuit of the common good.

One of our great British exports to America, Harvard historian Niall Ferguson, has a fascinating passage in his book *Civilization*,* in which he asks whether the West can maintain its primacy on the world stage or is it a civilisation in decline?

He quotes a member of the Chinese Academy of Social Sciences, tasked with finding out what gave the West its dominance. He said: At first, we thought it was your guns. Then we thought it was your political system, democracy. Then we said it was your economic system, capitalism. But for the last twenty years we have known that it was your religion.

It was the Judeo-Christian heritage that gave the West its restless pursuit of a tomorrow that would be better than today. The Chinese have learned the lesson. Fifty years after Chairman Mao declared China a religion-free zone, there are now more Chinese Christians than there are members of the Communist Party.

China has learned the lesson. The question is: will we?

* Niall Ferguson, *Civilization: The West and the Rest* (London: Penguin, 2018).

The 9/11 Attacks Are Linked to a Wider Moral Malaise

Published in The Times, *8 September 2011 to mark the ten-year anniversary of the terrorist attacks in New York on 11 September 2001.*

Two things have haunted me since 9/11. The first is the pain, the grief, the lives lost, and families devastated, the sheer barbaric ingenuity of evil. The scar in our humanity is still unhealed. The second is our failure to understand what Osama bin Laden was saying about the West. We did not hear the message then. I'm not sure we hear it now.

After the shock and grief subsided, two theories began to be heard. The first was that this was an event of epoch-changing magnitude. The terms of international politics had been transformed. The Cold War was over. Another war had begun. This time the enemy was not the Soviet Union and Communism. It was radical, political Islam.

The second was the opposite. 9/11 was terrifying and terrible but it changed nothing because acts of terror never do. Terrorist campaigns have been aimed at other countries. Britain suffered similarly from the IRA in the 1970s. The most important thing is not to overreact. Terror may bring dividends in local conflicts, but it never succeeds in its larger political aims.

There is something to be said for both theories. But there is a third, no less consequential. Why did al-Qaeda attack America? Because it believed that it could. Because it thought the United States was a power past its prime, no longer as lean and hungry as it believed it was.

Robert McNamara said that the first rule in politics is to understand your enemy's psychology. As I struggled to understand 9/11,

I began to suspect that the answer lay in the events of 1989. That is when the narratives of the West and the rest began seriously to diverge.

In the West, 1989 was seen as the collapse of Communism, the fall of the Berlin Wall, the implosion of the Soviet Union and the end of the Cold War. The Western narrative was triumphalist. It saw those events as heralding the victory of its values without a shot being fired. The free market and liberal democratic politics had won for the simplest of reasons. They delivered, while Communism did not. They would now spread across the world. It was, said Francis Fukuyama, the beginning of the end of history.

There was, though, another narrative that few were listening to. It said that the Soviet Union collapsed in 1989 not because of the triumph of liberal democracy but because of the Soviet withdrawal from Afghanistan earlier that year. It had invaded in 1979 and was forced to withdraw, not because of superpower politics but because of the determined resistance of a small group of highly motivated religious warriors, the Mujahideen and their helpers. That, historically, is the event that captured the imagination of Osama bin Laden.

According to this account, that one event, the humiliating retreat of the Soviet Army, set in motion a series of internal crises that resulted, months later, in the fall of a great power. If one of the world's two superpowers was vulnerable to asymmetric warfare – the war of the few against the many – why not the other, America itself? What 1989 represented was not the end of history but the end of a history dominated by the twin superpowers of Communist Russia and capitalist America.

Both were vulnerable because both were overripe and about to fall from the tree. Much excitement was felt in the West by the failure of Communism. Less attention was paid to what Daniel Bell called the cultural contradictions of capitalism.

Throughout this period there were voices that few seemed to be listening to. First and greatest was the philosopher Alasdair

MacIntyre in his 1981 masterwork, *After Virtue*.* He argued that the moral discourse of the West had broken down.

The 'Enlightenment project' of a purely rational ethic had failed – not because there was no such thing, but because there were too many. They clashed inconclusively and people were left with a sense that morality is whatever you think it is.

His minatory warning was: 'The barbarians are not waiting beyond the frontiers; they have already been governing us for quite some time.' That was a scary thing to hear from one of the world's great philosophers. I soon began to hear it from other leading intellectuals also, such as Philip Rieff, Christopher Lasch and Robert Bellah. That is what I heard in the echoes of 9/11: that all great civilisations eventually decline, and when they begin to do so they are vulnerable. That is what Osama bin Laden believed about the West. and so did some of the West's own greatest minds.

If so, then 9/11 belongs to a wider series of phenomena affecting the West: the disintegration of the family, the demise of authority, the build-up of personal debt, the collapse of financial institutions, the downgrading of the American economy, the continuing failure of some European economies, the loss of a sense of honour, loyalty and integrity that has brought once esteemed groups into disrepute, the waning throughout the West of a sense of national identity; even last month's riots.

These are all signs of the arteriosclerosis of a culture, a civilisation grown old. Whenever 'Me' takes precedence over 'We', and pleasure today over viability tomorrow, a society is in trouble. If so, then the enemy is not radical Islam, it is us and our, by now, unsustainable self-indulgence.

The West has expended much energy and courage fighting wars in Afghanistan and Iraq abroad and defeating terror at home. It has spent far less, if any, in renewing its own morality and the institutions – families, communities, ethical codes, standards in public life – where it is created and sustained. But if I am right,

* Alastair MacIntyre, *After Virtue* (London: Bloomsbury, 2013).

this is the West's greatest weakness in the eyes of its enemies as well as its friends.

The only way to save the world is to begin with ourselves. Our burden after 9/11 is to renew the moral disciplines of freedom. Some say it can't be done. They are wrong: it can and must. Surely, we owe the dead no less.

Has Europe Lost Its Soul to the Market?

Published in The Times *on 12 December 2011 to coincide with Rabbi Sacks' visit to the Vatican for a private audience with Pope Benedict XVI and a keynote lecture he delivered at the Pontifical Gregorian University in Rome on the state of Europe.*

As the political leaders of Europe come together to save the euro and European Union itself, I believe the time has come for religious leaders to do likewise.

The task ahead of us is not between Jews and Catholics, or even Jews and Christians, but between Jews and Christians on the one hand and the increasingly, even aggressively secularising forces at work in Europe today on the other, challenging and even ridiculing our faith.

When a civilisation loses its faith, it loses its future. When it recovers its faith, it recovers its future. For the sake of our children, and their children not yet born, we – Jews and Christians, side by side – must renew our faith and its prophetic voice. We must help Europe to recover its soul.

The idea of religious leaders saving the euro and the EU sounds absurd. What has religion to do with economics, or spirituality with financial institutions? The answer is that the market economy has religious roots. It emerged in a Europe saturated with Judeo-Christian values. In the Hebrew Bible, for instance, material prosperity is a divine blessing. Poverty crushes the human spirit as well as the body, and its alleviation is a sacred task.

The first financial instruments of modern capitalism were developed by fourteenth-century banks in Christian Florence, Pisa, Genoa and Venice. Max Weber traced the connections between the Protestant ethic and the spirit of capitalism. Michael Novak has done likewise for Catholicism. Jews, numbering one fifth of 1 per cent of the population of the world, have won more than 30 per cent of Nobel Prizes in economics. When I asked the developmental economist Jeffrey Sachs what drove him in his work, he replied without hesitation, *tikkun olam*, the Jewish imperative of 'healing a fractured world'. The birth of the modern economy is inseparable from its Judeo-Christian roots.

But this is not a stable equilibrium. Capitalism is a sustained process of creative destruction. The market undermines the very values that gave rise to it in the first place. The consumer culture is profoundly antithetical to human dignity. It inflames desire, undermines happiness, weakens the capacity to defer instinctual gratification and blinds us to the vital distinction between the price of things and their value.

Instead of seeing the system as Adam Smith did, as a means of directing self-interest to the common good, it can become a means of empowering self-interest to the detriment of the common good. Instead of the market being framed by moral principles, it comes to substitute for moral principle. If you can buy it, negotiate it, earn it and afford it, then you are entitled to it – as the advertisers say – because you're worth it. The market ceases to be merely a system and becomes an ideology in its own right.

The market gives us choices; so morality itself becomes just a set of choices in which right or wrong have no meaning beyond the satisfaction or frustration of desire. The phenomenon that characterises the human person, the capacity to make second-order evaluations, not just to feel desire but also to ask whether this desire should be satisfied, becomes redundant. We find it increasingly hard to understand why there might be things we want to do, can afford to do and have a legal right to do, that nonetheless we should not do because they are unjust, or dishonourable, or disloyal, or demeaning. When *Homo economicus* displaces *Homo sapiens*, market fundamentalism rules.

There is a wise American saying: never waste a crisis. And the current financial and economic crisis affords us a rare opportunity to pause and reflect on where we have been going and where it leads.

The financial instruments at the heart of the current crisis, subprime mortgages and the securitisation of risk, were so complex that governments, regulatory authorities and sometimes even bankers themselves failed to understand them and their extreme vulnerability. Those who encouraged people to take out mortgages they could not repay were guilty of what the Bible calls 'putting a stumbling block before the blind' (Leviticus 19:14).

The build-up of personal and collective debt in America and Europe should have sent warning signals to anyone familiar with the biblical institutions of the Sabbatical and Jubilee years, created specifically because of the danger of people being trapped by debt. Those who encouraged this recklessness protected themselves but not others from the consequences. Ultimately, financial failure is the result of moral failure: a failure of long-term responsibility to the societies of which we are a part, and to future generations who will bear the cost of our mistakes. It is a symptom of a wider failure: to see the market as a means not an end.

The Bible paints a graphic picture of what happens when people cease to see gold as a medium of exchange and start seeing it as an object of worship. It calls it the Golden Calf. Its antidote is the Sabbath: one day in seven in which we neither work nor employ, shop or spend. It is time dedicated to things that have a value, not a price: family, community, and thanksgiving to God for what we have, instead of worrying about what we lack. It is no coincidence that in Britain, Sunday and financial markets were deregulated at about the same time.

Markets need morals. We tend to forget that the keywords of a market economy are deeply religious. Credit comes from the Latin *credo*, meaning 'I believe'. Confidence comes from the Latin for 'shared faith'. Trust is a religious and moral concept.

Try running an economy without confidence or trust and you will soon see that it cannot be done. It was a breakdown of trust that led to the banking crisis. And trust cannot be created by systems. It depends on an ethic of honour and responsibility internalised by those who run the systems.

Stabilising the euro is one thing; healing the culture that surrounds it is another. A world in which material values are everything and spiritual values nothing is neither a stable state nor a good society. The time has come for us to recover the Judeo-Christian ethic of human dignity in the image of God. Humanity was not created to serve markets. Markets were created to serve humankind.

The Moral Animal

Published in The New York Times *on 24 December 2012 to coincide with the last day of the Jewish festival of Chanukah and the day before Christmas.*

It is the religious time of the year. Step into any city in America or Britain and you will see the night sky lit by religious symbols; Christmas decorations certainly and probably also a giant *menorah*. Religion in the West seems alive and well.

But is it really? Or have these symbols been emptied of content, no more than a glittering backdrop to the West's newest faith, consumerism, and its secular cathedrals, shopping malls?

At first glance, religion is in decline. In Britain, the results of the 2011 national census have just been published. They show that a quarter of the population claims to have no religion, almost double the figure ten years ago. And though the United States remains the most religious country in the West, 20 per cent declare themselves without religious affiliation – double the number a generation ago.

Looked at another way, though, the figures tell a different story. Since the eighteenth century, many Western intellectuals have predicted religion's imminent demise. Yet after a series of withering attacks, most recently by the new atheists, including Sam Harris, Richard Dawkins and the late Christopher Hitchens, still in Britain three in four people, and in America four in five, declare allegiance to a religious faith. That, in an age of science, is what is truly surprising.

The irony is that many of the new atheists are followers of Charles Darwin. We are what we are, they say, because it has allowed us to survive and pass on our genes to the next generation. Our biological and cultural makeup constitutes our 'adaptive fitness'. Yet religion is the greatest survivor of them all. Superpowers tend to last a century; the great faiths last millenniums. The question is why.

Darwin himself suggested what is almost certainly the correct answer. He was puzzled by a phenomenon that seemed to contradict his most basic thesis, that natural selection should favour the ruthless. Altruists, who risk their lives for others, should therefore usually die before passing on their genes to the next generation. Yet all societies value altruism, and something similar can be found among social animals, from chimpanzees to dolphins to leafcutter ants.

Neuroscientists have shown how this works. We have mirror neurons that lead us to feel pain when we see others suffering. We are hard-wired for empathy. We are moral animals.

The precise implications of Darwin's answer are still being debated by his disciples – Harvard's E. O. Wilson in one corner, Oxford's Richard Dawkins in the other. To put it at its simplest, we hand on our genes as individuals but we survive as members of groups, and groups can exist only when individuals act not solely for their own advantage but for the sake of the group as a whole. Our unique advantage is that we form larger and more complex groups than any other life-form.

A result is that we have two patterns of reaction in the brain, one focusing on potential danger to us as individuals, the other, located in the prefrontal cortex, taking a more considered view of the consequences of our actions for us and others. The first is immediate, instinctive and emotive. The second is reflective and rational. We are caught, in the psychologist Daniel Kahneman's phrase, between thinking fast and slow.

The fast track helps us survive, but it can also lead us to acts that are impulsive and destructive. The slow track leads us to more considered behaviour, but it is often overridden in the heat of the moment. We are sinners and saints, egotists and altruists, exactly as the prophets and philosophers have long maintained.

If this is so, we are in a position to understand why religion helped us survive in the past – and why we will need it in the future. It strengthens and speeds up the slow track. It reconfigures our neural pathways, turning altruism into instinct through the rituals we perform, the texts we read and the prayers we pray. It remains the most powerful community builder the world has known. Religion binds individuals into groups through habits of altruism, creating relationships of trust strong enough to defeat destructive emotions. Far from refuting religion, the Neo-Darwinists have helped us understand why it matters.

No one has shown this more elegantly than the political scientist Robert D. Putnam. In the 1990s he became famous for the phrase 'bowling alone': more people were going bowling, but fewer were joining bowling teams. Individualism was slowly destroying our capacity to form groups. A decade later, in his book *American Grace*,* he showed that there was one place where social capital could still be found: religious communities.

Putnam's research showed that frequent church- or synagogue-goers were more likely to give money to charity, do volunteer work, help the homeless, donate blood, help a neighbour with housework, spend time with someone who was feeling depressed, offer a seat to a stranger or help someone find a job. Religiosity as measured by church or synagogue attendance is, he found, a better predictor of altruism than education, age, income, gender or race.

Religion is the best antidote to the individualism of the consumer age. The idea that society can do without it flies in the face of history and, now, evolutionary biology. This may go to show that God has a sense of humour. It certainly shows that the free societies of the West must never lose their sense of God.

* Robert Putnam and David Campbell, *American Grace: How Religion Divides and Unites Us* (New York: Simon & Schuster, 2010).

What Makes Us Human?

Published in The New Statesman *on 29 April 2013 as the first in a series of articles on this topic, run in the magazine and in partnership with BBC Radio 2's Jeremy Vine.*

As an answer to the question what makes us human, even in the age of neuroscience, it's hard to improve on the Bible's answer.

First comes the good news of Genesis 1. We are each, regardless of class, colour or culture, in the image and likeness of God. This is the most important statement in Western culture of the non-negotiable dignity of the human person. It is the source of the idea of human rights, most famously formulated in the American Declaration of Independence, 'We hold these truths to be self-evident, that all men are created equal and are endowed by their Creator with certain inalienable rights.'

Like God, we are creative. Like God, we are free. All other life forms adapt to their environment. We alone adapt the environment to us, sometimes with disastrous results, but always extending our powers, making us ever less vulnerable to the random cruelties of fate and the indignities of powerlessness.

Then comes the complication from which all human history flows. 'It is not good for man to be alone' (Genesis 2:18). We are supremely the social animal – part cause, part effect of our ability to use language. What makes us human, according to Judaism, is the strength and quality of our relationships. Jean-Paul Sartre was never more wrong than when he said, 'Hell is other people.' Hell is the absence of other people. Solitary confinement is the worst punishment there is.

So the Book of Genesis is about relationships, focusing on the most important of them: husbands and wives, parents and children and sibling rivalries. Only in Exodus does the Bible turn to the politics of slavery and freedom. Much of the Bible is about what makes a good society, but it insists on the primacy of the personal over the political. As long as family feeling is alive, said Alexis de Tocqueville, the opponent of oppression is never alone. Without strong families standing between the individual and the state, freedom is eventually lost.

The centrality of the family is what gave Jews their astonishing ability to survive tragedy and centuries of exile and dispersion. I knew this in my bones long before I was of an age to step back and reflect on the human condition. My parents were not well off. My father had come to Britain as a refugee fleeing persecution in Poland. The family was poor, and he had to leave school at the age of fourteen to help his father earn a living.

He had a small shop in London's East End, but he was not made to be a businessman. My mother came from a religious family at a time when it was not considered seemly for a Jewish girl to continue in education after the age of sixteen. So, though we never knew poverty, our parents had little in material terms to give us, their four boys. But they took immense pride in us and wanted us to have the opportunities they lacked. We all duly went to university and on to good careers. Ours was a story shared by many of our contemporaries.

When it works, the family is the matrix of our humanity. It is where we learn love and self-confidence and the basic values that will serve as our satellite navigation system through the uncharted territory of life. It is where we learn responsibility and the choreography of turn-taking and making space for others. It is where we acquire the habits of the heart that help us take responsibility and risks, knowing there is someone to lift us if we fall. A childhood lived in the stable presence of two loving parents is the greatest gift anyone can have, which is why so much of Jewish ritual and celebration is centred on the home.

Family life isn't easy or straightforward. The Bible does not hide that fact from us. The stories of Genesis do not contain a single sentence saying, 'And they all lived happily ever after.' Families need constant work, sacrifice and mutual respect. But if you get home right, your children will have a head start in making their own fulfilling relationships, and relationships truly are what make us human.

Which is why I sometimes worry about the future. A recent report by the Mental Health Foundation found that one in ten Britons is lonely, and the proportion amongst the young is higher and rising. We invest immense time and energy in electronic communication: smartphones, texts and social networking software. But are virtual relationships the same as face-to-face ones? A 2012 survey carried out by Macmillan Cancer Support revealed that the average eighteen-to-thirty-year-old has 237 Facebook friends. When asked, though, on how many of these they could rely in a crisis, the average answer was two. A quarter said one. An eighth said none.

This is where, I believe, religion has an immense contribution to make at every level: spiritual, personal and collective. Spiritually, the Judeo-Christian ethic teaches us to see the trace of God in the face of the human other, the most sublime idea I know. Personally, it teaches the importance of love and forgiveness, the two great dimensions of a lasting relationship. Collectively, religions create strong and supportive communities where you have friends on whom you can rely.

Faith is the redemption of solitude, and this is its most humanising gift. God lives in the space between us when we come together in love and joy.

If I Ruled the World

Published in Prospect Magazine *on 18 July 2013 as part of a regular feature column by public figures where they are invited to outline what they would do if they ruled the world.*

If I ruled the world I would resign immediately. It's hard enough, individually and collectively, to rule ourselves, let alone others. But if offered an hour before I resigned I would enact one institution that has the power to transform the world. It's called the Sabbath.

The idea of a weekly day of collective rest was unprecedented in the ancient world. Months and years are natural ways of structuring time, based respectively on the appearance of the moon and the sun. But the seven-day week corresponds to nothing in nature; nor does a day of rest.

The Greeks and Romans could not understand the Sabbath at all. They wrote that the Jews kept it because they were lazy. The interesting fact is that within a relatively short space of time after making that judgment, Greece, and later Rome, declined and fell. Without institutionalised rest, civilisations, like individuals, eventually suffer from burnout.

Originally the Sabbath was conceived as a way of limiting slavery. One day a week, masters could not make their servants work. For Orthodox Jews today the Sabbath is a liberation from other kinds of slavery. Imagine a day without texts, tweets, emails or phone calls, without television, computers or electronic games, a day without the pressures of a consumer society, without cars, traffic, planes, noise and pollution, a day dedicated to family, community, study and collective expressions of gratitude. It's when we make space for the things that are important but not urgent.

The significance of the Sabbath is threefold. First it introduces into a culture in the most vivid way the idea of limits. We can't produce, consume and deplete our resources constantly with no constraints and no thought for future generations. A day without cars and planes would go a long way to cutting the carbon consumption that threatens the Earth's ecology. A failure to understand the idea of limits has, as Jared Diamond has chronicled in his books, brought about environmental devastation almost everywhere *Homo sapiens* has set foot.

Second, it creates for a day a week a world in which values are not determined by money or its equivalent. On the Sabbath you can't buy or sell or pay for someone's services. It is the most tangible expression of the moral limits of markets. Whether in the synagogue or home, relationships are determined by other things altogether, by a sense of kinship, belonging and mutual responsibility.

Third, the Sabbath renews social capital. It bonds people into communities in ways not structured by transactions of wealth or power. It is to time what parks are to space: something precious that we share on equal terms and that none of us could create or possess on our own.

Britain used to have its own Sabbath every Sunday. Then it was deregulated and privatised. Holy days became holidays, sacred time became free time and rest became leisure. The assumption was that everyone would benefit because we could all decide for ourselves how to spend the day. This was and remains a fallacy.

There are certain experiences, even states of being, you can't have unless they are 'out there', not just 'in here'. You can't have the peace and quiet that used to mark the English Sunday if, as now, the roads are crowded, the shops are open, and everything is for sale. To use Robert Putnam's famous analogy, ten-pin bowling becomes a different kind of experience if no one joins teams anymore and everyone goes bowling alone.

Émile Durkheim was among the first to diagnose the dangers of an era of individualism and the breakdown of community. He believed that Trade Unions might supply the *Gemeinschaft*, the strong togetherness, that was being lost in society as a whole. Perhaps they did once, but not now. Today you find the strongest forms of social capital in places of worship and the congregations they house, as Putnam himself has shown in his book *American Grace*.*

Societies need civic time when we cultivate the relationships that constitute the third realm that is neither the market nor the state, and that in effect means a Sabbath, whether or not it carries religious connotations. A secular Jewish writer, Achad Ha'am, once said, 'More than the Jewish people has kept the Sabbath, the Sabbath has kept the Jewish people.' A once-a-week sabbatical that is public, not private, rest would renew the social fabric, the families and communities that sustain our liberal democratic freedom today.

* Robert Putnam and David Campbell, *American Grace: How Religion Divides and Unites Us* (New York: Simon & Schuster, 2010).

A New Movement Against Religious Persecution

Published in The Wall Street Journal *on 12 December 2014 to highlight the growing threat to religious freedom, particularly in light of the violence in the Middle East as a result of the rise of the Islamic State terrorist organisation.*

In 1991, I lit Chanukah candles with Mikhail Gorbachev, then President of the Soviet Union. After the ceremony he asked, through his interpreter, what we had just done – what was the meaning of the ritual? I asked the interpreter to tell him that more than 2,000 years ago, under a repressive government, the Seleucid Greeks, Jews fought for the right to practise their faith in freedom. 'My people won,' I said, 'and ever since we have performed this ceremony in memory of that event.'

I then noted that for seventy years after the Russian Revolution, Jews also lived under a repressive government in the Soviet Union and were not allowed to practise their faith. 'You gave them back their freedom,' I said, 'so you too are part of that story.'

As the interpreter translated my reply, President Gorbachev blushed. He had recently made history with the dissolution of the Soviet Union, but I guess he wasn't accustomed to praise for the significance of his actions resonating quite that far back. It was true, though: he had liberated Soviet Jews from silence, and the Jews at that Chanukah celebration felt it. For Jews worldwide, it was one of the high points of recent history.

But of course, those were remarkable days for millions of people. As the Berlin Wall fell a quarter-century ago, Soviet Communism imploded and the Cold War came to an end, Francis Fukuyama's

*The End of History** made thrilling sense. The era of ideological conflict was over. The last great secular ideology, Communism, had failed. What had succeeded were liberal democracy and market economics, neither of them ideological, simply systems for liberating the energies of individuals and allowing them to live peaceably and creatively together despite their differences. Adam Smith and John Stuart Mill turned out to be greater prophets of the human spirit than Karl Marx.

Rarely has a dream been so rudely interrupted. Already in 1991, the Bosnian conflict had flared, and it was this event that was to prove the shape of things to come. Bosnians who had lived together for decades found themselves, under the toxic leadership of Slobodan Milošević and Radovan Karadžić , divided along ethnic and religious lines. Three years later in Rwanda came the massacre of Tutsis by Hutus. Tribalism had returned with a vengeance.

Religious freedom has been the casualty of the new global disorder. There is an onslaught against Christians in the Middle East, who are being butchered, crucified and beheaded in Syria and Iraq, and persecuted and threatened in sub-Saharan Africa, Iran, Pakistan, Indonesia and elsewhere. Muslims are dying at the hands of their fellow Muslims across the Sunni–Shiite divide. Baha'i are suffering persecution in Iran and Egypt, Buddhists in Vietnam, Myanmar and China and Hindus in Pakistan. And within living memory of the Holocaust, antisemitism has returned to Europe.

According to the Religious Freedom in the World Report 2014 by the Catholic Church's Aid to the Church in Need organisation, freedom of religion has deteriorated in almost half the countries of the world and sectarian violence is at a six-year high. Yet freedom of religion is one of the basic human rights, as set out in Article 18 of the Universal Declaration of Human Rights. More fundamentally, it was the cause for which the modern world established

* Francis Fukuyama, *The End of History and the Last Man* (London: Hamish Hamilton, 1992).

the concept of human rights in the first place. Revulsion at a century of religious wars in Europe helped spur Enlightenment thinking about the social contract, the moral limits of power and the centrality of human rights.

The world needs a new, enlightened movement: of people of all faiths working together for the freedom of all faiths. The record of religion in the past, and tragically also in the present, has not been good. Throughout history, people have hated in the name of the God of love, practised cruelty in the name of the God of compassion, killed in the name of the God of life and waged war in the name of the God of peace. None of the world's great religions has been exempt from this at one point or another. The time has come to say 'enough'.

The challenge is simple, and it is posed in the first chapter of the Bible. Can we recognise God's image in a person who is not in our image; whose colour, creed or culture is not our own? When Chanukah begins on Tuesday evening, I will light the first candle and pray that the day may come when people of all faiths light a *menorah* together to celebrate a new festival of religious freedom, when we finally have learned to honour the brotherhood and sisterhood of humankind under the love and forgiveness of God.

A Kingdom of Kindness

Published in The House Magazine *on 12 December 2014, reflecting on the growing political debate around immigration that was taking place within Britain.*

As a Jew, I am always deeply grateful that when fleeing antisemitism in Poland my late father found refuge in Britain. Like so many other Jews in Britain, I know in my heart, in my very bones, that had it not been for this country, my parents and grandparents would not have lived, and I would not have been born. My father had a Hebrew phrase for Britain; he called it a *malkhut shel chessed*, a 'kingdom of kindness', and indeed that it what it has been.

I will never forget the words of one of the members of our community who was rescued from Nazi Germany in 1939 by the operation known as Kindertransport. Many decades later, by now in her eighties, she spoke at the memorial erected to commemorate that operation outside Liverpool Street Station, where the children had arrived. She spoke of her surprise and joy at discovering that in Britain a policeman was a friend, not an enemy! That is the mark of a kingdom of kindness.

At first, life for my father and other immigrants was hard. Poor, concentrated in ghettoes, barely able to speak English, they were caricatured as alien elements in British life. Jews who remember those days can readily sympathise with Hindus, Sikhs and Muslims today.

Yet what the Jewish experience taught was that whilst there were conflicts and a long struggle to define an identity that was both British and Jewish, these were pains of adjustment, not permanent conditions. Today, our community thinks of itself as proudly British and Jewish. Integration and acceptance happened, but it did not happen overnight.

Today's debate around immigration – is it a good thing, a bad thing or a good thing gone too far? – is fraught and delicate. At its heart, however, should be a discussion beyond economic issues that addresses the fundamental questions of what defines British identity, what is loyalty to the nation, and what binds us in a bond of mutual responsibility as we work for the common good.

What previously held our society together and helped immigrants to integrate – a common language, a shared culture, a collective code of conduct – are now fragmented. The internet has added to the complexity, making it possible to physically live in one place but mentally somewhere else.

Recovering a sense of the common good requires steps from both sides. As a society, we need to have pride in our identity, our history and heritage and want newcomers to share it. On the other hand, those who come here from elsewhere would do well to heed the advice of the prophet Jeremiah to seek the 'peace and prosperity' (Jeremiah 29:7) of the country. To be a blessing to your faith while being a blessing to others regardless of their faith is the best formula I know for creating a collective sense of identity and community.

Immigration will always be an important part of our political discourse, but we must remain vigilant in the way we frame the issues and the rhetoric we use to debate them. There is no place in the debate for prejudice, xenophobia and the appeal to baser instincts of fear toward the stranger. The history of the twentieth century should remind us what can happen if we begin to blame this or that group for our misfortunes. Britain's greatness is that it did not go down that road at a time when mainland Europe was rife with antisemitism. Nations that are confident of their own identity have no need for the politics of fear, and we should avoid it at all costs, now and in the future.

We are living through an age of immense change, and change creates insecurities that are easily translatable into suspicion and hate. That is why it is so important that Britain remains a 'kingdom of kindness' to those who seek refuge in its shores. Britain gave much to those who came here, and they gave much in return. There is a genuine debate to be had about immigration, but it must be conducted with wisdom, generosity and restraint.

Nostra Aetate: Fifty Years On

Published in First Things *on 28 October 2015 to mark the fiftieth anniversary of* Nostra Aetate, *the declaration of the Catholic Church to non-Christian religions that was proclaimed by Pope Paul VI on 28 October 1965.*

It was, on the face of it, a minor theological gesture, yet it brought about one of the greatest revolutions in religious history. *Nostra Aetate,* the Catholic Church's 1965 statement of relationships with non-Christian faiths, declared that 'the Jews should not be spoken of as rejected or accursed as if this followed from Holy Scripture'. Today as a result, Jews and Catholics meet not as enemies but as cherished and respected friends.

Vatican II, the international meeting of Catholic bishops from which *Nostra Aetate* emerged, owes its genesis to two remarkable men, Pope John XXIII and the French-Jewish historian Jules Isaac. Isaac survived the Holocaust, during which he lost his wife and daughter in the death camps. He then set himself to discover the roots of the antisemitism that had infected swathes of Europe in the nineteenth and twentieth century.

He traced it back to the early history of the Church. Isaac did not believe, nor should we, that the Holocaust, or antisemitism itself, were inspired by Christianity. Hitler's hate had altogether different roots, and antisemitism as such predates the birth of Christianity. But Isaac charted the tendency of early Christian texts after the opening of the Church to Gentiles to blame Jews collectively for the death of Jesus and to see Judaism as a failed relationship between God and humanity. This became especially pronounced in the writings of the Church Fathers in what he called 'the teaching of contempt'.

Much of this was due to internal tensions within the early church. Yet it led to a painful history, during which Jews were at times massacred, expelled, publicly humiliated, forcibly converted, accused of poisoning wells, spreading the plague and killing Christian children for religious purposes, the so-called Blood Libel. Though such behaviour was often condemned by popes, and in some cases in violation of Christian doctrine, it left a legacy of suspicion, fear and hate.

Isaac's work was read by John XXIII, a man of courage who, as Archbishop Roncalli in Istanbul during the war, had saved thousands of Jewish lives. In June 1960 the two men met, and the Pope resolved to re-examine the Church's attitude to other faiths, Judaism in particular. Thus began the process of Vatican II, though John XXIII, who died in 1963, did not live to see its completion. Though the doctrinal development eventually adopted was small, it brought a completely new spirit to the relations between the two faiths that has persisted to this day.

Events once inconceivable have taken place, among them Pope John Paul II's 1986 visit to the synagogue in Rome where he spoke of the Jewish people with profound fraternal respect and even love, and his prayer in 2000 at the Western Wall in Jerusalem. Most remarkable of all, though, was Pope Francis' 2013 statement in the course of his reply to an open letter by an Italian journalist, Dr Eugenio Scalfari, which was critical of the Church, not least for its attitude to Jews.

Referring to Vatican II, Francis wrote that 'God has never neglected his faithfulness to the covenant with Israel, and that, through the awful trials of these last centuries, the Jews have preserved their faith in God. And for this, we, the Church and the whole human family, can never be sufficiently grateful to them.' This is the most positive statement ever uttered by a pope about Judaism and the Jewish people, and it is eloquent testimony that even in the face of religious difference, broken relationships can be mended and ancient wounds begin to heal.

Rarely has this been more important, because our world faces formidable challenges in which it is essential that Jews and Christians stand together, if possible expanding that embrace to include other faiths, not least the other Abrahamic monotheism, Islam.

Religiously motivated violence has brought chaos and destruction to great swathes of the Middle East, parts of sub-Saharan Africa and Asia. Christians are suffering the religious equivalent of ethnic cleansing in countries where they have been a presence for centuries. Peaceful Islam is being subverted by radical jihadists, leading to barbarism and slaughter, often of other Muslims, on an ever-widening scale. Meanwhile, antisemitism has returned in full force within living memory of the Holocaust.

Few foresaw that religion would once again become a major force in the global political arena, and it has returned not as a still, small voice but as a whirlwind destroying all that lies in its path. We need, if anything, another and larger *Nostra Aetate*, binding together the great world religions in a covenant of mutuality and responsibility. The freedom and respect we seek for our own faith we must be prepared to grant to others. We need a global coalition of respected religious leaders with the vision John XXIII had in his day and the honesty to admit that much that is done in the name of faith is in fact a desecration of faith and a violation of its most sacred principles.

It took the Holocaust to bring about *Nostra Aetate*. What will it take now for religious leaders to stand together in opposition to the religiously motivated hatreds spreading like contagion through our interconnected world? The need is great, the risk immense, and the time is now.

The Road Less Travelled

Published in The Islamic Monthly *on 10 March 2016, reflecting on the relationship and history between Judaism and Islam.*

We in the Jewish community sometimes forget how much we owe Islam. It was the great Islamic theologians and thinkers – among them al-Farabi, Ibn Sina (Avicenna) and Ibn Rushd (Averroes) – who recovered the classical tradition of philosophy, leading the West out of the Dark Ages.

Maimonides, one of the greatest Jewish thinkers in the past 1,000 years, was also deeply indebted to them. Throughout his masterwork, *The Guide for the Perplexed*, he is in constant dialogue with the *Mutakallimun*, or the Muslim Kalamists. Even his great religious law code, the *Mishneh Torah*, was inspired by Sharia codes. Maimonides, in turn, influenced Christian thinkers like Aquinas. Thus, both Judaism and Christianity are deeply indebted to the thinkers of Islam.

Furthermore, Maimonides' son, Rabbi Abraham, felt a deep kinship with Islamic mystical traditions. Speaking personally, I learned much from Ibn Khaldun, who is sometimes described as the world's first sociologist. His insights into the processes of social decline remain deeply relevant to the West today.

Some years ago, I wrote an article in *The Times* telling the story of how Averroes became the first person to make a religious argument for freedom of speech. He influenced the sixteenth-century Jewish sage, Rabbi Judah Loew of Prague, who quotes him on the subject. John Milton, a Christian writer, made the same point in his 1644 defence of free speech, *Areopagitica*. Two centuries later, secularist John Stuart Mill reiterated the argument in his 1859 classic, *On Liberty*. I found it moving how first a Muslim, then a

Jew, then a Christian, then a secular humanist, came together to agree on the importance of free speech and the dignity of dissent.

Today, however, all religions face a challenge. The world is changing at an ever-accelerating pace. Meanwhile, societies in the West are abandoning the religious ethic that once made them great. The dominant culture in Europe today is secular, consumerist, individualist and relativistic, offering little by way of moral guidance and still less in terms of a sense of the sacred.

Oscar Wilde once defined a cynic as a person who knows the price of everything and the value of nothing. In that sense, ours is a cynical age. That is why in all the great faiths, the most rapidly growing groups are those most opposed to the secular mainstream. In one sense, this is good news. It means that religion still has a voice in the twenty-first century, and an important one, reminding us of the things that have value, but not a price. In another sense, though, it is very dangerous indeed, because religion has become a source of strife throughout the world in the Middle East, Africa, Asia and even Europe. That is why I wrote *Not in God's Name*.*

It is a religious protest against religiously motivated violence, against those who kill in the name of the God of life, hate in the name of the God of love, wage war in the name of the God of peace and practise cruelty in the name of the God of compassion. For this is not the way of Abraham and those who count themselves among his heirs.

The Abrahamic monotheisms – Judaism, Christianity and Islam – have all had violent periods in their history, but in the long run, these experiences have turned out to be disastrous. They begin by fighting the 'Other,' but they end by fighting people of their own faith: Jew against Jew, Christian against Christian, Muslim against Muslim. That is when serious believers – at first only a few, but an important few – come to the conclusion that

* Jonathan Sacks, *Not in God's Name* (London: Hodder & Stoughton, 2015).

this cannot be what God really wants from us. They know that every life is like a Universe, that the murder of the innocent is a sin as well as a crime, and that terror in the name of God is a desecration of the name of God.

The great faiths consecrate the name of God when they honour human dignity, practise justice and compassion, lead people to feed the hungry and help the homeless and teach their children to love, not hate. Those who respect others are respected, while those who practise violence eventually perish through violence.

Jonathan Swift once said, 'We have just enough religion to make us hate one another, but not enough to make us love one another.' Let that not be said of us. We each have the responsibility to offer an alternative to the violent voices within our own faith. Only Jews can do this for Judaism, Christians for Christianity, and Muslims for Islam. I wrote *Not in God's Name** to encourage others to do the same within their own faiths. Real change only comes from within.

In an age of extremes, it is easy to be an extremist. The real religious hero is the one who takes the road less travelled, showing that faith heals, not harms. That is what Islam did in the great age of Al-Andalus and *La Convivencia* in Spain, and it won the admiration of the world. Who will do it today?

* Ibid.

Beyond the Politics of Anger

Published in The Daily Telegraph *on 11 November 2016 to reflect on the rising levels of extreme political debate in light of the British public's decision on 23 June 2016 to leave the European Union and the election of Donald Trump as President of the United States on 9 November 2016.*

This is not politics as usual. The American Presidential election, the Brexit vote and the rise of extremism in the politics of the West are warnings of something larger, and the sooner we realise it, the better. What we are witnessing is the birth of a new politics of anger. It is potentially very dangerous indeed.

No civilisation lasts for ever. The first sign of breakdown is that people stop trusting the ruling elite. They are seen as having failed to solve the major problems facing the nation. They are perceived as benefiting themselves, not the population as a whole.

They are out of touch and surrounded by people like themselves. They have stopped listening to the grass roots. They underestimate the depth and breadth of popular anger. That happened in both Washington and Westminster. The governing class fail to see the blow coming. That is how the party of the status quo is defeated by the candidate of the angry party, however incoherent his or her policies actually are.

Therein lies the danger because anger is a mood, not a strategy, and it can make things worse not better. Anger never solves problems, it merely inflames them. The danger down the road, as it has been throughout history, is the demand for authoritarian leadership, which is the beginning of the end of the free society. We shouldn't forget Plato's warning that democracy can end in tyranny.

There is only one viable alternative. It is not a return to the status quo. It is bigger than traditional divisions between the parties. It is the creation of a new politics of hope.

Hope is not optimism. It begins with a candid acknowledgment on all sides of how bad things actually are. Vast swathes of the population in Britain and America have not benefited from economic growth. They have seen their living standards fall, relatively and absolutely. They have watched while traditional jobs have been outsourced to low-wage economies, leaving once-thriving industrial centres as demoralised wastelands.

We need a new economics of capitalism with a human face. We have seen bankers and corporate executives behaving outrageously, awarding themselves vast payments while the human cost has been borne by those who can afford it least. We have heard free-market economics invoked as a mantra in total oblivion to the pain and loss that come with the global economy. We have acted as if markets can function without morals, international corporations without social responsibility, and economic systems without regard to their effect on the people left stranded by the shifting tide. We who are grandparents know only too well that life is harder for our children than it was for us, and for our grandchildren it will be harder still.

We need to rebuild our social ecology. When a civilisation is in good order it has institutions that provide support and hope in hard times. In the West these have traditionally been families and communities. Neither is in a good state throughout the West today. Their breakdown led two of the most important thinkers in America, Charles Murray on the right and Robert Putnam on the left, to argue that, for large sections of the population, the American dream lies broken beyond repair. The sooner we abandon the politically correct but socially disastrous view that marriage is outmoded, the better.

We need to recover a strong, inclusive sense of national identity if people are to feel that those in power care about the common good, not simply the interests of elites. The West is still suffering from the damage done by multiculturalism, living proof that the road to Hell is paved with good intentions. Unless we can restore what George Orwell called patriotism as opposed to nationalism, we will see the rise of the far right, as is happening already in Europe.

The religious voice is important also, and I say this not because I am religious but because historically the great faiths have given people a sense of dignity and worth that was not tied to what they earned or owned. When religion dies and consumerism takes its place, people are left with a culture that encourages them to buy things they don't need with money they don't have for a happiness that won't last. It is a bad exchange, and it will end in tears.

All this is big and deep and serious, and it will need us to move beyond the confrontational politics and divisive zero-sum thinking that have so brutalised public debate. Anger is always a hazard of politics in ages of rapid change, but it has not always been as dangerous as it is now. The revolution in information technology has transformed the entire tone of global culture in the twenty-first century. Smartphones and the social media empower groups that might otherwise lack a collective voice. The internet has a disinhibition effect that encourages indignation and spreads it like contagion.

A politics of hope is within our reach. But to create it we will have to find ways of strengthening families and communities, building a culture of collective responsibility and insisting on an economics of the common good. This is no longer a matter of party politics. It is about the very viability of the freedom for which the West fought for so long and hard. We need to construct a compelling narrative of hope that speaks to all of us, not some of us, and the time to begin is now.

Morality Matters More Than Ever in a World Divided by Fear and Faithlessness

Published in The Daily Telegraph *on 1 September 2018 to highlight the launch of Rabbi Sacks' landmark five-part BBC Radio 4 series exploring 'Morality in the Twenty-first Century'.**

What happens to national identity when everything holding a nation together disintegrates or disappears? What happens to society when the focus of a culture is on the self and its icon, the 'selfie'? What happens when Google filters and Facebook friends divide us into non-communicating sects of the like-minded? And what happens to morality when the mantra is no longer 'We're all in this together', but rather 'I'm free to be myself'?

These were some of the questions that prompted me to undertake a five-part series on morality in the twenty-first century to be broadcast on BBC Radio 4 next week. It was thrilling to engage in dialogue with some of the finest minds in Britain and North America as well as with some stunningly articulate sixth-formers from London and Manchester.

What emerged from this journey into the state of Western culture is that morality matters more than we commonly acknowledge. It's all we have left to bind us into shared responsibility for the common good. Morality is our oldest and most powerful resource for turning disconnected 'I's into a collective 'We'. It's

* 'Morality in the Twenty-first Century', Rabbi Sacks' BBC Radio 4 series, is available to listen to on BBC Sounds. In addition to the five main programmes, you can also listen to extended conversations between Rabbi Sacks and the participants: Nick Bostrom, David Brooks, Melinda Gates, Jonathan Haidt, Noreena Hertz, Jordan Peterson, Stephen Pinker, Robert Putnam, Michael Sandel, Mustafa Suleyman and Jean Twenge.

the alchemy that turns selfish genes into selfless people, egoists into altruists, and self-interested striving into empathy, sympathy and compassion for others.

It is no accident that the word 'demoralisation' means what it does: a loss of confidence, enthusiasm and hope. Without a shared morality, we are left as anxious individuals, lonely, vulnerable and depressed, struggling to survive in a world that is changing faster than we can bear and becoming more unstable by the day.

One symptom of this was starkly revealed this week in the news that almost a quarter of fourteen-year-old girls in Britain had self-harmed in the course of a year. This is a deeply disturbing trend, but it will have come as no surprise to readers of *iGen*,* the thoroughly researched study of American children born in or after 1995: the first generation to have grown up with smartphones. Jean Twenge, its author, is one of the participants in the radio series. She told me about her discovery that rates of self-ascribed life satisfaction among American teenagers plummeted after 2012, while depression and suicide rocketed upward. Again, it was girls who were the more vulnerable.

Her view is that social media and smartphone addiction have played a significant part in this pathology. Young people were spending between seven and nine hours a day on their phones. The result has been a loss of social skills, shortened attention spans and sleep deprivation, but, above all, anxiety. Seeing their friends' posts, they are subject to Fear of Missing Out (FOMO) and constantly comparing themselves with the burnished images of their contemporaries. iGeners, she says, are 'scared, maybe even terrified'. They are 'both the physically safest generation and the most mentally fragile'.

* Jean Twenge, *iGen: Why Today's Super-connected Kids Are Growing Up Less Rebellious, More Tolerant, Less Happy – and Completely Unprepared for Adulthood – and What That Means for the Rest of Us* (New York: Atria Books, 2017).

The second result, charted by another participant in the series, the American social psychologist Jonathan Haidt, is the assault on free speech taking place in university campuses. His new book, published next week, is called *The Coddling of the American Mind*,* subtitled, 'How good intentions and bad ideas are setting up a generation for failure.'

It tells of how the new ideas of 'safe spaces', 'trigger warnings' and 'no platforming', despite their good intentions, can screen out from university life views and voices that fail to fit the prevailing canons of political correctness. This is being done in the name of the right not to be offended – a right that would have terrified George Orwell, whose dictum, engraved on the walls of the new BBC Broadcasting House, states: 'If liberty means anything at all, it means the right to tell people what they do not want to hear.'

This is closely related to a third phenomenon playing an ever-larger part in the liberal democracies of the West, namely identity politics. There was a time, until recently, when politics aspired to be about what is best for the nation. One of the lasting unintended consequences of multiculturalism is that we no longer think of the nation as a whole. Instead, the electorate has been fragmented into a series of subcultures, defined by ethnicity, religion, gender or sexual orientation. These can easily become competitive interest groups, less concerned with the common good than with what is good for those-like-me.

Each group can be encouraged, by the mood of our time, to see itself as a victim and to identify an oppressor who can be blamed for their current predicament. This gives rise to a divisive and rancorous politics that divides society, like the dualisms of old, into the children of light and the children of darkness. It also provides a justification for the use of social media to manipulate public opinion by fake news and 'alternative facts'. When it comes

* Jonathan Haidt and Greg Lukianoff, *The Coddling of the American Mind: How Good Intentions and Bad Ideas Are Setting Up a Generation for Failure* (New York: Penguin, 2019).

to defending your group against oppressors, people think that the end justifies the means.

These are dangerous tendencies at both an individual and collective level. You can see this in the spate of best-selling self-help books about anxiety and depression on the one hand, and, on the other, a string of books with titles such as *How Democracies Die*,[*] *Suicide of the West*[†] and *The Retreat of Western Liberalism*.[‡]

What connects the personal and the political was given a name more than a century ago by the great sociologist Émile Durkheim. He called it anomie: a state of instability, in societies and individuals, resulting from the breakdown of a shared set of moral beliefs and attitudes. This would lead, he thought, to a rise in suicides as well as a loss of social cohesion.

Since the 1960s, we have come to believe that you can outsource morality to the market and the state. The market is about wealth, the state about power. The market gives us choices and the state deals with the consequences of those choices. Within those parameters we can do whatever we like so long as it does not directly harm others.

We are learning that this only works in the short term. In the long term, when all that matters is wealth and power, the wealthy and powerful gain and the poor and powerless suffer. That's what has happened for at least a generation. Hence the anger and loss of trust that today divide societies throughout the West.

There is an alternative. Since civilisation began, morality has been humanity's internal satellite navigation system as we have journeyed towards the undiscovered country called the future. It has taken different forms, but it is always about caring for the

* Steven Levitsky and Daniel Ziblatt, *How Democracies Die: What History Reveals About Our Future* (New York: Penguin, 2019).

† Jonah Goldberg, *Suicide of the West: How the Rebirth of Tribalism, Populism, Nationalism, and Identity Politics Is Destroying American Democracy* (New York: Crown Forum, 2018).

‡ Edward Luce, *The Retreat of Western Liberalism* (London: Little, Brown, 2017).

good of others, not just ourselves; about decency, honesty, faithfulness and self-restraint, treating others as we would wish to be treated. It's the world of 'we', not 'I'.

While the market and the state are about competition, morality is about co-operation. It is born and sustained in families, communities, voluntary organisations and religious congregations. Altruism, Viktor Frankl taught us, is the best cure for depression. Virtue, as Aristotle noted, is the basis of strong societies. And we can each make a contribution. As Melinda Gates reminds us in the last programme of the series: change one life for the better and you've begun to change the world.

Morality is the redemption of our solitude. With it we can face the future without fear, knowing we are not alone.

Part Four

The House of Lords

Queen's Speech (Maiden Speech)

26 November 2009

'If there is one insight above all others to be gained from Jewish history, it is that freedom depends on education. To defend a country you need an army, but to defend a civilisation you need schools.'

My Lords, when I entered this Chamber for the first time, I did so from the Moses Room, and I thank my Lordships for the lengths they went to make a rabbi feel at home.

Today I feel the other side of that occasion, for it was Moses at the Burning Bush who felt so overwhelmed by emotion that he told God he could not speak; he was 'not a man of words' (Exodus 4:10).

Mind you, that did not stop him speaking a great deal thereafter. In fact, on one occasion, when pleading with God to forgive the people for making the Golden Calf, he spoke for forty days and forty nights.

However, on another occasion, when asking God to heal his sister Miriam, he limited himself to a mere five words. I am told by your Lordships that, when making a maiden speech, it's better to err on the side of the latter than the former; and that I will try to do.

The powerful emotion I feel today is simply explained. My late father came here as a child fleeing persecution in Poland. My mother's family had arrived here somewhat earlier. And the love they felt for Britain was intense.

It took me a while to understand it, but eventually I came to realise what so many Jews in Britain know in their hearts and their very bones, that had it not been for this country, their parents or grandparents would not have lived, and they would not have been born.

That visceral sense of indebtedness is what made Jews in this country want to give back, to contribute to society as a whole, which they did with all their heart. They contributed to its arts and sciences, its law and medicine, its business and finance, its Armed Forces and its public life, its charities and voluntary associations. And they wanted us to do the same, to be proud of being British and proud of being Jewish, seeing no contradiction between the two but on the contrary, a mutual reinforcement. And I believe the same is true for other minority groups in this country.

My late father had to leave school at the age of fourteen to help support the family, and he wanted us, his four sons, to have the education he lacked. And for that too I am deeply grateful. We were able, all four of us, to go to university, the same university that educated a foreign secretary of Israel, Abba Eban, who began his speech, when he returned there many years later to receive an award, with the words: 'It was here that I learned the honesty, integrity and love of truth that have been such a disadvantage to me in my political career.'

I too learned lessons there that I will never forget. I was religious; my doctoral supervisor, the late Sir Bernard Williams, was Britain's most intellectually gifted atheist. Yet never once did he deprecate or even challenge my religious faith. For we were both equal participants in that collaborative pursuit of truth that Judaism's sages, long ago, called 'argument for the sake of heaven'.

And it is this that I have rediscovered in your Lordships' House. What extraordinary things happen here! When somebody speaks, other people listen. When people disagree, they do so politely. What special gifts these are in this age of clashing sound bites, diminishing attention spans, angry voices and gladiatorial politics. And I hope that, whatever constitutional changes are in store for this House, those things will always be preserved. For what I have found in your Lordships' House, and what I learned at university, are the foundations of the virtues that made Britain the country my parents loved: its tolerance, its decency, its undemonstrative yet indomitable sense of fairness and justice.

And with this I come to my point. Democratic freedom is not just a matter of political arrangements, of constitutions and laws, elections and majorities. It depends too on what Alexis de Tocqueville called 'habits of the heart': on civility, the willingness to hear the other side, respect for those with whom you disagree and friendships that transcend the boundaries between different parties and different faiths. And those things must be taught again and again in every generation.

If there is one insight above all others to be gained from Jewish history it is that freedom depends on education. To defend a country you need an army, but to defend a civilisation you need schools. Abraham was chosen, says the Bible, so that he would teach his children to practise righteousness and justice. Moses commanded, in what has become the most famous of our prayers, 'You shall teach these things diligently to your children' (Deuteronomy 6:7). In ancient times the Egyptians built pyramids, the Greeks built temples, the Romans built amphitheatres. Jews built schools. And because of that, alone among ancient civilisations, Judaism survived.

I wonder whether even now we value teachers sufficiently highly, for they are the guardians of our liberty. Schools teach us theories and facts. They help us answer the question, 'What do I know?' Schools teach us skills. They help us answer the question, 'What can I do?' But they also teach us the story of our nation, what freedom is and how it was fought for, and what battles those who came before us had to fight. They help us to answer the questions: 'Who am I? Of what story or stories am I a part? And how then shall I live?' They teach us about keeping faith with the past while honouring our obligations to the future. At best, they teach us collective responsibility for the common good.

Sadly today, schools have to fight against a culture that sometimes overvalues material success. Some years ago, I visited a school many of whose children came from very affluent backgrounds. They told me that, the previous week, an inspector had visited the school and tested the children – they were seven or eight years old – on their vocabulary. He asked them: 'Who can tell me the meaning of the word "economy"?' One child put up his hand and said, 'Please sir, that's where the other people sit on a plane.'

Thankfully such things are rare. Therefore, with your Lordships' permission, I simply wish to say: let us value our teachers, celebrate our schools, keep education at the top of our priorities, and we will raise a generation of British children who will make us proud.

Faith Communities

29 May 2012

'We are enriched by our religious diversity. Each faith is a candle; none is diminished by the light of others; and together they help banish some of the darkness in the human heart.'

My Lords, it is a great privilege to have the opportunity of initiating this debate . . . Given that this weekend, we will celebrate Her Majesty's Diamond Jubilee, I hope that your Lordships will allow me to focus the majority of my time on the second portion of the question today, that of the relationship between faith communities and the Queen, and to draw attention to the gracious way in which she has guided and sustained this nation through one of its most challenging transitions, into a multi-ethnic, multicultural and multi-faith society.

Many tributes have been and will be rightly paid to Her Majesty for the six decades of her sustained and dedicated service to the nation, but one in particular should not be forgotten. It is not easy for any society to undergo change, least of all when that change touches on such fundamental markers of identity as religion, ethnicity and culture. It is even harder in a nation where there is an established Church, to make the members of other faiths feel welcomed, valued and at home.

But that is precisely what her Majesty has done, and I believe I speak for all of us if I say that we are lifted, blessed and enlarged by the generosity of spirit in which she has done so. Many noble Lords will wish to add their perspectives, and we will be hearing today from Christian, Muslim, Hindu, Sikh, Zoroastrian and other Jewish members of this house, as well as being honoured by the Most Reverend Primate, the Archbishop of Canterbury, who, together with his predecessors, has done so much personally to contribute to our national ecology of tolerance and mutual respect.

Let me simply therefore say on behalf of the Jewish communities of Britain and the Commonwealth how much we have appreciated Her Majesty's kindness to us and to others. This is something of a miracle in itself since Jews rarely agree on anything; but on this we are united. It is in fact astonishing how far this spreads. For the past year wherever I have travelled to Jewish communities throughout the world, one of the first questions I have been asked, is 'How was the Royal wedding?' And in the United States in several synagogues I visited in February of this year, to my astonishment, they sang 'God save the Queen'. This may be the first time since 1776 they have done so! Each week in all our synagogues we say a prayer for the Queen and the Royal Family, and this week we will be saying a special prayer of thanksgiving to mark Her Majesty's Diamond Jubilee and the great gift of her leadership and service. There are rare individuals whose greatness speaks across all ethnic and religious divides. Her Majesty is such an individual and we are truly blessed by her.

She has spoken often of her personal faith and of the Church of England of which she is the head. But she has spoken equally of the contribution all other faith communities have made to the life of the nation. At Lambeth Palace, in February, in one of the first official engagements of the Jubilee year, she reminded us of how faith itself, not just Christian faith, recalls us to the responsibilities we have beyond ourselves, and about how, together with the Church of England, other faith communities were increasingly active in helping the sick, the elderly, the lonely and the disadvantaged.

In 1952, in the first year of her reign, Her Majesty became the patron of the Council of Christians and Jews, the organisation founded ten years earlier, in the Holocaust years, by Archbishop William Temple and Chief Rabbi Joseph Hertz. That was one of the first great interfaith organisations in Britain, and today there are hundreds of such groups, creating friendships across the boundaries between faiths, where otherwise there might have been suspicion and fear. One of the greatest of them, the Interfaith Network, is this year celebrating its silver jubilee; and as we speak, another new initiative, Interfaith Explorers, is being launched at the Regent's Park Mosque in the presence of HRH The Duke of York. That too is a reminder of how greatly other members of the Royal family like HRH The Duke of Edinburgh, HRH The Prince of Wales, and others, have done in their own right to make all nine of the major faith communities in Britain feel recognised and respected.

We are enriched by our religious diversity. Each faith is a candle; none is diminished by the light of others; and together they help banish some of the darkness in the human heart. I know of few places in the world where friendship across faiths is more vigorously pursued than Britain; and for the way she has led and encouraged this great opening of hearts and minds to one another, as for so much else, Her Majesty has lifted our spirits and earned our thanks.

Religion in the United Kingdom

22 November 2012

'Religion is often misunderstood in secular ages and societies like ours . . . Religion is the redemption of our solitude.'

My Lords, I thank the noble Lord for initiating this important debate, for his distinguished contribution to the religious life of this country, and for the part he has played as a founding member and vice chair of the Interfaith Network, which is celebrating its twenty-fifth anniversary this year. It has helped to ensure that religious groups that may elsewhere find themselves in conflict, here, in Britain, meet in friendship and peace. That is a great blessing to us all.

My Lords, religion is often misunderstood in secular ages and societies like ours. It is seen as a set of strange beliefs and idiosyncratic rituals, both of which we could lose without loss. A better way of understanding religion even from the outside is as a shaper of character, a sustained education in a life lived beyond the self. Many, perhaps all, of the world's great religions teach their adherents the importance of making sacrifices for the sake of others, through charity, hospitality, visiting the sick, helping the needy, giving comfort to those in crisis, bringing moments of moral beauty into what might otherwise be harsh and lonely lives. Religion is the redemption of our solitude.

Long before these functions were taken over by the state, religious groups here and elsewhere were building schools and hospitals and networks of support. According to the extensive research carried out by Harvard sociologist Robert Putnam, today in America, and here in Britain, regular worshippers are more likely than others to give to charity, regardless of whether the charity is religious or secular, do voluntary work, give money to a homeless person, donate blood, help a neighbour with housework, spend time with someone who is feeling depressed or help someone find a job. They are more active citizens, significantly more likely to belong to community organisations and neighbourhood groups. They get involved, turn up and lead. I do not say that to be good you need to be religious, but religiosity as measured by attendance at a house of worship turns out to be a better predictor of altruism and empathy than education, age, income, gender or race.

My Lords, if this is so, the social implications are immense. Just as religions were building a welfare state before there was a welfare state, so now and in the future they may help sustain a welfare society in areas where the need for help is greater than the ability of governments to provide it. They act as a counter-voice to the siren song of a culture that sometimes seems to value self over others, rights over responsibilities, getting more than giving, consumption more than contribution, and success more than service to others.

I therefore congratulate the Government for its support in bringing Britain's many faiths together in acts of volunteering through local congregations and businesses. I urge it to consider further ways of harnessing the formidable altruistic energies of our faith communities for the common good of all of us together.

Business and Society

12 June 2013

'In Judaism we believe that work is fundamental to human dignity. We believe that everyone should be able to say: I made a contribution to the common good. I gave; I did not just receive.'

I thank your Lordships for this opportunity to ask the Government about its views on the relationship between business and society, and I welcome in particular the opportunity short debates like this provide to step back from the specifics of policy to take a larger and longer view of the moral dimensions of economic policy. This is a very large subject indeed, and I will hazard just a few words about it in general and then turn to one aspect, confident that other speakers will touch on others.

In the light of the G8 protests and so much else that has been said in recent years, it is often assumed that when religious leaders speak about business it is to be critical of capitalism and all its works. That is not the case in the tradition from which I speak. The Hebrew Bible, after all, records perhaps the world's first economist, Joseph, who invented the theory of trade cycles (seven years of plenty followed by seven lean years), which has thus far proved to be a more accurate guide to the twenty-first century than most other economic forecasts.

We believe that business, and the market economy generally, plays a moral role in society. It is the greatest stimulus we know to human creativity. It increases the common wealth. It reduces poverty, and poverty is profoundly humiliating. Economic liberty has a deep association with political liberty. Trade, as

Montesquieu pointed out in the eighteenth century, is the deep alternative to war. And throughout history, trading centres, like the city of London, have been at the forefront of tolerance and respect for difference.

But economics is always subject to an overarching moral law. According to the Talmud, the first question we are asked in heaven is: 'Were we were honest in business?' It doesn't say what happens if the answer is 'no', but in my mind's eye I see an angelic figure like Lord Sugar with wings, saying, 'You're fired!'

However, I wish to express my concern at one specific aspect of our current situation, namely youth unemployment. Today unemployment is high throughout Europe, and youth unemployment far higher still. In Britain the current figure is 20.7 per cent. This by no means the worst. In Greece the figure is 58 per cent, in Spain 55 per cent, in Italy 37 per cent, and in France 25 per cent. These are all disturbing figures.

And the real question hovering in the background is, is this a mere temporary feature of a low point in the economic cycle, or is it likely to become a permanent feature of economies in the West as virtually everything to do with business becomes increasingly globalised, as we continue to outsource manufacturing and service industries to low-wage economies elsewhere in the world?

It used to be thought that high unemployment was the price we paid for low interest and inflation rates. Is it now to be the price we pay for global free trade? Are we condemning a significant proportion of young people to a future in which they will never find work?

If so, the price we pay is likely to be very high indeed. There is the economic danger of an increasingly small working population supporting an ever-larger non-working population, something already happening because we are living so much longer. There is a political danger. Historically, and in many parts of the world today, youth unemployment is a prime cause of political instability. Above all, though, we should be mindful of the moral, psychological and, dare I say it, spiritual hazard at stake.

In Judaism we believe that work is fundamental to human

dignity. We believe that everyone should be able to say: 'I made a contribution to the common good. I gave; I did not just receive. I earned my daily bread. I did not depend on the generosity of others.' Our ancient sages said: 'Do even the most menial work rather than be dependent on others.' Maimonides, our most eminent medieval scholar, held that the highest form of charity was job creation, because it enabled the recipient to become independent of charity. These remain compelling ideas.

A Jewish economist, David Ricardo, formulated one of the most morally beautiful of all economic theories, the law of comparative advantage, which states that even if you are better than me at everything, still, if you are better at some things than others, and I am better at some things than others, then if we both concentrated on what we are best at, and trade, we are both better off. Which means that every one of us has a contribution to make to the common wealth. We all have something to give.

In a very moving article a few months ago Matthew Parris wrote about the experience of life on welfare benefit which he had once undertaken to do for a television documentary. He discovered that the real issue was not so much material as psychological. Without minimising the deep financial hardship, he wrote, 'What I'll never forget was the slow, quiet, killing quality of a life without purpose, a life where you depend but no one depends on you; a life where all the people around you, too, are without occupation.' He spoke of the 'shame' and 'indignity' of worklessness. That is precisely what drives Jewish economic ethics.

My Lords, there is an inescapable moral dimension to economic policy because it is, in the end, not about abstractions like GDP but about people. There could be no more dispiriting prospect than the thought that a significant proportion of young people in this country will grow up without prospect of employment, without contributing to the nation's economy, without having the chance to say: 'I made this, I contributed, I helped this to happen.' Employment is a moral issue, because dignity comes from what we do to enhance the lives of others.

Middle East and North Africa

30 October 2014

'When ancient theologies are used for modern political ends, they speak a very dangerous language indeed.'

My Lords, I too thank the noble Lord, Lord Risby, for initiating this important debate. And at the outset I declare an interest. I am a Jew. Israel is therefore for me the place where my people were born almost 4,000 years ago, the place to which Abraham and Sarah travelled, where Amos voiced his vision of social justice and Isaiah dreamed of a world at peace, where David composed the Psalms and Solomon built the Temple – and this had consequences not only for Jews but also for Christians and Muslims, who claim Abraham as their ancestor in faith, and whose God they take as their own.

This had tragic repercussions throughout the Middle Ages because Christians and Muslims claimed, each in their own way, to have replaced Jews as the people of God and thus as heirs to the Holy Land. The otherwise saintly Augustine declared that Jews were cursed with the fate of Cain, destined to be restless wanderers on Earth without a home. Islam held that any land that ever came under Muslim rule was henceforth and for ever Dar al-Islam, that is, land that rightly belongs to the Ummah, the Muslim people, any other rule being illegitimate. On both of these theologies, Jews had no right to their ancestral home.

A half-century ago, these theologies would have been considered irrelevant. The West had moved on. After a century of religious wars following the Reformation, it recognised the need for the secularisation of power. This allowed the United Nations, in the Partition vote of 1947, to grant Jews the right to a nation state of their own after 2,000 years of exile and persecution. Eventually there were peace agreements with Egypt and Jordan and an intensive process with the Palestinians. When power is secularised, peace is possible.

Today, though, the Middle East and parts of Asia and Africa are undergoing a seismic shift in precisely the opposite direction. People are de-secularising. They feel betrayed by secular nationalist governments that failed to deliver prosperity and national pride. They consider the national boundaries imposed by colonial powers to be artificial and obsolete. They are uninspired by the secular culture of the West with its maximum of choice and minimum of meaning. And they have come to believe that salvation lies in a return to the Islam that bestrode the narrow world like a colossus for the better part of a thousand years.

And though their faith is hostile to modernity, they sometimes understand modernity better than its own creators in the West. They know that because of the internet, YouTube and the social media, communication, indeed politics itself, has gone global, and they also know that the great monotheisms are the most powerful global communities in the world, far broader and deeper in their reach than any nation state. And the religious radicals are offering young people the chance to fight and die for their faith, winning glory on Earth and immortality in Heaven. They have started recruiting in the West and they have only just begun.

But when ancient theologies are used for modern political ends, they speak a very dangerous language indeed. So, for example, Hamas and Hezbollah, both self-defined as religious movements, refuse to recognise the legitimacy of the State of Israel within any boundaries whatsoever and seek only its complete destruction.

The Islamists also know that the only way they can win the sympathy of the West is by demonising Israel. They know you can't win support for ISIS, Boko Haram or Islamic Jihad, but if you can blame Israel, you will gain the support of academics, unions and the media and you will distract attention from the massacres in Syria and Iraq, the slow descent of other countries into chaos and the ethnic cleansing of Christians throughout the region.

They are thus repeating the very failure of the regimes they have risen against, who for fifty years suppressed dissent by demonising Israel as the cause of everything wrong in the Arab or Islamic world. When you blame others for your failures you not only harm them, you harm yourself and your people. To be free, you have to let go of hate. And if you let hate speech infect the West, as has already happened in some of our campuses, prisons and even schools, then our freedom too will be at risk.

My Lords, I and the vast majority of the Jewish community care deeply about the future of the Palestinians. We want Palestinian children, no less than Israeli children, to have a future of peace, prosperity, freedom and hope. Which is why we oppose those who teach Palestinian children to hate those with whom they will one day have to live; who take money given for humanitarian aid and use it to buy weapons and dig tunnels to take the region back to a dark age of barbarism.

More generally, we say in the name of the God of Abraham, the Almighty, merciful and compassionate God, that the religion in whose name atrocities are being carried out, innocent people butchered and beheaded, children treated as slaves, civilians turned into human shields and young people into weapons of self-destruction, is not the Islam that once earned the admiration of the world, nor is its God the God of Abraham. It was Nietzsche not the prophets who worshipped the will to power. It was Machiavelli not sacred scripture who taught that it is better to be feared than to be loved.

Every religion must wrestle with its dark angels, and so today must we: Jews, Christians and Muslims alike. For we are all children of Abraham, and it will only be when we make space for one another as brothers and sisters that we will redeem the world from darkness and walk together in the light of God.

Freedom of Religion and Belief

16 July 2015

'Religious freedom is about our common humanity, and we must fight for it if we are not to lose it.'

I thank the noble Lord, Lord Alton, for enabling us again to address this vital issue of religious freedom, and indeed Baroness Berridge for chairing the APPG [All-Party Parliamentary Group] on International Religious Freedom and Belief, and I salute their courage in confronting perhaps the single greatest humanitarian issue of our time.

Three things have happened to change the religious landscape of the world. First, the secular nationalist regimes that appeared in many parts of the world in the twentieth century have given rise to powerful religious counter-revolutions.

Second, these counter-revolutions are led by religion in its most extreme, adversarial and anti-Western form.

Third, the revolution in information technology has allowed these groups to form, organise and communicate to actual and potential followers throughout the world with astonishing speed. The internet is for radical political religion what printing was for Martin Luther. It has allowed them to circumvent and outflank all existing structures of power.

The result has been the politicisation of religion and the religionisation of politics; and throughout history this has been a deadly combination. In the long run it will threaten us all, because in a global age no country or culture is an island.

We must do minimally three things. First, given that religious freedom is enshrined as Article 18 in the United Nations

Universal Declaration of Human Rights, there should be, under the auspices of the United Nations, a gathering of religious leaders and thinkers to formulate an agreed set of principles that are sustainable theologically within their respective faiths, and to which member nations can be called to account. Otherwise Article 18 will continue to be a utopian ideal.

Second, we must do the theological work. That is fundamental. That is what happened in Europe after the wars of religion of the sixteenth and seventeenth centuries. A group of thinkers, among them John Milton, Thomas Hobbes, John Locke and Benedict Spinoza, sat down, re-read the Bible, and formulated some of the most important ideas ever formulated about state and society: the social contract, the moral limits of power, liberty of conscience, the doctrine of toleration and the very concept of human rights.

These were religious ideas based on the Bible, which is what John F. Kennedy meant when he said in his Inaugural Address, 'the same revolutionary beliefs for which our forebears fought are still at issue around the globe – the belief that the rights of man come not from the generosity of the state, but from the hand of God'.

We have not yet done the theological work for a global society in the information age; and not all religions in the world are yet fully part of that conversation. If we neglect the theology, all else will fail.

Third, we must stand together, people of all faiths and of none, for we are all at risk. Christians are being persecuted throughout the Middle East. Jews are facing a new and resurgent antisemitism. Muslims who stand on the wrong side of the Sunni/Shia divide are being killed in great numbers. Hindus, Sikhs, Buddhists, Baha'i and others face persecution in some parts of the world.

There must be some set of principles that we can appeal to, and be held accountable to, if our common humanity is to survive our religious differences. Religious freedom is about our common humanity, and we must fight for it if we are not to lose it. This, I believe, is the issue of our time.

National Life: Shared Values and Public Policy Priorities

2 December 2016*

'When people in a society share a strong moral code, there is greater trust and solidarity . . . there is a sense of collective pride and common purpose that activates and empowers the better angels of our nature.'

I am deeply sorry that illness prevents me from being present at the important House of Lords debate, initiated by the Archbishop of Canterbury, on the shared values underpinning our national life. Few subjects have been more neglected in recent decades, and the results are palpable, damaging and dangerous.

You cannot have a society without a shared moral code. The point was made eloquently by Lord Devlin: 'If men and women try to create a society in which there is no fundamental agreement about good and evil they will fail; if, having based it on common agreement, the agreement goes, the society will disintegrate.'

Lord Devlin was speaking at a fateful moment in the history of the West, in 1958. Over the next ten years his argument was in effect rejected, and one after another of the moral principles we have come to call the Judeo-Christian heritage were abandoned, at least as far as the law was concerned. Since then, most people have come to believe that we are entitled to do whatever we like so long as it is within the law, and that the law itself should be limited to the prevention of harm to others.

* Rabbi Sacks was unwell on the day of this debate and therefore was unable to deliver these prepared remarks in the Chamber.

But what does harm others is not always immediately obvious. The breakdown of marriage and stable families has caused immense harm to several generations of children, psychologically, socially and economically. The breakdown of codes of honour and responsibility have led to appalling behaviour on the part of at least some senior figures in business and the financial sector, who have served themselves while those they were supposed to have served have borne the cost. There has been a palpable collapse of trust in one institution after another – an inevitable consequence of our failure to teach the concepts of duty, obligation, altruism and the common good.

We have begun a journey down the road to moral relativism and individualism which no society in history has survived for long. It was the road taken in Greece in the third pre-Christian century and Rome in the first century CE: two great civilisations that shortly thereafter declined and died. Britain has begun along the same trajectory, and it is bad news for our children, and for our grandchildren worse still.

Some elements of morality are universal: justice-as-fairness and the avoidance of inflicting harm. But others are particular. They are what give a country and culture its colour, its distinctive handwriting in the Book of Life. The Britain I grew up in had extraordinary values and virtues. It honoured tradition but was open to innovation. It valued family and community but also left space for eccentricity and individuality.

People did not need to shout to make a point. There was a coolness, a dignity, a sense of propriety and protocol, that allowed people of very different views to get along with minimum abrasion. Even if you lost, you took pride in playing the game. If you were successful, you were not ostentatious. If you were unsuccessful, you were still accorded dignity.

I was a Jew and Britain was a Christian country, but it wore its religion lightly and its embrace was inclusive and warm. Generations of Jews who came here fleeing persecution elsewhere saw these virtues as wondrous, as something deeper and stronger than mere abstract tolerance, and wanted us, their children, to acquire them. For them and for us Britain was not just where we were but a vital part of who we were.

Britain today is far more diverse, but there is no reason to think that we do not need a strong sense of shared morality and collective responsibility, all the more so now that Britain has chosen to go its own way into the future and not simply as part of Europe as a whole.

When people in a society share a strong moral code, there is greater trust and solidarity: people become more active citizens, they help others, fewer people are left abandoned and alone, the successful share their blessings with those who have less, and there is a sense of collective pride and common purpose that activates and empowers the better angels of our nature.

Achieving such a state cannot be done by government alone, but the Government can encourage civil, communal, charitable and religious groups to deliberate together to envision the Britain we would like to create for future generations, and then work together to help bring it about. I can think of no more important, urgent and uplifting task for all of us right now than to work together to create a society of justice, fairness, kindness and compassion that honours the dignity of each and the welfare of all.

Balfour Declaration Centenary

5 July 2017

'I urge Her Majesty's Government to acknowledge the State of Israel as living testimony to the power of hope to triumph over hate.'

My Lords, the Balfour Declaration in 1917 was a significant moment in history for three reasons.

First it was a momentous reversal of imperialism. It gave back to the Jewish people the home that had been seized by empire after empire, the Assyrians, Babylonians, Persians, Greeks, Romans, and the Christian and Muslim empires that fought one another for centuries for control of the Jewish land.

Second, what eventually became the State of Israel was the only non-artificial creation among a host of artificial states, among them Jordan, Lebanon, Syria, Iraq and Libya, that had never been states before and thus still exist in a state of ethnic, religious and tribal strife. Only Israel had previously existed as a nation state, which it had done 3,000 and 2,000 years ago.

Third, it was a brave, if failed, attempt to prevent what later became clear at the Evian Conference in 1938, when the Jewish people, facing what Hitler called *Vernichtung* ('extermination'), had not one square inch they could call 'home' in the sense defined by the poet Robert Frost as the place where, when you have to go there, they have to let you in.

No people should lack a home, not Palestinians and not Jews. Which is why it is tragic that a century after the Balfour Declaration, significant groups still seek to deny the Jewish people a home, among them Iran and Hezbollah and Hamas, two groups that the leader of Her Majesty's Opposition [the Labour Party, led by Jeremy Corbyn MP] has in the past called 'friends'. Friends of violence and terror, yes. Friends of humanity, no.

My Lords, it is shameful that the Jewish people still has to fight for the right to exist in the land that for thirty-three centuries it has called home. Yet, constantly threatened though it is by missiles, terror and delegitimation, it has achieved so much in science, medicine, technology and humanitarian aid that I urge Her Majesty's Government to acknowledge the State of Israel as living testimony to the power of hope to triumph over hate.

Education and Society

8 December 2017

'We need to teach our children the story of which we and they are a part, and we need to trust them to go further than we did, when they come to write their own chapter.'

My Lords, I am grateful to the Most Reverend Primate for initiating this debate on a subject vital to the future flourishing of our children and grandchildren. My Lords, allow me to speak personally as a Jew. Something about our faith moves me greatly and goes to the heart of this debate. At the dawn of our people's history, Moses assembled the Israelites on the brink of the Exodus.

He didn't talk about the long walk to freedom. He didn't speak about the land flowing with milk and honey. Instead, repeatedly, he turned to the far horizon of the future and spoke about the duty of parents to educate their children. He did it again at the end of his life, commanding: 'You shall teach these things repeatedly to your children, speaking of them when you sit in your house, when you walk on the way, when you lie down and when you rise up' (Deuteronomy 6:7).

Why this obsession with education that has stayed with us from that day to this? Because to defend a country you need an army. But to defend a civilisation you need schools. You need education as the conversation between the generations.

Whatever the society, the culture or the faith, we need to teach our children, and they theirs, what we aspire to and the ideals we were bequeathed by those who came before us. We need to teach our children the story of which we and they are a part, and we need to trust them to go further than we did when they come to write their own chapter.

We make a grave mistake if we think of education only in terms of knowledge and skills – what the American writer David Brooks calls the 'résumé virtues' as opposed to the 'eulogy virtues'.

And this is not woolly idealism. It's hard-headed pragmatism. Never has the world changed so fast, and it's getting faster each year. We have no idea what patterns of employment will look like in two, let alone twenty years from now, what skills will be valued, and which done instead by artificially intelligent, preternaturally polite robots.

We need to give our children an internalised moral satellite navigation system so that they can find their way across the undiscovered country called the future. We need to give them the strongest possible sense of collective responsibility for the common good, because we don't know who will be the winners and losers in the lottery of the global economy and we need to ensure its blessings are shared. There is too much 'I' and too little 'We' in our culture and we need to teach our children to care for others, especially those not like us.

We work for all these things in our Jewish schools. We give our children confidence in who they are, so that they can handle change without fear and keep learning through a lifetime. We teach them not just to be proud Jews, but proud to be English, British, defenders of democratic freedom and active citizens helping those in need.

Schools are about more than what we know and what we can do. They are about who we are and what we must do to help others become what they might be. The world our children will inherit tomorrow is born in the schools we build today.

Antisemitism

13 September 2018

'It pains me to speak about antisemitism, the world's oldest hatred. But I cannot keep silent.'

My Lords, I am grateful to the noble Lord, Lord Popat, for initiating this debate, and I want to explain why. The greatest danger any civilisation faces is when it suffers from collective amnesia. We forget how small beginnings lead to truly terrible endings. A thousand years of Jewish history in Europe added certain words to the human vocabulary: forced conversion, inquisition, expulsion, ghetto, pogrom, Holocaust. Once hate goes unchecked, the road to tragedy is short.

My Lords, it pains me to speak about antisemitism, the world's oldest hatred. But I cannot keep silent. One of the enduring facts of history is that most antisemites do not think of themselves as antisemites. 'We don't hate Jews,' they said in the Middle Ages, 'just their religion.' 'We don't hate Jews,' they said in the nineteenth century, 'just their race.' 'We don't hate Jews,' they say now, 'just their nation state.'

Antisemitism is the hardest of all hatreds to defeat because, like a virus, it mutates, but one thing stays the same. Jews, whether as a religion or a race or as the State of Israel, are made the scapegoat for problems for which all sides are responsible. That is how the road to tragedy begins.

Antisemitism, or any hate, become dangerous when three things happen. First, when it moves from the fringes of politics to a mainstream party and its leadership. Second, when the party sees that its popularity with the general public is not harmed thereby. And third, when those who stand up and protest are vilified and abused for doing so. All three factors exist in Britain now. I never thought I would see this in my lifetime. That is why I cannot stay silent. For it is not only Jews who are at risk. So too is our humanity.

Part Five

Speeches and Lectures

A Decade of Jewish Renewal

In London's St John's Wood Synagogue on 1 September 1991, Rabbi Sacks delivered this installation address after formally being inducted as the sixth Chief Rabbi of the United Hebrew Congregations of the Commonwealth.

I have had more than a year to contemplate this moment, but the closer it has come the more overwhelmed I have been. The greatest leader the Jewish people has ever known, Moses, trembled when he contemplated the burden of leadership, and said *Mi anochi:* 'Who am I?' (Exodus 3:11) What then shall I say, who until the age of twenty-five never dreamed of becoming a rabbi, let alone a Chief Rabbi? Thirteen years ago, almost exactly to the day, I began a journey as rabbi of the Golders Green Synagogue, and today, on my bar mitzvah in the rabbinate, you have bestowed on me the honour of one of the great positions of leadership in the Jewish world. Now as then, I am determined never to rely on my own merits. Instead, I pray to God, in the words of King Solomon, for a *lev shomea lishpot et amcha,* 'a listening and discerning heart' (1 Kings 3:9), attentive to the needs of His community and ever obedient to His word. *Ana avdah dekudsha brikh hu:* 'I am a servant of the Holy One, blessed be He.' No Jew can say less; no Jew can aspire to more.

Let me begin by paying tribute to my distinguished predecessor Lord [Immanuel] Jakobovits. Here in this pulpit, nearly a quarter-century ago, he spoke at his own installation of the three crowns of rabbinic leadership: the crowns of kingship, priesthood and Torah. Since then, no one has done more to raise those crowns to their proper glory: kingship, in addressing and securing the admiration of the wider public, recognised in his elevation to the peerage and the award of the Templeton Prize; priesthood, in his great work for Jewish education; and Torah, in his adoption of the mantle of the prophets as the voice of Jewish ethics in confused times. Lord Jakobovits, you have raised the standing of the Chief Rabbinate in both Jewish and non-Jewish eyes; and for you and Lady Jakobovits, may your years of retirement be as long and as creative as your years of office.

At this emotional moment let me express my thanks to those in whose merit I stand here today: to my teachers, especially to Rabbi Nachum Rabinovitch, from whom I learned that love of Torah and moral courage go hand-in-hand; to the distinguished Dayanim of our Beth Din [Judges of the Rabbinical Court], for their constant encouragement and advice; to my revered colleagues in the rabbinate without whom I could not hope to achieve what must be achieved in the coming years; and to all those with whom I had the privilege of working at Jews' College, and in the Golders Green and Marble Arch synagogues – true friends who made each of those experiences memorable.

Above all, my heart goes out today to my family. Elaine and I married young, and little did she know then where this strange journey of ours would one day lead. But she has been with me every inch of the way, as have our children Joshua, Dina and Gila, giving strength and support and love. Most of all on this day of days I thank my parents, who gave me a *Yiddisher neshomo*, 'a Jewish soul', and who made me realise that the greatest love parents can have for a child is to want him always to grow. To you all: I pray that I may be worthy of your hopes.

I want today to set out the direction of my Chief Rabbinate, and to share with you the vision that lies behind it. Let me begin with the vision.

Time and again this past year, as I sat in Jerusalem, breaching its inspiration, one saying came into my mind, the saying of one of the great heroes of Judaism, Akavia ben Mahalalel. He said: *histakel bishloshah devarim ve-ein atah ba lidei averah* ('Reflect on three things, and you will not transgress, go wrong, lose your way'). *Da meayin bata* ('know from where you came'), *ulean ata holekh* ('and where you are going'), *velifnei mi atah atid liten din vecheshbon* ('and know before whom you will have to give an account') (Ethics of the Fathers 3:1).

Akavia was suggesting something daring and fundamental. We can go wrong as individuals or as a people, not necessarily because we are driven by malice, but simply because of a failure of imagination. For a moment we lived for the moment; and we forgot what the past should have taught us, what the future consequences would be, and we forgot that there is always an accounting, a moral price to pay. We can go astray simply because of a failure of imagination. A failure of *historical* imagination: we forgot where we came from. A failure of *prophetic* imagination: we forgot where we were travelling to. Or a failure of *spiritual* imagination: we forgot before Whom we stand. Akavia spoke of individuals. But I want today to apply his three great questions to the Jewish people as a whole, because it is there that my vision belongs.

How does Jewish history begin? With a journey. *Lech lecha* ('get thee out') (Genesis 12:1). The very first words of God to Abraham set him on a journey, *el haaretz asher areka* ('towards a land'), *ve'escha legoi gadol* ('towards nationhood'), *va'avarecherha va'agadla shemecha vehyeh berakhah* ('towards being blessed and becoming a blessing unto others') (Genesis 12:1–2). The whole of the Torah from Genesis to Deuteronomy is the story of that journey. But what happens?

And here we come to a mystery which haunts the whole of Jewish existence. The story the Torah tells about Israel begins with the journey of Abraham to the land. But by the time it ends his children still have not arrived. The book of Devarim ends with Moses on the mountain looking down on Israel from afar but still not having crossed the Jordan. *Meayin bata ulean atah holech.* Where have the children of Israel come from and to where are they going? From a small family to a great nation. From exile to a land. From slavery to freedom. The five books of Moses tell that story. What they do not tell is what happened when Israel finally arrived.

We are an ancient people, older than almost any other. We have seen one civilisation after another rise to power and then decline and fall. But in almost 4,000 years of our history, only three times have we stood on the brink of our destination. Only three times have we been a great nation with freedom and a land. Once, in the days of Joshua. A second time when Cyrus of Persia gave the Babylonian exiles permission to return. And the third time today. The whole of Jewish history has been a journey to those three moments. What happened when we arrived?

On the first occasion, Israel fell apart. There was the period of the judges, when *ish hayashar be'enav yaaseh* ('each person did what was right in his own eyes') (Judges 21:25). Then, after only three kings – Saul, David and Solomon – the country split into two with the ultimate loss of 80 per cent of the people of Israel, the lost ten tribes. Those that remained were too few and weak to overcome the might of Babylon. And so, the First Temple was destroyed, the first arrival failed.

On the second occasion, Israel fell apart. Under Ezra and Nehemiah they renewed the covenant. But then they succumbed to Hellenisation, what we would today call assimilation. There were fierce divisions within Jewry, even at times civil war. It was, said the rabbis, a time of *sinat chinam*, of 'groundless hatred' between Jew and Jew. And by the time Vespasian and Titus marched on Jerusalem, Jews were too disunited to resist. And so, the Second Temple was destroyed; the second arrival failed.

And at that moment a great question mark was raised over the Jewish people. We have an unparalleled capacity to travel hopefully. Abraham, Isaac, Jacob, Moses, all of them spent their lives travelling in hope. But do we have the capacity to arrive? That is the single most crucial question facing Jewry today. Because, for only the third time in the annals of our people, we stand as Moses stood at the end of his life: within sight of the destination to which the whole of Jewish history has been a journey.

For nearly 2,000 years of exile, we longed for freedom. We have it now. We prayed for a land. We have it now. We prayed to stand within thy gates, O Jerusalem. We have it now. We prayed for the ingathering of exiles from the four corners of the world. We have it now. Nothing stands between us and the realisation of the greatest dream ever dreamed by our grandparents or theirs all the way back to Abraham: to be a *mamlechet kohanim vegoi kadosh* ('a people dedicated to God in freedom and sovereignty') (Exodus 19:6). We stand at the threshold of millennial longings. And only one thing stands in our way: a failure of imagination. Of historical imagination, remembering where we came from. Of prophetic imagination, remembering where we are travelling to. Or of spiritual imagination, remembering before Whom we stand.

Consider this. For 2,000 years we were the People of the Book. No nation has ever cherished Jewish learning, education, as did we. Against every other civilisation, Jews said education is not for an elite but *morashah kehillat yaakov,* the heritage of every Jew. It isn't just for the young but *chayenu veorech yamenu* – it is our whole lives and the length of our days. Only one people ever predicated its very survival not on might or power but on a book: education is the link that binds the generations.

And today? Despite the great advances in Anglo-Jewish education, how many of our children have been to a Jewish school? How many of them can understand Hebrew, the one language that connects us to the Jewish people? How many of them carry on studying about Judaism beyond the age of twelve or thirteen, perhaps the earliest age that it begins to make sense? How often do we study a Jewish book?

Or consider this. Since the time of Abraham and Sarah, if there was one thing Jews guarded as the very fulcrum of their survival it was the family. What did they pray for more than anything else? For children to carry on the covenant. When the prophets rose to the climax of religious passion, how did they describe the relationship between God and Israel? In the language of the family. *Bni bechori Yisrael* (Exodus 4:22). We are God's children, and He is our father. *Ve'erastich li leolam* (Hosea 2:21). We are God's betrothed, and He is our beloved. The family was where Jews learned who they were, where they came from and to where they were going. The family was where Jews learned to love. The family was the crucible of Jewish survival.

Today we know that in Anglo-Jewry there are too few synagogue marriages. Divorce has become an epidemic. Non-marriages, mixed marriages and broken marriages have become not the rare exception but the rule. How can we, almost within a single generation, have taken perhaps the Torah's greatest single contribution to human happiness and simply thrown it away?

Or consider this. For the last 1,800 years Jews were scattered across every country of the globe, from Babylon to Birmingham, from Buenos Aires to Berditchev. And yet they knew, and their neighbours knew, that they were an extended family, a single nation *Yeshno am echad mefuzar umeforad bein ha'amim* (Esther 3:8). Though they were dispersed, they were united: by a common past, a common hope and a common faith. They knew where they had come from, to where they were going and before Whom they stood. Though they had no land, they were one people.

And today: we have a land, but are we one people? We are more deeply divided than at almost any time in our history. Israel is divided. We in the Diaspora are divided. A few years ago, Jewish thinkers asked the question: Will there be one Jewish people in the year 2000? Today there are already many prepared to give the answer 'no'. These are fundamental rifts which threaten the very integrity of Jewry as *am echad*, a single people.

The Jewish people has lost its way. For generations we travelled hopefully; but do we now have the courage to arrive? For generations we prayed; but can we live with the answer to our prayers? We survived slavery; but can we handle freedom? We have eaten the bread of affliction; but can we handle affluence? We learned to live with Israel as a dream; can we live with Israel as a reality?

Can it be that on the very brink of the fulfilment of the hopes of generations, our strength of will might desert us at the last moment yet again? It cannot be. The first failure brought us an exile of seventy years. The second failure brought us an exile of 1,870 years. There can be no third failure.

In this fifty-eighth century, Jewish time, Jews have passed through the *Shoah,* the greatest human tragedy ever to befall our people, and the rebirth of the State of Israel, our greatest collective miracle in 2,000 years. In Israel during the Gulf War, I could not believe what was happening, that even through the missiles and the danger, Russian and Ethiopian Jews kept on coming; and I knew that though Jews had said these words for thousands of years, it was our generation that had been privileged to see them come true: *im yihyeh nidachacha bikzei hashamayim,* 'Though you are scattered to the ends of the world, from there the Lord your God will gather you and bring you back' (Deuteronomy 30:4). And within the last two weeks we have witnessed Soviet Communism, one of the greatest attempts ever made to eliminate God, Judaism and the biblical value of individual freedom, bring upon itself its own destruction. Can any of us believe that we live in ordinary times?

A Jewish writer once said, 'The number of Jews in the world is smaller than a small statistical error in the Chinese census. Yet . . . big things seem to happen around us and to us.' This century things have happened to us, for evil and for good, so big that they have no precedent since the days of the Bible; and they summon us to greatness. I pray: let our imagination not fail us now.

We must work together to renew the Jewish world. For nearly 2,000 years we travelled in hope; and now on the brink of arrival let us not lose our way. We have suffered from complacency and religious underachievement. We have injured ourselves by divisions and petty rivalries. A section of our community is slowly drifting away. We are losing our most precious possessions – Jewish identity, the Jewish family, above all our commitment to the Torah which inspired generations to lead lives of holiness and moral beauty. Are we, who once heard the call of destiny, deaf to it now? Are we, who taught the world that religious faith is a journey from slavery to freedom, unable to cope with the challenges of freedom? God forbid. We have lost our prophetic vision.

But we who live at this momentous time can recover it together.

Because – *meayin bata*. Where did we come from? From a hundred generations of Jews who suffered because of their faith and people yet remained loyal to both. *Le'am atah holekh*. Where are we going to? To the day when, living our faith in freedom and pride, *verau kol amei ha'aretz ki sham Hashem nikra alecha,* 'all the nations of the Earth shall see that we are called by the name of God' (Deuteronomy 28:10). *Velifnei mi atah atid liten din vecheshbon*. And to whom are we responsible? To God, and to all the generations of Jews who came before us and prayed for what we have; and to all those generations yet unborn whose Jewish fate is in our hands.

I was sitting one Shabbat afternoon watching children playing in the streets of Jerusalem. There was a stillness and a peace which exists only on Shabbat in Jerusalem as the sun begins to set and the houses turn red and gold. And then I remembered how almost 2,000 years ago Rabban Gamaliel and Rabbi Elazar ben Azariah and Rabbi Yehoshua had seen this city in ruins and they wept. But Rabbi Akiva, that giant of faith, said: 'One day Zechariah's prophecy will come true. "Old men and women will once again sit in the streets of Jerusalem . . ." *urechovot ha'ir yimalu yeladim viyladot mesachakim birchovoteha,* "and the streets of the city will be filled with children playing"' (Zechariah 8:4–5). And I thought, *Ribbono shel olam,* how long we waited; how many exiles, expulsions, persecutions and pogroms we endured; but we never lost that vision.

Here was Israel, the oldest of lands, renewed; here was Jerusalem, the oldest of cities, made new again; here were Jewish children giving an ancient faith new life. I understood as never before what the rabbis meant when they said that when God gave us the Torah *chayei olam nata betochenu,* He planted everlasting life in our midst. And at that moment I knew what it was I had come to Jerusalem to learn. That in each generation the

Shehkinah, the Divine presence, rests with those who take our old faith and make it new again. It rested with the builders of Israel; with the builders of *yeshivot* and Jewish schools; with those who lived not for the moment but for the sake of future generations of Jewish children. It is they who gave us, as a people, new life.

And I no longer doubted what I had to do in Anglo-Jewry. I had to begin by calling on you to join with me in creating a Decade of Jewish Renewal.

Let us cease to be a community whose institutions and attitudes are growing old. Let us start this day and for the next ten years a process of working together to build a community where Jewish children can stand proud and free, knowing where they came from, where they are going to and before Whom they stand.

I call on you to join with me in renewing our *ahavat Yisrael,* our categorical commitment to the love of every Jew. We must reach out to every Jew with open arms and an open heart. If we must disagree, and sometimes we must, let us do so with love and dignity and respect. We can prove the Torah's greatness only by inspiration, not by negation. We are a divided community. But let us work to lessen those divisions by coming closer to one another and to God. We have suffered enough from antisemitism. Let us practise philosemitism. We have suffered enough from the assaults of others. Let us never inflict them on ourselves.

Help me to renew *ahavat Torah:* a love of the way of life which is our one claim to distinctiveness as a people, and above all a love of learning. Let us renew Jewish learning at every level, formal and informal, child and adult, in every context and every form. There is no more radical idea than *vedibarta bam,* 'You shall speak words of Torah, when you sit in your house and when you walk on the way, when you lie down and when you rise up' (Deuteronomy 6:7). That we should never stop learning. That we should continually grow. That we should serve God not only with our hearts but also with our minds. The greatest single renewal of Anglo-Jewry will come about if we make learning the heritage of every Jew.

Help me to renew *ahavat Hashem,* love of God who brought the Jewish people into being and lifted us above the shifting winds of history to make us an eternal people. We have become secularised. There are times when we believe that Jews can survive without beliefs, as an ethnic group sustained on nostalgia. But faith is not a luxury we can live without. It is the air we breathe. If we can speak to God in prayer; if we can give to God through charity or service to the community; if we can create in our private lives a home for the Divine presence, and in our public lives a *kiddush Hashem,* a sanctification of God's name, we gain that one sense without which there can be no human happiness. That in this fleeting transitory span of years we did something great. We walked in *derekh Hashem,* the path of God.

Let us renew our contribution to British society. Here in this country we love, we have found freedom, tolerance and respect for our traditions. Britain was and is a moral giant among nations; and we must play our full part in carrying it forward as a caring and compassionate society. As Jews we must care about the environment, about social, medical and business ethics and about the image of God in our fellow human being, Jew and non-Jew alike.

Let us renew our attachment to the land and State of Israel. For there, in the land where we were born as a people, we have been reborn as a people. Because of Israel, after 2,000 years Jews have taken up their destiny once again as a sovereign people. Because of Israel there is some place that every Jew whose life or liberty is threatened can call home. Because of Israel, Jewish learning flourishes as never before and as nowhere else. Without sidestepping any of the dilemmas Israel faces, let our love for it be unequivocal and our attachment to its people unbreakable.

A Decade of Jewish Renewal: Let me be quite clear what I mean. I do not mean that I have a personal programme which I am determined to impose on the community with or against its will. That is not how I understand leadership. I want to encourage leadership in others; to be a catalyst for creativity; to open closed doors and let in the fresh air of initiative and imagination. I want to start a process that will gather momentum over time. I want to listen to and involve everyone willing to work with me in three great areas – leadership, education and spirituality.

And so, I call, first and foremost, to our rabbis: my colleagues. Let us lead from the front. Let us be driven by our calling to reach out, bring close, enthuse and inspire. If there is only one great leader in Anglo-Jewry and it is the Chief Rabbi, I will have failed. Because my greatest ambition is not my success but your success.

I call to our educators: let us see how we can make the whole of Anglo-Jewish education greater than the sum of its constituent parts. Let us see how we can bring the school, the synagogue and the Jewish home closer so that they reinforce one another.

I call to our lay leaders: let us work together to plan, not for today or even tomorrow but for the next generation. Let us start now to recruit the leaders of ten and twenty years' time. Let us be less cautious, less insular, less afraid of experiment and open debate. Above all I call to every member of Anglo-Jewry to join me in the task of renewing this great community. I cannot, nor will I ever try to, lead alone. I call not for your appreciation but for your participation. I will only succeed if you will join the ranks of the doers. I call on every group in the community to begin this year the process of defining objectives and constructing plans. Let us become joint architects of the Anglo-Jewish future.

A Decade of Renewal: I choose the word renewal carefully. Judaism recognises not *shinui* but *chiddush,* not change but revitalisation. And if we do not renew our institutions, they will die the slow death of increasing irrelevance. There is more than one way of building a shul, or conducting a service, or teaching Torah, or constructing a communal institution. Every year Rosh Hashanah tells us that we are living now, not a century ago. We must search out a hundred new ways of letting prayer speak to our souls, learning to our minds and *mitzvot* to our lives; and if they fail, we must search for the hundred-and-first way. Our community has been immeasurably enriched in recent years by *yeshivot*, Chassidic groups, outreach movements, new ventures in adult and informal education. I see in each of these developments a priceless source of spiritual energy; and I want above all to liberate spiritual energy so that Judaism lives as if it were given new this day.

What then should we hope to achieve?

An Anglo-Jewry in which we reach out in love and with respect to every Jew.

An Anglo-Jewry in which we do not pretend that all is right with our community so long as there are groups who feel neglected; and there *are* groups who feel neglected: women, the young, intellectuals, the less well-off, the provinces, the small communities.

An Anglo-Jewry in which Judaism challenges us at the highest levels of our minds, hearts and souls.

An Anglo-Jewry in which we praise the successes of others, because we are not threatened but enlarged by the many ways of serving God.

An Anglo-Jewry in which, precisely as committed Jews, we make a distinctive contribution to Britain as a compassionate society.

An Anglo-Jewry in which we bring all our powers of leadership, creativity and energy to the service of God.

An Anglo-Jewry in which we are never afraid to grow as Jews.

An Anglo-Jewry of open doors, open hearts and open minds. Open to the love of God, Torah and the Jewish people.

A small agenda. Can it be done? *Ein hakodosh barukh hu ba betyrunia im beriyotav.* God never sets us tasks that cannot be done. Never for one moment believe that it cannot be done.

You have given me, as Chief Rabbi, one precious gift above all: the gift of time. One of my great predecessors of blessed memory once said: 'Chief Rabbis never retire and only very rarely die.' Well: all men are mortal, and nowadays Chief Rabbis retire as well. And yet since 1845 there have been only five Chief Rabbis, and I am the sixth. You have given me the mandate to build for the future. What I cannot achieve one year, I will work for the next. I recognise the problems. We are a declining and ageing community.

We are in the midst of a recession. We must work with limited resources. There are in our community attitudes and divisions which will take a long time to change. I approach my task with open eyes. I will make mistakes, but I will learn from them. I will have failures, but I will try again, another way, another time. But I will never give up or relax or despair. And if it is not for us to complete the task, neither are we free to desist from it.

Together we have great things to do. For this is a rare and special moment in the history of the Jewish people. Only twice before in our long life as a people have we had the chance to practise Judaism in freedom and against the background of a sovereign State of Israel. For 2,000 years we prayed for it to come again, and now that it has, we must not fail the challenge of this *et ratson,* this window of opportunity. We will not fail. Because *haba letaher mesayin oso;* because God helps those who turn toward Him; and never does He allow those who seek Him to fail. We will succeed because *ein bererrah:* this time there is no choice but to succeed.

Let us work together to plan and create a Decade of Renewal of Jewish leadership, education and spirituality. And may God, who will not forsake His people, cause His spirit to rest in the work of our hands.

Markets and Morals

On 2 June 1998, Rabbi Sacks was invited to deliver the annual Hayek Lecture at the Institute of Economic Affairs in memory of the Nobel prize-winning economist Fredrich Hayek.

In 1978, Friedrich Hayek, whose work and influence we commemorate tonight, proposed a great debate. He was by then almost eighty years old, but the passion with which he sought to defend the market order against what he saw as the heresy of collectivism was undiminished. So, as if hoping to settle the issue once and for all, he suggested nothing less than an international disputation that would discuss the question, 'Was socialism a mistake?' The event did not take place, but Hayek nonetheless produced a large manuscript setting out his beliefs, which was published in an abridged form under the title *The Fatal Conceit*.* What interests me in particular about this work is the title of the book's last chapter, namely 'Religion and the Guardians of Tradition'. What led Hayek, who had devoted a lifetime to the study of economics and politics, to set the seal on this work with a reflection on religion and tradition?

The Fatal Conceit is a difficult book, but if I have understood it correctly, its argument is this. For the free market and its 'extended order' to emerge, so too did a certain kind of morality. For many thousands of years, human beings had lived in small bands of hunter-gatherers, and it was during that long pre-history of *Homo sapiens* that our instincts were formed. Those instincts – of solidarity and altruism – allowed our ancestors to live together

* F. A. Hayek, *The Fatal Conceit: The Errors of Socialism* (London: Routledge, 1998).

in close face-to-face groups and without them no isolated individual could have survived for very long.

However, a significant change had to take place in the way people related to one another for mankind to be able to make the transition from the small group or tribe to the larger and more open associations needed for complex societies and economies. Instincts were no longer sufficient. Instead their place had to be taken by rules such as those relating to private property, honesty, contract, exchange and so on. For Hayek, the question of how these rules first appeared is irrelevant. What matters is that they emerged and spread, not because people were able to decide in advance what their consequences would be, but simply because the groups who adhered to them found themselves able to grow and spread more successfully than others.

Often, they involved people acting against their instincts, so they had to be taught through habit rather than by appeal to inclination. Moral education became a matter of imitation, learning by doing, the handing on of tradition by habituation. Morality itself consisted largely of 'Thou shalt not's', prohibitions that served as boundaries within which free human action could be directed and contained, much as the banks of a river contain and direct the flow of water. It was this kind of morality that, for Hayek, made possible the fateful transition of humanity from tribal society to a market economy in which ever larger associations of individuals and groups could develop their specialisations and yet meet their needs through the peaceful process of trade and exchange.

So it was in the past. But Hayek, having lived through some of the great dislocations of the twentieth century, could never take the market order or its associated phenomenon, the free society, for granted. It was, he believed, vulnerable on two counts. On the one hand there was the perennial danger of a retreat into the primitive instinct of group solidarity with its attendant hatred of the outsider. On the other there was the seductive voice of reason, the 'fatal conceit' that by conscious intent and deliberate planning we can improve on the morality of the past, and as it were re-design our basic human institutions. This, he felt, was the error of socialism, but not only socialism. It was also the mistake of liberals such as John Stuart Mill who regarded traditional moral constraints as, for the most part, eminently dispensable, the unwanted baggage of a more superstitious age. Morality – as Hayek never tires of reminding us in the course of the book – occupies a place *between* instinct and reason and cannot be reduced to either.

This line of thought brought Hayek to reflect on the role of religion – in particular the great monotheistic faiths – in preserving moral traditions. In part this was a matter of history. We owe it to religions, he said, 'that beneficial traditions have been preserved and transmitted at least long enough to enable those groups following them to grow, and to have the opportunity to spread by natural or cultural selection'.*

But it was not only a matter of history; it was a matter of the present as well. To understand why, we have to remind ourselves again of Hayek's understanding of the 'extended order' of complex societies. They come about, he argues, because of repeated applications of simple rules. They develop in ways which none of us can predict in advance. Each one of us plays a minute but significant part in that process. We participate, in his powerful phrase, in 'those spontaneous social forces through which the individual creates things greater than he knows'. Only with hindsight and historical perspective can we see what, through an almost infinite number of individual acts, we have achieved. None of us, not the wisest of sages or the most informed of central agencies, could have planned it in advance.

The striking feature of religion, for Hayek, is its attitude of humility, even reverence, towards the great moral institutions without which our 'extended order' could not have developed. It guards against what he calls 'the rationalist delusion that man, by exercising his intelligence, invented morals that gave him the

* F. A. Hayek, ibid., p. 136.

power to achieve more than he could ever foresee'. Of course it does so by insisting that our morals were given by God. For Hayek, they were arrived at by the evolutionary forces of history. What these two views held in common, though, was a strong and principled opposition to the idea that individually or collectively we can devise a better system rationally constructed to maximise happiness or some other good.

It is a fascinating argument, and it places Hayek in a line of thinkers – such as Edmund Burke, Max Weber, and most recently Francis Fukuyama – who have reflected not only on the internal morality of markets (what we call nowadays 'business ethics') but on the wider question of what kind of society gives rise to and is able to sustain a market economy. The answer which each of them gave – an answer that has been given new salience by the rise of the economies of Southeast Asia – is that they tend to be societies with a strong respect for certain kinds of tradition.

Like Burke, Hayek combines liberalism in economics and politics with a marked conservatism in morality. Free institutions, they seem to say, are best preserved by a certain piety towards the past. Traditions encode the accumulated discoveries of earlier generations in a way that no single generation, however sophisticated, could discover for itself; and it is through learning those traditions and passing them on to our children that we avoid extremely costly mistakes. Paradoxically, it may be just those societies that have strong religious and moral habits, which form the best environment for economic development and technological innovation. It may be that those who are most secure in their past are the most confident and energetic in shaping the future.

Thus far Hayek; and it is an argument that is worth revisiting, for the very opposite reason than the one he contemplated. *The Fatal Conceit* was written in 1978 and published in 1988. Twenty years ago, he could still see socialism as the dragon to be slain. Within a year, though, of the book's publication, the Berlin Wall came down. In rapid succession, the Cold War ended, East European Communism was abandoned and the Soviet Union was disbanded. It was one of the most decisive victories in the history of ideologies, all the more striking for having taken place without a shot being fired. Hayek's great debate never took place, but it is fair to say, as of now, that he won the argument after all. As Raymond Plant put it, 'Central economic planning is now not on the political agenda of any country seeking to be part of the global economy.'*

It is therefore all the more important for us to bear in mind the caveat Hayek himself insisted on, namely that the market economy can only be sustained by certain habits of behaviour and restraint which he called traditions. He believed that the threat to these traditions was socialism. Doubtless, in his day it was. But what he paid far less attention to was the possibility that they might be undermined not by anti-market ideologies but by the very power of the market itself. For the market is not only an institution of exchange. It is also a highly anti-traditional force, at least in advanced consumer societies. The stimulation of demand, for example, depends on a culture, even a cult, of the new, the product that improves on the past and renders it obsolete in an increasingly short space of time. It encourages a view of human life itself as a series of consumer choices rather than as a set of inherited ways of doing things.

One of the most fateful developments is the displacement of human identity as something given by the history into which I am born. Instead it becomes something like a suit of clothes which I can choose, wear for a while, and then discard in favour of the new season's fashion – the move graphically illustrated by our change of terminology from 'life' to 'lifestyle', with its suggestion that there is nothing of substance that defines who I am; there is merely the supermarket of ideas from which I can choose what I happen to be into for the time being, from Buddhism to therapy to aerobics to the environment to organic vegetables to the internet

* Lord Plant, 'Market, Morals and Community', Twentieth Annual Lecture, St George's House, Windsor, 1997, p. 3.

to *The Little Book of Calm*.* In the process, religion itself is transformed from salvation to a branch of the leisure industry, and we are transformed, as one writer put it, 'from pilgrim to tourist'.

That is why it is sometimes useful to do what Hayek advised us to do in *The Fatal Conceit*, namely, to reflect on the role of religion in sustaining a particular kind of moral order. That is what I want to do, taking the experience of Jews and Judaism as an example. It was of course Max Weber, in his famous work *The Protestant Ethic and the Spirit of Capitalism*,† who made us familiar with the idea that religion – in particular Calvinism – was one of the great shaping forces of the modern economy. More recently Michael Novak has written powerfully about the same subject from a Catholic perspective. But few writers have doubted the contribution Jews made to the development of finance, business and industry, a contribution that can be traced far back into the Middle Ages and beyond.

I vividly recall a talk given by the master of my college [Gonville & Caius, University of Cambridge], the late Joseph Needham, describing the role Jews had played in bringing the inventions of China to the West. Christopher Columbus in his great journey of 1492, the year in which Jews were expelled from Spain, made use of tables drawn up by one Jew, Abraham Zacuto, instruments made by another, Joseph Vecinho, and took a third, Luis de Torres, as his interpreter. At about the same time, one of the great rabbis and bible commentators of the Middle Ages, Don Yitzhak Abarbanel, served as financial advisor to King Alfonso V of Portugal and Ferdinand and Isabella of Castile, and later made important contributions to the economic life of Naples and Venice. Wherever they were able to, Jews played a significant role in the development of trade and finance. Indeed in 1844, in

* Paul Wilson, *The Little Book of Calm* (Hawthorn: Penguin Putnam, 1996).

† Max Weber, *The Protestant Ethic and the Spirit of Capitalism* (London: Penguin Modern Classics, 2014).

a notoriously antisemitic tract, Karl Marx argued that Jews were the very embodiment of the capitalist system.

It would be quite wrong to identify a great religious tradition with any particular set of economic institutions. It was, after all, the biblical Joseph who instituted the first known example of centralised economic planning, using the seven years of plenty to prepare for the seven years of famine, and whose ability to forecast trade cycles is probably still the envy of economists. Jewish history contains some of the great experiments in socialist utopias, from the property-sharing communities of the Essenes in the Second Temple period to the modern Israeli kibbutz. But there is no doubt that for the most part, Jews and Judaism itself found free competition and trade the system most congruent with their values.

What was it about Judaism that led to this elective affinity between it and the market economy? In his stimulating recent book *The Wealth and Poverty of Nations*,* David Landes identifies a number of factors. First there was the biblical respect for property rights. This he sees as nothing less than a revolution against the ancient world and the power it gave rulers to regard the property of the tribe or the people as their own. By contrast, when Moses finds his leadership challenged by the Israelites during the Korach rebellion, he says about his relation to the people, 'I have not taken one ass from them nor have I wronged any one of them' (Numbers 16:15).

For a ruler to abuse property rights is, for the Hebrew Bible, one of the great corruptions of power. Judaism is the religion of a people born in slavery and longing for redemption; and the great assault of slavery against human dignity is that it deprives me of the ownership of the wealth I create. At the heart of the Hebrew Bible is the God who seeks the free worship of free human beings, and two of the most powerful defences of freedom are private property and economic independence. The ideal society envisaged by the prophets is one in which each person is able to sit

* David Landes, *The Wealth and Poverty of Nations* (London: Little Brown, 1998), pp. 29–59.

'underneath his own vine and fig tree' (Micah 4:4). The prophet Samuel in his famous speech on the dangers of monarchy – which might almost be subtitled 'The Road to Serfdom' – warns against the constant temptation of kings to expropriate persons and property for the public good. Government, he seems to argue, may be necessary, but the less of it there is, the better.

Beyond this, Landes identifies in the Judeo-Christian tradition, an openness to invention and innovation. In part this has to do with the biblical respect for labour. God tells Noah, for example, that he will be saved from the Flood, but it is Noah who has to build the Ark. The high value Judaism sets on work can be traced throughout the biblical and rabbinic literature. If not itself a religious act, it comes close to being a condition of the religious life. 'Six days shall you labour and do all your work, but the seventh day is a Sabbath to the Lord your God' (Exodus 20:9–10) – meaning that we serve God through work as well as rest. By our labour we become, in the striking rabbinic phrase, 'partners with God in the work of creation'.

The Jewish liturgy for Saturday night – the point at which the day of rest ends – culminates in a hymn to the values of work: 'When you eat of the labour of your hands, you are happy, and it shall be well with you' (Psalm 128:2). On this, the rabbis commented, 'You are happy' refers to this life; 'It shall be well with you' refers to life in the world to come. Work, in other words, has spiritual value, because earning our food is part of the essential dignity of the human condition. Animals *find* sustenance; only mankind *creates* it. As the thirteenth-century commentator Rabbeinu Bachya put it, 'The active participation of man in the creation of his own wealth is a sign of his spiritual greatness.'

As a result, Judaism never developed either an aristocratic or a cloistered ethic that was dismissive of the productive economy. The great rabbis were themselves labourers or businessmen or professionals. They knew that the Jewish community needed an economic as well as a spiritual base. Accordingly, the Talmud lists as one of the duties of a parent, to teach one's child a craft or trade through which he can earn a living. Maimonides rules that one who is wise 'first establishes himself in an occupation which supports him, afterwards he buys a home, and after that he marries'. More powerful still is his ruling that to provide someone with a job is higher than any other form of welfare benefit:

> The highest degree of charity, exceeded by none, is that of a person who assists a poor Jew by providing him with a gift or a loan or by accepting him into a business partnership or by helping him to find employment – in a word, by putting him where he can dispense with other people's aid. With reference to such help it is said, 'You shall strengthen him, be he a stranger or a settler, he shall live with you' (Leviticus 25:35), which means to strengthen him in such a manner that his falling into want is prevented.*

All other forms of charity leave the recipient dependent on charity. Work alone restores his self-respect and independence. 'Flay carcasses in the market-place,' said the third century teacher Rav, 'and do not say: I am a priest and a great man and it is beneath my dignity.'

No less important than the value placed on work is Judaism's positive attitude to the creation of wealth. The world is God's creation; therefore it is good, and prosperity is a sign of God's blessing. Asceticism and self-denial have little place in Jewish spirituality. What is more, God has handed the world over to human stewardship. The story of man's creation begins with the command, 'Be fruitful and multiply, fill the Earth and subdue it' (Genesis 1:28). God, taught Rabbi Akiva in the second century, deliberately left the world unfinished so that it could be completed by the work of man. Industry is more than mere labour. It is the arena in which we transform the world and thus become, in the striking rabbinic phrase, 'partners with God in the work of creation'.

* Maimonides in Mishneh Torah, Laws of Charity, 10:7–14.

It was Max Weber who observed that one of the revolutions of biblical thought was to demythologise, or disenchant, nature. For the first time human beings could see the condition of the world not as something given, sacrosanct and wrapped in mystery, but as something that could be rationally understood and improved upon. This perspective, central to Judaism, even today makes rabbinical authorities surprisingly open to new medical technologies such as genetic engineering and cloning, and tends to make religious Jews among the most dedicated users of the internet and multimedia for purposes of education.

Above all, from a Jewish perspective, economic growth has religious significance because it allows us to alleviate poverty. Judaism's early sages had the sanest view of poverty I know, and they did so because most of them were poor men. They refused theologically to anaesthetise its pain. They would utterly have rejected Marx's description of religion as the opium of the people. Poverty is not, in Judaism as in some faiths, a blessed condition. It is, the rabbis said, 'a kind of death' and 'worse than fifty plagues'. They said, 'Nothing is harder to bear than poverty, because he who is crushed by poverty is like one to whom all the troubles of the world cling and upon whom all the curses of Deuteronomy have descended. If all other troubles were placed one side and poverty on the other, poverty would outweigh them all.'

What concerned the sages was not so much the elimination of poverty through redistributive taxation. Instead, what they sought to create was a society in which the poor had access to help when they needed it, through charity to be sure, but also and especially through job creation. Hence with wealth came responsibility. *Richesse oblige*. Successful businessmen (and women) were expected to set an example of philanthropy and to take on positions of communal leadership. Conspicuous consumption was frowned upon, and periodically banned through local 'sumptuary laws'. Wealth was a Divine blessing, and therefore it carried with it an obligation to use it for the benefit of the community as a whole.

Not the least significant of Judaic contributions to the development of Western civilisation was its emphasis on, perhaps even invention of, linear time. Ancient cultures tended to think of time as cyclical, seasonal, a matter of eternal recurrences to an original and unchanging nature of things. The Hebrew prophets were the first to see time in a quite different way – as a journey towards a destination, a narrative with a beginning and middle, even if the end (the Messianic society) is always beyond the horizon. It is ultimately to this revolution that we owe the very notion of progress as a historical category, the idea that things are not predestined always to remain what they were. Hope, even more than necessity, is the mother of invention.

And to this we must add one further idea. The great philosophical advocates of the market, Bernard Mandeville, David Hume and Adam Smith, were struck by a phenomenon that many considered to be scandalous and amoral. This was their discovery that the market produced benefits to all through a series of actions and transactions that were essentially selfish in their motivation. As Adam Smith put it bluntly, 'It is not from the benevolence of the butcher, the brewer, or the baker, that we expect our dinner, but from their regard to their own interest.'[*] Within the system of free trade, as Smith put it most famously, the individual 'intends only his own gain, and he is, in this, as in many other cases, led by an invisible hand to promote an end which was no part of his intention'.[†] This fact, that markets and their associated institutions tend to work on the basis not of altruism but of somewhat earthier motives, has always led to a high-minded disdain for everything suggested by the word 'commercial'.

Not so within Judaism. Long before Mandeville and Adam Smith, Judaism had accepted the proposition that the greatest advances are often brought about through quite unspiritual

* Adam Smith, *An Inquiry into the Nature and Causes of the Wealth of Nations* (New York: Modern Library, 1937), p. 14.

† Smith, ibid., p. 423.

drives. 'I saw', says the author of Ecclesiastes, 'that all labour and all achievement spring from man's envy of his neighbour' (Ecclesiastes 4:4). Or as the Talmudic sages put it, 'Were it not for the evil inclination, no one would build a house, marry a wife, have children, or engage in business.' Purity of heart was essential to the relationship between man and God. But in relations between man and man, what mattered was the result not the sentiment with which it was brought about. Jews would find it easy to agree with the remark of Sir James Frazer that 'it is better for the world that men should be right from wrong motives than that they would do wrong with the best intentions'.*

In general, then, the rabbis favoured markets and competition because they generated wealth, lowered prices, increased choice, reduced absolute levels of poverty and in the course of time extended humanity's control over the environment, narrowing the extent to which we are the passive victims of circumstance and fate. Competition releases energy and creativity and serves the general good. Admittedly, Jewish law permitted protectionist policies in some cases to safeguard the local economy, especially when the outside trader did not pay taxes. There were also times when rabbinic authorities intervened to lower prices of essential commodities. But in general, they favoured the free market, nowhere more so than in their own professional sphere of Jewish education. An established teacher could not object to a rival setting up in competition. The reason they gave for this ruling illustrates their general approach. They said simply, 'Jealousy among scholars increases wisdom.'

Needless to say, in a faith as strongly moral as Judaism, alongside the respect for markets went a sharp insistence on the ethics of business. At one of the critical points of the Jewish calendar, on the Sabbath before the Ninth of Av when we recall the destruction of the two Temples, we read in the synagogue the great first

* Quoted in Hayek, *The Fatal Conceit*, op. cit., p. 157.

chapter of Isaiah (Isaiah 1:17, 22–23) with its insistence that without political and economic integrity, religious piety is in vain:

> Seek justice, encourage the oppressed,
> Defend the cause of the fatherless,
> Plead the case of the widow . . .
> Your silver has become dross,
> Your choice wine is diluted with water,
> Your rulers are rebels, companions of thieves,
> They all love bribes and chase after gifts.

The same message is carried through into the teachings of the rabbis. According to Rava, when a person comes to the next world for judgment, the first question he is asked is, 'Did you deal honestly in business?'. In the school of Rabbi Ishmael it was taught that whoever conducts himself honestly in business is as if he fulfilled the whole of Jewish law. The perennial temptations of the market – to pursue gain at someone else's expense, to take advantage of ignorance, to treat employees with indifference – needed to be fought against. Canons of fair trading had to be established and policed, and much of Jewish law is taken up with these concerns. The rabbis recognised that a perfect market would not emerge of its own accord. Not everyone had access to full information, and this gave scope for unscrupulous practices and unfair profits, against which they took a strong stand.

Perhaps the best summary of the way Judaism differed from Christianity, at least in its pre-Reformation guise, was given by Michael Novak, himself a Catholic:

> In both its prophetic and rabbinic traditions Jewish thought has always felt comfortable with a certain well-ordered worldliness, whereas the Christian has always felt a pull toward otherworldliness. Jewish thought has had a candid orientation toward private property, commercial activity, markets, and profits, whereas Catholic thought – articulated from an early period chiefly

> among priests and monks – has persistently tried to direct the attention of its adherents beyond the activities and interests of this world to the next.*

So much, then, by way of an overview of Jewish economic ethics, much of which bears a strong kinship with views Hayek tirelessly espoused. But it is just here that I want to enter into the spirit of *The Fatal Conceit*, in which Hayek warned us to look, not just at markets, but also at the moral environment in which they are sustained. I want to draw attention briefly to five features of Judaism, essential to its way of life, which on the face of it stand utterly opposed to the market ethic.

The first, of course, is the Sabbath and its related institutions, the Sabbatical year and the Jubilee. The Sabbath is the boundary Judaism draws around economic activity. 'Six days shall you labour and do all your work, but the seventh day is a Sabbath to the Lord your God' (Exodus 20:9–10). What marked the Sabbath off from all other religious celebrations in the ancient world was its concept of a day of rest. So unintelligible was this to the writers of ancient Greece that they accused Jews of observing it merely out of laziness. But of course, what was at the heart of the Sabbath was and is the idea that there are important truths about the human condition that cannot be accounted for in terms of work or economics. That Sabbath is the day on which we neither work nor employ others to do our work, on which we neither buy nor sell, in which all manipulation of nature for creative ends is forbidden, in which all hierarchies of power or wealth are suspended.

The Sabbath is one of those phenomena – incomprehensible from the outside – which you have to live in order to understand. For countless generations of Jews it was the still point in the turning world, the moment at which we renew our attachment

* Michael Novak, *This Hemisphere of Liberty* (Washington DC: AEI Press, 1992), p. 64.

to family and community, during which we live the truth that the world is not wholly ours to bend to our will but something given to us in trust to conserve for future generations, and in which the inequalities of a market economy are counterbalanced by a world in which money does not count, in which we are all equal citizens. The Jewish writer Achad Ha'am was surely correct when he said that more than the Jews have kept the Sabbath, the Sabbath has kept the Jews. It was and is the one day in seven in which we live out all those values which are in danger of being obscured in the daily rush of events; the day in which we stop making a living and learn instead simply how to live.

Or second, consider marriage and the family. Judaism is one of the great familial traditions, and this despite the fact that in strict legal terms a Jewish marriage has the form of a contract; that Judaism has never prohibited divorce by mutual consent; and that it is quite relaxed about that modern development, the prenuptial agreement, and indeed sees it as a useful device in alleviating the stress of separation. The reason Judaism has often succeeded in sustaining strong marriages and families has little to do with the structure of Jewish marriage law, and a great deal to do with its ritual life, the way in which many of the supreme religious moments take place in the home as a dialogue between husband and wife, or between parents and children. Ultimately, Judaism saw marriage not as a contract but as the supreme example of a covenant, namely a commitment based not on mutual benefit but on mutual belonging, whose key value is fidelity, holding fast to one another especially during difficult times, because you are part of who I am. The Jewish family survived because, in the graphic phrase of the sages, it was surrounded by 'a hedge of roses', an elaborate network of rituals that bound individuals together in a matrix of mutual giving that was utterly at odds with a market ethic.

Or third, consider education. I have already mentioned that Jewish law favours competition in the provision of teaching. What it did not do, however, was to leave access to education to the market and to the ability to pay. Even in the days of Moses, Jews were instructed to set the highest religious value on education – as one of our most famous prayers (the *Shema*), taken from the book of Deuteronomy, puts it, 'You shall teach these things diligently to your children, speaking of them when you sit at home or travel on the way, when you lie down and when you rise up' (Deuteronomy 6:7). And by the first century, Jews had constructed the world's first system of universal compulsory education, funded by collective taxation. Education, the life of the mind, an ability to follow a train of thought and see the alternative possibilities that give rise to argument, are essential features of Jewish spirituality, and ones to which everyone, however poor, must be given access.

Or fourth, the concept of property. I mentioned earlier that Judaism has a high regard for private property as an institution governing the relations between human beings. At the same time, though, governing the relationship between humanity and God, there has been an equal insistence that what we have, we do not unconditionally own. Ultimately everything belongs to God. What we have, we hold in trust. And there are conditions to that trust – or as the great Victorian Jew Sir Moses Montefiore put it, 'We are worth what we are willing to share with others'.*

The effect of this idea on Jewish society has been profound. I was recently at a ceremony to mark the opening of a new Jewish school in one of our provincial communities. The project had been made possible by the great generosity of one of the local members. Over dinner I leaned over to him to express my thanks for his gift. He said, without a moment's reflection, 'What else could I do? The money wasn't mine. God lent it to me, and I invested it as wisely as I could in the next generation.' That kind of unreflective response lies at the foundation of the long tradition of Jewish philanthropy and explains much of how Judaism

* Lawrence J. Epstein, *A Treasury of Jewish Anecdotes* (New Jersey: Jason Aronson, 1989), p. 162.

has been able to encourage the creation of wealth without giving rise to class resentments.

And finally, there is the Jewish tradition of law itself. It was a non-Jew, William Rees-Mogg, who first drew my attention to the connection between Jewish law and the control of inflation, a link that I confess I never thought of making. His argument is contained in a book he wrote during an era of high inflation (in 1974), entitled *The Reigning Error*.* It was simply this: 'Inflation is a disease of inordinacy'. It comes about through a failure to understand that energy, to be channelled, needs restraints. It was the constant discipline of law, he says, that provided the boundaries within which Jewish creativity could flow. The law, to quote his words, 'has acted as a bottle inside which this spiritual and intellectual energy could be held; only because it could be held has it been possible to make use of it. It has not merely exploded or been dispersed; it has been harnessed as a continuous power.' Jews, for him, were a model of acquired self-restraint, and it was the failure of societies to practise self-restraint that led to runaway inflation.

And with this I come back to Hayek and *The Fatal Conceit*. It was Hayek's view that moral systems produced their results, not directly or by conscious intention, but rather in the long run and often in ways that could not have been foreseen. Certainly, Jews believed that their way of life would lead to the blessings of prosperity. That, after all, is the substance of many of Moses' prophecies. But there was no direct connection between institutions like the Sabbath and economic growth. How could there be? The Sabbath, the family, the educational system, the concept of ownership as trusteeship and the disciplines of the law were not constructed on the basis of economic calculation. To the contrary, they were ways in which Judaism in effect said to the market: thus far and no further. There are realms in which you may not intrude.

* William Rees-Mogg, *The Reigning Error* (London: Hamish Hamilton, 1974).

The concept of the holy is precisely the domain in which the worth of things is not judged by their market price or economic value. And this fundamental insight of Judaism is all the more striking given its respect for the market within the marketplace. *The Fatal Conceit* for Judaism, as for Hayek, is to believe that the market governs the totality of our lives, when in fact it governs only a limited part of it, that which concerns goods which we think of as being subject to production and exchange. There are things fundamental to being human that we do not produce; instead, we receive from those who came before us and from God Himself. And there are things which we may not exchange, however high the price.

What then might be the lesson of *The Fatal Conceit* for our time? That socialism is not the only enemy of the market economy. Another enemy, all the more powerful for its recent global triumph, is the market economy itself. When everything that matters can be bought and sold, when commitments can be broken because they are no longer to our advantage, when shopping becomes salvation and advertising slogans become our litany, when our worth is measured by how much we earn and spend, then the market is destroying the very virtues on which in the long run it depends. That, not the return of socialism, is the danger that advanced economies now face. And at such times as now, when markets seem to hold out the promise of uninterrupted growth in our satisfaction of desires, the voice of our great religious traditions needs to be heard, warning us of the gods that devour their own children, and of the temples that stand today as relics of civilisations that once seemed invincible.

The market, in my view, has already gone too far: not indeed as an economic system, but as a cast of thought governing relationships and the image we have of ourselves. A great rabbi once taught this lesson to a successful but unhappy businessman. He took him to the window and asked him, 'What do you see?' The man replied, 'I see the world.' He then took him to a mirror and asked, 'What do you see?' He replied, 'I see myself.' 'That', said the rabbi, 'is what happens when silver covers glass.' Instead of seeing the world you see only yourself. The idea that human happiness can be exhaustively accounted for in terms of things we can buy, exchange and replace, is one of the great corrosive acids which eats away the girders on which societies rest; and by the time we have discovered this, it is already too late.

Hayek's final contribution to the great debate about economic systems was to remind us that the market does not survive by market forces alone. It depends on respect for moral institutions, which are themselves expressions of our reverence for the human individual as the image and likeness of God.

Forgiveness and Reconciliation

On 28 August 2000, Rabbi Sacks was invited to the United Nations in New York to deliver an address to the Millennium World Peace Summit of Religious and Spiritual Leaders.

Two millennia ago, the rabbis asked a question. *Eizehu gibbor?* Who is strong? Who is a hero? The simple answer is obvious. Who is a hero? One who defeats his enemies. But the rabbis did not give a simple answer. Instead they gave an answer so powerful that it still moves me today. Who is a hero? One who turns an enemy into a friend.

And they were right. If I defeat you, I win and you lose. But in truth, I also lose, because by diminishing you, I diminish myself. But if I forgive you, and if, in that moment of truth, you forgive me, then forgiveness leads to reconciliation; reconciliation leads to friendship; and in friendship, instead of fighting one another, we can fight together the problems we share – poverty, hunger, starvation, disease, violence, injustice and all the other injuries that still scar the face of our world. You gain, I gain, and all those with whom we are associated gain as well. We gain economically, politically, but above all spiritually. My world has become bigger because it now includes you. Who is a hero? One who turns an enemy into a friend.

So simple, and yet so hard. This time last year, I stood in the streets of Pristina, in Kosovo, amidst the wreckage of war. The NATO operation had just come to an end. The Kosovo Albanians had returned home. But in the air there was an atmosphere of bitterness and anger. Months earlier the Albanians were in terror of the Serbs. Now the Serbs feared reprisals from the Albanians. There was peace, but not real peace. War had ended, but reconciliation had not begun. Most of the soldiers with whom I spoke feared for the future. They thought that someday – perhaps not tomorrow, not next year, but some day – the conflict would begin again, as it has so often in that part of the world.

And then I knew, standing there surrounded by broken buildings and broken lives, that one word has the power to change the world. The word *forgiveness*. If we can forgive others, and act so that others can forgive us, then we can live with the past without being held as a prisoner by the past. But only if we forgive. Without that we condemn ourselves and our children to fight old battles again and again, with the same bloodshed, the same destruction, the same waste of the human spirit, the same devastation of God's world.

It takes courage to forgive – because forgiving means letting go: letting go of the pain, letting go even of our sense of justice, our feeling that we or our people have been wronged. In war, even ordinary people become heroes. But in pursuit of peace, even heroes are often afraid to take the risk. I think of the exceptions. I think of the late Anwar Sadat of Egypt, and of the late Yitzhak Rabin of Israel. Both had the courage to make peace, and both were assassinated. Why is reconciliation so hard?

Let me answer personally. I am a Jew. And as a Jew, I carry with me the tears and sufferings of my grandparents, and theirs, through the generations. The story of my people is the story of a thousand years of exiles and expulsions, persecutions and pogroms, beginning with the First Crusade and culminating in the murder of two-thirds of Europe's Jews. For centuries, Jews knew that they, or their children, risked being murdered simply because they were Jews. How can I let go of that pain when it is written into my very soul?

And yet I must. For the sake of my children, I must. Will I bring one victim of the Holocaust back to life by hating Germans? Will I bring my people one step nearer freedom by denying that same freedom to others? Does loving God more entitle me to love other people less? If I ask God to forgive me, does He not ask me to forgive others? The duty I owe my ancestors who died because of their faith is to build a world in which people no longer die because of their faith. I honour the past by learning from it, by refusing to add pain to pain, grief to grief. That is why we must answer hatred with love, violence with peace, and conflict with reconciliation.

Today God has given us no choice. There was a time when we could live surrounded by people who were like us. We could afford to say, 'We are right. The rest of the world is wrong.' We can't do that any more. In every city, every street, we live among people who are not like us. Our lives, our safety, our environment, our very future, is bound up with countries far away and cultures unlike our own. God has brought us eyeball to eyeball with the diversity of His world – and right now He is asking us: Can we recognise God's image in someone who is not in my image? Can strangers, even enemies, become friends?

Never have the stakes been higher. Never have we had more power to heal or to wreck the world. Which will it be? Today I can communicate instantly across the world. But can I communicate with the Muslim, or Hindu or Sikh who lives in my street? We have conquered every distance except one – the distance between human beings. It won't be technology that decides the future of our planet, but us, you and I and the people we lead. And that is where we, as religious leaders, bear a unique responsibility.

Look at the conflict zones in today's world, and you will see that they coincide almost exactly with regions of religious tension. The question is: is religion part of the solution, or is it part of the problem? Let none of us doubt the difference we can make. Politicians have power, but religion has something greater than power. It has influence. Politics moves the pieces, but religion changes lives. Politicians sign peace agreements, but it our people, out there, on the ground, who will determine whether peace is real, or just a breathing space between wars. Religion is fire. And fire gives warmth and light, but it also burns. And we are the guardians of the flame.

It took the death of six million people to bring Jews and Christians together in mutual dignity and respect. How many more people will have to die in the Middle East, Kashmir, Northern Ireland, the Balkans, before we understand that God has given us many faiths but only one world in which to live together. I call on the leaders of the great faiths unequivocally to dissociate themselves from violence even when, especially when, it is done in the name of God. I believe the time has come to for the United Nations to invite the religious leaders of the world to form a global peace coalition, ready to travel to any conflict zone in the world, armed with the only thing more powerful than weapons of destruction, namely, words of forgiveness and reconciliation. We have suffered, and inflicted suffering, for too long. The time has come for us to turn enemies into friends.

The Good Society

Rabbi Sacks was invited by HRH The Duke of Edinburgh to deliver the St George's Lecture in St George's Hall at Windsor Castle on 5 June 2000.

Your Royal Highness, Ladies and Gentlemen, I am honoured and moved by the invitation to address you tonight. I thank you, not just for the invitation but also for the institution under whose auspices we meet – St George's House. A great philosopher, Alasdair MacIntyre, once said that the importance of an institution lies not only in what it does but in *the conversations of which it is the arena*. Over the years, St George's House has been the home of one of the most important conversations we can have, namely about where we are going as a society and why. Its creation took wisdom and foresight, and I wish to pay tribute to it and its work.

Let me also add a personal note as the first member of the Jewish community to deliver this lecture. I do so by way of a story. Three years ago, I was invited to give the first Jewish Heritage lecture at Cambridge University's Divinity School. After the lecture was over, since I was in the year of mourning for my late father, I asked the Jewish students to stay behind so that we could say the evening prayers and I could recite *Kaddish*, the Jewish prayer associated with mourning. I then went down to the reception held to mark the lecture, where I saw an elderly Jewish academic in tears. I asked him why he was crying. 'Surely', I said, 'the lecture wasn't *that* bad!' 'No,' he said, but he wondered whether I had understood the significance of that night.

What he went on to tell me was this: that part of Cambridge had been the site of the Jewish community prior to its expulsion in 1290. The alleyway at the back of the School, now called All Saints' Passage, was then known as Jews' Lane, and the spot on which the Divinity School now stands was, in all probability, where the synagogue had stood in the thirteenth century. Tonight, he said, was the first time that Jews had prayed there in 700 years. That was why he wept, thinking of how he had lived to see Jews return in honour to the place from which they had once been banished. Tonight I feel the same emotion, standing here in this ancient home of England's kings and queens, and I thank God *shehecheyanu ve-kiyemanu ve-higiyanu la-zeman ha-zeh,*' who has kept us alive and sustained us and brought us to this day.'

In thinking about where we are going as a society, I begin by way of another story, one of my favourites, told to me by an Oxford academic when I was a student. He had asked me what I was studying, and when I replied, 'Philosophy', he tutted with disapproval. 'Awful subject, philosophy. Philosophers never know what day of the week it is. Who's your favourite philosopher?' 'Wittgenstein', I replied, as most philosophers did in those days. 'Just proves my point,' he said, and proceeded to tell the following tale. Wittgenstein was standing one day with two of his disciples, Elizabeth Anscombe and H. L. A. Hart, on the platform of Oxford station, waiting for the London train. Deeply immersed in metaphysical speculation, they entirely failed to notice the train as it steamed into the platform. Eventually they looked up and saw that the train had begun to move. Professor Hart ran and heaved himself on board. Elizabeth Anscombe ran and heaved herself on board. Wittgenstein ran but could not catch up and stood watching the train disappear from view. He looked so disconsolate that a woman came up to him and said, 'Don't worry. There's another train due in an hour's time.' 'But you don't understand,' said Wittgenstein in his heavy Viennese accent. '*Zey came to see me off!*' From this I learned: don't ask how fast the train is going. Ask whether it is going to where you want to be.

We enter the twenty-first century on the brink of extraordinary possibilities. A hundred years ago there had been no successful effort at one of mankind's oldest dreams, powered flight. That came with the Wright brothers in 1903. There had been no radio transmission. That was achieved by Marconi in 1901. In a single century there has been more scientific and technological progress than in all the millennia since man first walked on Earth. Ours has been the age of the computer, the laser beam, the credit card, micro-surgery and interactive CD-ROMs. We have sent rockets into deepest space, photographed the birth of galaxies and decoded the human genome, the book of life itself; and it has happened at dazzling speed. Today the average shopper in the average supermarket has a range of choices that, a century ago, would have been beyond the dreams of kings. Journeys that would have taken months now take hours. We have better health, longer life expectancy and more possibilities of almost every kind than any previous generation of mankind.

Yet, coincidentally with these changes in the past fifty years there has been – especially among children – a quantum leap in rates of depressive illness, suicide attempts, stress-related syndromes, drug and alcohol abuse, and other symptoms of psychological dysfunction. To take one particularly striking example: in 1940, teachers were asked what were the seven most serious problems they faced in school. They replied: talking out of turn, chewing gum, making noise, running in corridors, cutting in line, not wearing school uniform, and dropping litter. In 1990, teachers were asked the same question. Their replies were: drug abuse, alcohol abuse, teenage pregnancy, suicide, rape, robbery and assault.

Contemplating these facts, I am reminded of the fabled Russian politician who began his speech with these words: 'Friends, yesterday we stood on the edge of the abyss, but today we have taken a giant step forward!' How has there been so striking a disjunction between human possibility on the one hand and human happiness on the other? That is a central question of our time.

The simplest answer is that in pursuit of progress, we have valued science over ethics. We have focused on technical mastery rather than on the question, 'To what end?' The result is that we have unparalleled knowledge of what is, and unprecedented doubts as to what ought to be. We are moving at great speed without being altogether sure where we want to go. Let me give some examples.

Imagine an anthropologist from some future century, studying our urban landscape and trying to infer from it the shape of our culture. She would notice the great cathedrals and churches that still mark our skyline. She would note that the buildings, though magnificent, were mostly old. She would conclude, rightly, that religion once played a central part in British society but no longer, and she would search for their functional equivalent today. She would find it in today's shopping centres and hypermarkets, the cathedrals of our time. The analogy goes deep. They are the places where people congregate on Sundays, where they engage in ritual behaviour ('retail therapy'), and worship the icons of our age, whose initials we wear, like stigmata, on our clothes. Sometimes it even becomes Puritanical: 'Shop until you drop'. Its credo is summed up in the American bumper sticker that reads, 'The guy with the most toys when he dies, wins.'

The question is: can we translate houses of worship into shopping arcades without loss? To this, the psychologist Oliver James, concerned about the huge rise in depressive illness in the course of two generations, gave a telling answer.* His thesis is that a society predicated on increasing consumer expenditure must necessarily be sustained on the basis of artificially created dissatisfaction. So, advertising surrounds us with images of models who are impossibly thin, women unattainably beautiful, men absurdly well dressed, cars and computers that make us embarrassed to still be using last year's model. Marketing intentionally creates a tension between what we have and what we see, a dissonance that can only be eased by buying this or wearing that. Perpetual dissatisfaction is good for business. It just happens to be bad for people. Compare this to the world within a place of worship,

* Oliver James, *Britain on the Couch* (London: Century, 1997).

whose message is that we are valued, not for what we earn or own or spend, but for who we are.

Let me illustrate this point by travelling back in time to a comparable moment in the history of civilisation. It is a story about translation, because I believe that one of the simplest ways of understanding the differences between cultures is to identify the words that are untranslatable from one language to another. Some 2,300 years ago there occurred a famous moment in the history of translation, when the Hebrew Bible was translated for the first time into Greek, the so-called 'Septuagint'. Jewish tradition records that the translators found themselves unable to translate literally the verse, 'On the seventh day, God completed the work that He had done' (Genesis 2:2). Evidently, they felt that the sentence, in that form, would have been unintelligible to the Greeks; so instead they wrote, 'On the *sixth* day, God completed . . .'

What did they believe was unintelligible? The idea that *rest* is a creation, an achievement, a work of art. As it happens, we have independent evidence that their intuition was correct. Several Greek and Latin writers of antiquity say that the Jews kept the Sabbath because they were lazy. The concept of a holy day was familiar to every ancient culture. What was unique about the Sabbath was that it was a *day of rest*, a time whose holiness was expressed in cessation from work.

The Sabbath meant and means many things. It was a protest against slavery. One day in seven, every individual shared the same freedom, breathed the same air of liberty. It was a reminder that there are limits to our exploitation of natural resources. Like the Sabbatical and Jubilee years, it was a time when the Earth rested as a reminder that we are not only creators but also creations, charged with conserving the natural world for future generations. But it has something, too, to do with the nature of happiness. The story is told of the eighteenth-century mystic Rabbi Levi Yitzhak of Berditchev who looked out of his window one day and saw people rushing in the town square below. 'Why are you running?'

he asked one passer-by. 'To make a living,' he replied. 'What makes you so sure', said the rabbi, 'that your living is ahead of you, and you have to run to catch it up? Perhaps it's behind you, and you need to stand still to let it catch up with you!' The Sabbath is the time when we stand still and let our blessings catch up with us.

Greece, at the time of the Bible translation, was at the height of its powers. Its achievements in art, architecture, drama and philosophy remain awe-inspiring. Yet within two centuries it had begun its decline, to be replaced by the power of Rome, while Judaism, despite its tragic history, survived. I wonder whether that episode does not contain the explanation. Might it be that civilisations, like individuals, are prone to burn-out, to exhaustion? Might the Sabbath not be one of the great elements in the sustainability of a culture? Is this why Judaism and its daughter monotheisms, Christianity and Islam, survived while so many other civilisations faded and disappeared?

The Hebrew writer Achad Ha'am once said that more than the Jewish people kept the Sabbath, the Sabbath kept the Jewish people. Jews are not opposed to the market economy or technological advance; we welcome them. But in the Sabbath there is a necessary counter-affirmation, best expressed by one of our ancient sages who said, 'Who is rich? One who rejoices in what he has' (Ethics of the Fathers 4:1). The remorseless pressure of consumerism to define ourselves in terms of what we lack, not what we have, takes a heavy toll in a culture which has no counter-voice. The translation of Sunday from a day of rest to a day of shopping is not a minor, but a major, transformation and, in my view, a great mistake.

Let me take another example, this time from bioethics. There is no doubt that the discovery of DNA and the decoding of the human genome are among the most exciting advances in human knowledge ever made. Their potential benefits are vast. Genetic screening and gene-splicing may allow us in the future to treat hitherto incurable conditions, among them Huntington's disease, Tay-Sachs disease, cystic fibrosis and Down's syndrome. The question is: will we know where to stop? Will we be able to draw the essential line between therapeutic and eugenic interventions? Will we recognise the moral limits of biotechnology?

Certain concerns are, I believe, misplaced. It is not wrong to pursue new ways of curing disease. Judaism does not contain a prohibition against 'playing God'. To the contrary, it sees us as 'God's partners in the work of creation'. Nor does it see infertility as a condition to be accepted, but rather as one, if possible, to be cured. Genetic engineering, even cloning, may well be acceptable if these are the only ways of treating illness or enabling a couple to have a child. Nor is cloning, in and of itself, merely replicating a human being. Identical twins are both persons in their own right and display differences when they grow up, whether raised separately or together. We should resist any tendency to genetic determinism, as the Judeo-Christian ethic has resisted every other form of determinism in the past. We are creatures of will and choice, of upbringing, culture, reflection and imagination. Our fate is not written in our genes.

Yet, for all that, we are right to have qualms. How will we differentiate, for example, between curing impaired learning ability and enhancing intelligence? At what point will we halt the right of parents to determine their child's genetic endowment? At what stage does childbirth shade over into manufacture? When does a child – produced, let us say, as a clone of a parent, or as a replacement for another child who has died – become a means to someone else's end rather than as an end in his or her own self? What, in the long run, will happen to our concepts of personal identity, relationship and individuality, and to the idea – fundamental to the sanctity of life – of life as God's gift?

These are not theoretical questions. Already we are moving into disturbing territory. Take the following case, which I owe to the philosopher Anthony O'Hear.* An Italian businessman and his Portuguese wife, who already had two children through

* *Daily Mail*, 8 May 2000.

surrogacy, decided that they wanted a third: a boy who was tall, athletic and blond. They went to an agency in Denmark, who found a sperm donor in the United States, an egg donor in Britain and a surrogate mother, also in Britain. The operation was performed in Athens. After twenty-one weeks of pregnancy, it was discovered that, instead of a boy, the surrogate mother was carrying twin girls. The couple demanded that she have an abortion. She refused. The twins were born and were eventually adopted by a lesbian couple in California, where they are now being raised by a nanny from Puerto Rico.

What are those children if not commodities produced to order and then traded across the world? Who are their parents? The couple who initiated the project? The sperm- and egg-donors? The surrogate mother? The two adoptive mothers? What story will the girls be able to tell themselves about their identity when they grow up? What in this case has become of the idea of persons as beings sacred in themselves rather than the gratification of someone else's desire? Once again, as in the previous example, we are allowing the market (this time, in co-operation with medical technology) to substitute for ethical principle, as if all that matters is the maximal freedom to do what we choose so long as we can afford it. At some stage, a civilisation must be able to say: *not everything we can do, should we do*. Without this, technology drives values instead of values directing technology; and if that happens, then truly we are travelling blind. Of any technological advance, the primary question must be: Does this enhance or diminish human dignity? In many cases it enhances it, but not in all. When it does not, we must call a halt.

Consider this declaration, made, in 1997 by the International Academy of Humanism and signed by some of the most distinguished scientists of our time. It said:

> Some world religions teach that human beings are fundamentally different from other mammals . . . Human nature is held to be unique and sacred . . . As far as the scientific enterprise can

> determine [however] . . . [h]uman capabilities appear to differ in degree, not in kind, from those found among the higher animals. Humanity's rich repertoire of thoughts, feelings, aspirations and hopes seems to arise from electrochemical brain processes, not from an immaterial soul that operates in ways no instrument can discover . . . Views of human nature rooted in humanity's tribal past ought not to be our primary criterion for making decisions about cloning.*

This is scientific reductivism at its worst. If human aspirations are no more than electrochemical brain processes, then a Rembrandt is a mix of pigments on canvas, and a Beethoven quartet mere marks on paper. Of course, this is nonsense. We are *both* physical beings whose movements can be described in terms of cause and effect, *and* intentional, self-conscious agents whose acts can only be understood in the language of purpose, meaning, imagination and aims. We are, as the Bible puts it, 'dust of the Earth' but within us is the 'breath of God' (Genesis 2:7). These two languages – one constructed in terms of physical causes in the past, the other in terms of aspirations for the future – are irreducible to one another. Morality belongs to the second. It is about the world to which we aspire – the world of 'ought' – and about its realisation in the here-and-now, the world of 'is'. A language which reduces humanity to electrochemical brain processes is one in which not only morality will become radically unintelligible; so too will be the ideas on which our essential humanity depends. We do well to heed the words of one of the great scientists of our time, E. O. Wilson, who says this about our current state:

> [W]e are learning the fundamental principle that ethics is everything . . . We are adults who have discovered which covenants are necessary for our survival, and we have accepted the necessity of

* Quoted in Leon Kass, 'The Moral Meaning of Genetic Technology', *Commentary* 108:2, September 1999.

> securing them by sacred oath . . . [I]f we should surrender our genetic nature to machine-aided ratiocination, and our ethics and art and our very meaning to a habit of careless discursion in the name of progress, imagining ourselves to be god-like and absolved from our ancient heritage, we will become nothing.*

Wilson's reference to 'our ancient heritage' brings me to my final example, and to the fundamental question: 'What is society?' Let me approach the issue obliquely by thinking about this building, Windsor Castle itself. I try to imagine what it must be like to inherit such a building. To live in such a place, so steeped in history, is to want to know how it came to be and why. In the course of asking such a question I would learn about how it began, in the days of William the Conqueror, on the legendary site of King Arthur's Round Table. I would find that it had been rebuilt several times over the course of the ensuing centuries, in the days of Henry II, Henry III and Edward III. In the course of learning this history I would do more than discover facts. I would also know that I had entered into a set of obligations – a moral relationship – with its past and future. I would know that I was part of a story. The very fact that the castle was here would tell me that its previous owners had endeavoured to preserve it, protect it, and at times enhance it so that it could be handed on to future generations. They had vested their hopes in me, that I too would guard it and hand it on in turn to those who come after me. The result is that when disaster strikes, as it did in the great fire of 1992, I would know that I had to restore the damaged buildings (including the great Hall we are in tonight), not necessarily exactly as it was before, but in keeping with the whole. That is what it is to live in the context of history.

Now compare the castle to a five-star hotel not far from here. My relationship to it is quite different. It does not tell a story that speaks of *this* place, *this* building, *this* history. To the contrary,

* E. O. Wilson, *Consilience* (London: Abacus, 1999, p. 332–333).

if the hotel is part of an international chain, it may only be the weather that reminds me, when I wake up, that I am in Britain and not Bali, Bangkok or Buenos Aires. My relationship with the hotel is purely *contractual*, meaning that the hotel provides me with certain services, in return for which I pay the bill. Beyond that, it makes no demands on me, nor I on it. That is the difference between a hotel and a home.

By now, of course, you will have realised that I am talking, not about two buildings, but about two conceptions of society. I will never own a building like Windsor Castle, but I do own something not less significant, namely a story. It was given to me by my parents when I was a child. Every Jewish child receives such a gift on the festival of Passover. It tells me that my ancestors were once slaves; that they were then set free; that they wandered in the desert for forty years, and then later across the Earth for 2,000 years. I know, just as does the heir of a physical inheritance, that I am a link in the chain of generations, with a duty of loyalty to the past and to the future. That is the conception of society Edmund Burke had in mind when he called it a 'partnership not only between those who are living, but between those who are living, those who are dead, and those who are to be born'.* I am part of a story whose earlier chapters were written by my ancestors, and whose next chapter I must now write and then hand it on to my children and they to theirs. That is society as a home with a history extended through time.

That, however, is not the view that prevails today. Instead, we have moved towards the idea that a State is purely procedural. It embodies no particular history or set of values. It exists in a purely contractual relationship with its members, whereby in return for certain payments in the form of taxes, we receive specific benefits and services. Beyond that each of us is free to do what we like so long as we do not scare the horses. This is society, not as a home,

* Edmund Burke, *Reflections on the Revolution in France* (Oxford: Oxford University Press, 1993) p. 96.

but as a hotel. It is therefore, at its very roots, not something from which I could derive an identity, a set of ideals, a story that helps me to understand who I am, or a sense of obligation toward the past or guardianship for the sake of the future. It is deeply problematic as to whether I could feel *loyalty* to such a society. Indeed, I suspect that the word 'loyalty', like so many other words in our vocabulary, is a mere survival, a relic, of an earlier age.

It is therefore not surprising, in the light of these three examples – to which one could add so many others – that our happiness has not kept pace with the advance in knowledge, technology and gross national product. That is because we are in the process of systematically deconstructing the bases on which happiness rests: our sense of being valued for what we are, of the uniqueness and sanctity of a human life, and of being part of a story that confers meaning and significance to our lives. With this, I come to the point to which we have been travelling all along.

Professor Stephen Hawking once wrote a 200-page bestseller called *A Brief History of Time*.* Here is an even briefer history of time, in three sentences: in the beginning, people believed in many gods. Then came monotheism and reduced them to one. Then came science and reduced them to none. Or in other words, first there was myth. Then there was monotheism, which demythologised the world. Then came the moment when Laplace said the famous words, '*Je n'ais pas besoin de cette hypothese*' ('I no longer need to invoke God to explain the world'). On this view, monotheism – Judaism, Christianity and Islam – was a mere halfway stage on the long road to science.

That is how we have come to tell the story, but it is not the only, or even the most interesting, way. I want to suggest an alternative: ever since *Homo sapiens* stopped beating the tribal drums long enough to express a thought, we have reflected on our place in the Universe. We know that, compared to all there is, we are

* Stephen Hawking, *A Brief History of Time: From the Big Bang to Black Holes* (London: Bantam, 1989).

each infinitesimally small. At best, we are a ripple in the ocean, a grain of sand on the shore. The Universe preceded us by billions of years, and it will survive for billions of years after we are gone. How then is our life, that fleeting shadow, related to the totality of things? To this there have been two answers, and they are fundamentally opposed.

There have been cultures, ancient and modern, that have seen reality in terms of vast impersonal forces. To the ancients they were the sun, the sea, the storm, the flood. Today they are the global economy, international politics, the environment and the internet. What they have in common is that they are indifferent to us, just as a tidal wave is indifferent to those it sweeps away. Global warming does not choose its victims. Economic recession does not pause to ask who suffers. Genetic mutation happens without anyone deciding to whom. On this view, the forces that govern the world are essentially blind. They are not addressed to us. We may stand in their path, or we may step out of the way, but they are unmoved by our existence; they do not relate to us as persons. In such a world, human hope is a prelude to tragedy. The best we can do is to combine hedonism with stoicism: seize what pleasures come our way and take Prozac to anaesthetise the pain. That is a coherent view. Its greatest expression is to be found in Greek tragedy. It is where our culture is heading today.

At some stage in the history of ancient Israel a different vision was born: one that saw in the cosmos *the face of the personal*. Without denying any of the world's appearances, it saw beyond them to a deeper reality: a God who brought the Universe into being, not as a scientist in a laboratory, but as a parent, in and through love. In this vision, we are not insignificant, nor are we alone. We are here because someone willed us into being, who wanted us to be, who knows our thoughts and values us in our uniqueness, whose breath we breathe and in whose arms we rest, someone in and through whom we are connected to all that is.

This was not a minor discovery, nor was it simply a religious one. It was as much about mankind as about God. To put it simply: by discovering God, our ancestors discovered man. For the first time a momentous concept began to take shape: the concept of the human person – *every* human person – as a being of unique dignity. It is not too much to say that in the words, 'Let us make man in our image, after our likeness,' were born all the great ethical and political concepts that have shaped Western civilisation for the past thousand years, among them, human rights, the free society, the sanctity of life and the dignity of difference.

Finding God singular and alone, our ancestors discovered the human person, singular and alone. Hearing God reach out to us, they discovered the importance of human beings reaching out to one another. Haltingly at first, then with growing confidence, they began to realise that God is not about power but about relationship. He is found, therefore, not just in heaven but in society, in the structures we make to honour His presence by honouring His image in other human beings. Faith is not a primitive form of science. It is about *the ultimate reality of the personal* and how we translate that into our shared and social world.

That is why we need, not only supermarkets and laboratories and hotels, but also places like St George's Chapel and the many other houses of worship where we sustain and give expression to our vision of the personal. That is the necessary counter-voice to all those forces – economic, scientific, political – whose glory and greatness is that they are *im*personal. We are not opposed to these things. To the contrary, they have given us economic growth, scientific advance and democratic government, three of the treasures of the modern world. It is simply that we *also* need the texts and contexts that remind us of the sacred stories and ethical principles that articulate our humanity, and that have been driven, in recent decades, to the very margins of the public square.

The pages of history are littered with the debris of civilisations that were, in their time, technologically supreme: from ancient Mesopotamia and Egypt to the Third Reich and the Soviet Union. I find it awe-inspiring to realise that the social orders that survived were those that valued, not power, but the powerless; not economic and military but spiritual strength; not the mass but the individual, in whose features they discerned the image of God. That is what will always constitute the good society, and if today this has become a counter-cultural view, so be it. Religions were always at their best when they were counter-cultural, when they challenged the consensus instead of running after it. Today we need to hear that voice again, loudly, fearlessly, unequivocally – for the sake of our children, our future, and God, in whose reflection alone we see ourselves as we are called on to become.

The Five Cs Essential to Our Shared Future

On 4 February 2002, Rabbi Sacks was invited to address the Global Leaders of Tomorrow Summit at the World Economic Forum in Davos, Switzerland.

The events of 11 September reminded us of an often-forgotten truth. Our knowledge of the Universe is vast. Scientific knowledge doubles in every generation. Computing power doubles every two years. Yet there remains one undiscovered country. Its name is – the future. We can know everything else, but there is one thing we do not know and never will: what tomorrow will bring. That is why leadership in any field is a close relative of faith. *Faith is not certainty. Faith is the courage to live with uncertainty*. To be a leader is to have that courage.

Since 11 September we have lived in the conscious presence of uncertainty. Part of what we mean by 'globalisation' is precisely the enormous increase of uncertainty that is now an inescapable feature of our lives – because of the sheer pace of technological change, the volatility of financial markets, the mobility of capital and employment and the sheer interconnectedness that makes almost every aspect of our lives vulnerable to unexpected developments from unforeseen directions. That is why a dialogue is so necessary between global leaders and religious leaders. The great religions are our richest resource of wisdom and the databases of our collective memory.

What might emerge from such a dialogue? My guess is that we would converge on what I call the five Cs that are essential to our shared future:

1 **Creativity.** The first axiom of the Bible is that a creative God made mankind in His image, and thus made *man the creator*.

Fostering human creativity will be crucial in the twenty-first century, in which for the first time in history the most potent form of capital will be intellectual capital.

2 **Co-operation.** Sociobiology and the 'iterated prisoner's dilemma' have taught us that humanity's unique evolutionary advantage is co-operation. One man versus one lion: lion wins. Ten men versus one lion: lion loses. Religions create habits of co-operation. The word 'religion' comes from the Latin word meaning 'to bind'. Religions bind us to one another. Economists nowadays call this *social capital*, and it too is vital to economic and social progress.

3 **Compassion.** Economic superpowers come and go: Venice in the sixteenth century, the Netherlands in the seventeenth, France in the eighteenth, Britain in the nineteenth, the United States in the twentieth. Religions come and stay. Judaism has lasted for 4,000 years, Christianity for 2,000, Islam for 1,400. What makes faith-systems endure while economic powers decline and fall? Because what makes a civilisation last is not power but concern for the powerless, not wealth but concern for the poor, not strength but concern for the weak. Civilisations become invulnerable precisely when they care for the vulnerable. Unless that essentially religious message is heard, global capitalism too will decline and fall.

4 **Conservation.** According to the Bible mankind was placed in the garden to 'serve and protect' it. We are guardians of the natural world for the sake of future generations. Without this religious insight, we will have growth without sustainability.

5 **Co-existence.** Here is a value that business leaders must teach religious leaders. Every businessperson knows that human difference is the key to the non-zero-sumness of trade. If each of us were perfect and complete we would never need anyone else. The fact that we are all different, that we have some things but not others, means that what we lack, someone else has, and what we have, someone else needs. That is the basis of trade: the understanding of the value of difference. That must now

> be applied to religion. Religious conflicts occur when religious people believe that they possess the totality of truth. In fact, the totality of truth can never be perceived from a single vantage point. That is why each great faith contributes something unique to the totality of knowledge because of its particular perspective. That is what I call *the dignity of difference*. By being what we uniquely are, we give humanity what we alone can contribute. That means that religions must now value, not fight against, diversity. This is the new paradigm we need if we are to avoid the 'clash of civilisations'.

If we can develop a shared language around these five Cs it will be good news for global development, good news for religion, but better still – good news for our children not yet born.

Insights from the Bible into the Concept of Criminal Justice

Rabbi Sacks was invited to deliver a lecture at Inner Temple on 1 December 2003 in London.

Master, the Princess Royal, Master Treasurer, fellow students of the Inn, this evening is for me both an honour and a pleasure, because it grants me one of those rare moments in life when one is able to complete an unfinished chapter of one's youth.

One of my great ambitions was to be a Member of the Bar, and to that end I joined Inner Temple. However, I never completed the course of study. Indeed, I lasted for a mere two hours, realising after the first lecture I attended that the law was made for far higher minds than mine. Instead, I was seduced by the siren voices, first of philosophy, and then of faith, and therefore I technically remain a student, which I regard as an honourable state.

I am therefore not sure this evening whether you are my reward, or I am your punishment!

You have already heard from the politician, Oliver Letwin, and the policeman, Sir John Stevens. There is certainly nothing I can add to what they have already said, and what you already know. Perhaps then the only thing I can do is to step back and look from a distance in time at this ancient and yet never-old subject of crime and punishment, seeing it as part of a history of ideas as to what society is and what we as human beings are.

Let me therefore begin with the Hebrew Bible. The Bible recognises many dimensions of punishment. For instance, it recognises its role in *deterrence*. The Book of Deuteronomy mentions certain punishments about which it says, 'Others will hear and be afraid, and such evil things will not again be done in your midst'

(Deuteronomy 19:20). It knows, too, about *rehabilitation* of the offender. As God says through the prophet Ezekiel: 'I take no pleasure in the death of the wicked, but rather that he turn from his ways and live' (Ezekiel 18:23). Ancient Jewish law establishes many provisions directed at the rehabilitation of the offender.

However, one central idea of the Hebrew Bible has fallen on hard times in recent years, namely *justice as retribution*. To be sure, this is clearly only one half of the biblical picture. One of the earliest of rabbinic sayings is that 'Initially God sought to create the Universe under the attribute of justice, but He saw that it could not thereby survive. What did He do? He joined to it the attribute of mercy.' In Judaism, justice is always tempered by compassion. However, from biblical times to the philosophy of Immanuel Kant, criminal justice has been seen primarily in terms of retribution. Why has this idea suffered an eclipse in modern times?

The reason, it seems to me, is confusion between two quite different ideas, namely *retribution* and *revenge*. So, for example, one textbook on punishment published in 2001 heads its chapter on retributivism, 'Retribution as Vengeance'. In Gordon (1994) it was said, 'retribution or the taking of vengeance for the injury which was done by the offender'. In Roberts (1963) punishment was regarded as 'vengeance or retribution' against the wrongdoer.

Why do I say that retribution is not revenge? Because the Bible categorically forbids revenge: 'Do not seek revenge or bear a grudge against one of your people, but love your neighbour as yourself; I am the Lord' (Leviticus 19:18). Confusion injures our ability to think clearly about the problems that face us, and when it affects language, it becomes a collective disability. Today the word *retribution* has become so infected that it is difficult to use it without generating emotion, so I will use instead a more neutral phrase: *justice-as-reciprocity*.

The first appearance of the idea occurs in God's covenant with Noah after the Flood: 'Whoever sheds the blood of man, by man shall his blood be shed' (Genesis 9:6). This sentence (in both Hebrew and English) is a chiasmus, a literary structure of the form ABCCBA. Nor is this accidental. Form mirrors content. In a chiasmus, the second half of the sentence is a mirror-image of the first. It describes a world in which what happens to you is a mirror-image of what you do. This is justice as what Shakespeare calls 'measure for measure'. As you treat others, so shall you be treated.

Stated thus, there is an intimate connection between justice-as-reciprocity and the great biblical command, 'You shall love your neighbour as yourself' (Leviticus 19:18). Together they represent the two faces of the moral life. The first is the command of love: do to others as you would wish them to do to you. The second is the command of justice: as you do to others, so shall it be done to you.

Behind both is a profound idea that we seem to have lost in recent centuries, namely that the world is a place in which God creates order, but humanity has a tendency to create chaos. That is why we need law, lawyers, police, courts and judges. Central to the biblical vision is an ordered Universe where everything has its integrity and place. Hence the significance of (moral) *boundaries*. The reason why God tells Adam and Eve not to eat from one of the trees in the Garden of Eden is to establish that even in paradise there are boundaries.

That is why the Hebrew word for wrongdoing, like its English translation, 'transgression', means to cross a boundary, to enter forbidden territory. That is also why punishment in the Bible usually takes the form of *exile*, of which the contemporary form is prison – exile from home, from normal freedoms to a place of not-at-homeness. If a crime is an act in the wrong place, reciprocity consists in placing the wrongdoer in the wrong place, as a result of which, we hope, he or she will experience something of the harm he has done to others. The anticipated result is that he or she will then show remorse, acknowledge wrongdoing and be restored to home. Biblical justice is a matter of reciprocity, not retaliation or revenge. It is an attempt to restore order after crime has disturbed the moral order of the world.

Why does this concept of justice appear in the history of the West at the same time as the birth of monotheism? This is not just a historical question; it has some bearing on the world we inhabit in the twenty-first century. In a polytheistic Universe the world is constituted by a multiplicity of forces which clash and conflict in unpredictable ways – with only this in common, that they are unconcerned with who they are affecting and whether the person affected *deserves* his or her fate. In the ancient world, the forces were the sun, the sea, the Earth, the storm, the wind, the rain. Today we would speak of the global economy, the environment, the march of technology and international conflict. In such a world, what matters is power. Might wins out against right. Justice, as Glaucon says in Plato's *Republic*, 'is whatever is in the interest of the stronger party'.

What threatens to destroy such a world, now as then, is precisely *retaliation* and *revenge*, the cycle of violence, the Montagues and the Capulets of the age. To the cycle of mutual destruction there is no natural end. It is against such a world that a new concept is born in an attempt to find order in the Universe, not just random cruelty. That is when monotheism is born, and with it a new concept of justice, not as revenge but as the *principled rejection of revenge*.

What is revenge? Its essence is that it is *personal* – one person or group restoring their honour after it has been assaulted. Revenge is what Martin Buber called an I–Thou relationship. It is intensely personal.

What criminal justice from the outset seeks to do is *to move from the personal to the impersonal*, from revenge to the due process of law – law whose very glory is that it is impartial, that it treats all alike, the rich and poor, the powerful and powerless. So profound is this idea that it leads to the astonishing scene in Genesis 18 where Abraham, calling himself mere 'dust and ashes' (Genesis 18:27), is nonetheless able to summon God Himself to the bar and say, 'Shall the Judge of all the Earth not do justice?' (Genesis 18:25). Even the Lawgiver is subject to the law.

This fact is important, as we will see later when we turn to 'restorative justice', a contemporary attempt to bring back an I–Thou dimension to criminal law. But I hope this brief sketch of justice-as-reciprocity may make us think again about retributive justice, because without it we will lose the essential connection between punishment and justice.

Beginning in the late eighteenth century, a new mood swept over the West. One of its founding fathers was Jeremy Bentham, and it reached practical expression in the 1960s. A profound shift took place in the moral landscape of the West in the course of which our understanding of punishment moved from justice-as-reciprocity to punishment as prevention, deterrence and rehabilitation – punishment as *social engineering*. It happened against a background of the rise of science, the dethronement of religion and 'the birth of the modern'.

Three major changes took place in Western civilisation at that time. The first was a *temporal reorientation from past to future*. Raymond Williams in his book *Keywords** shows us how in the course of the eighteenth century a whole series of words that until then had been neutral or negative came to signify positives: words like 'modern', 'original', 'creative', 'progressive' and many others. Western culture no longer turned to the past for wisdom, but to the future. The new, it was assumed for the first time, would be better than the old. The concept of punishment too changed – from being a response to a past act, to one measured by future consequences (deterrence, rehabilitation and so on). That was the first change.

The second was that in the eighteenth century, for the first time, ethics aspired to the condition of science. Following the achievements of Copernicus, Galileo and Newton, science became the benchmark of legitimacy. One result was *utilitarianism*, the attempt to turn ethics into the scientific calculation of consequences ('the greatest happiness for the greatest number'),

* Raymond Williams, *Keywords* (London: Fourth Estate, 1988).

using this as a decision procedure in matters of public policy. Utilitarianism is notoriously indifferent to the claims of justice.

The third and most ironic development was that – at the very time people were searching for political and moral freedom – doubt was cast on the very existence of human freedom, that is to say freedom as choice, free will and moral responsibility. In its place came a succession of determinisms: scientific determinism (Pierre-Simon Laplace), economic determinism (Karl Marx), psychological determinism (Sigmund Freud), and most recently genetic determinism. Following the decoding of the human genome, it is widely expected that we will eventually locate genes for crime, antisocial behaviour, violence and so on.

Clearly, if we are not free, then we cannot be held responsible for our acts. If human will is an illusion, then we cannot be *guilty* of our crimes, nor can we *deserve* punishment. The entire concept of moral agency (and with it justice-as-reciprocity) becomes incoherent. That is why the concept of retribution has been displaced, not because it means revenge (which it does not), but because it is predicated on human free will, which has been undermined by the assumptions of the human and social sciences. The danger is then that criminal law begins to lose its anchorage in the idea of justice.

This is a fearful prospect for many reasons. Notoriously, utilitarianism is the logic of totalitarian regimes because one of the best forms of *deterrence* is the show trial in which the guilt of the accused is irrelevant; what matters is the public confession of guilt. As far as *prevention* is concerned, Steven Spielberg's recent film *Minority Report* envisages a world in which crimes can be detected before they are committed and can thus be prevented before they happen. If the logic of punishment is prevention, then pre-emptive punishment is by definition better than punishment after the event. As for *rehabilitation*, we can surely speculate that in the not-too-distant future someone will argue that criminals should not be punished, but instead should have to undergo a form of genetic engineering that will remove the gene responsible for violence and replace it with something more pacific.

Of course, these are horror stories, but the serious point is that *there is nothing in the logic of utilitarianism, of judging acts by consequences, to rule out on principle any of these options* because they may be the most effective forms of deterrence, prevention or rehabilitation. That is why I am concerned that we never lose the logic of punishment-as-justice (retribution), because it is our sole defence of the idea that each of us is a responsible agent, a *subject* not just an object, and that punishment is ultimately an education in responsibility, meaning that the way we learn what it means to harm others is by undergoing harm ourselves.

Which leads me to the relatively new idea of *restorative justice*. This has been tested in various forms in New Zealand and Canada as well in Britain, especially in relation to young offenders. Restorative justice covers a variety of approaches, among them victim–offender mediations, family group conferences and sometimes the involvement of local community leaders or groups. Restorative justice represents an attempt to bring back a *personal* dimension to crime and punishment, the kind of personal dimension it had in its earliest phases in the history of society.

Restorative justice is thus both postmodern and premodern. Usually it involves confronting the criminal with his victim so that he can understand the effect his crime has had on a real life or a set of real lives. No less significant is that it is a way of enabling the victim (or his or her family) to feel that their voice has been heard. This too is part of the process of healing. The third motif is that restorative justice is intended to let us see crime not just as a moral wrong and a form of deviant behaviour, but also as a kind of injury, a wound within the fabric of families and communities that needs to be healed. Restorative justice seeks *reintegration* of both criminal and victim within the community, knitting up society's ravelled sleeve.

As one who has written on the politics of community, I am interested in and intrigued by restorative justice, which is an attempt, as it were, to bring back *community* as opposed to the State into the criminal justice system – especially since, as I have indicated, justice originally was a form of restoration, a different kind, but nonetheless a form of restoration.

However, one point must be made clear if we are to evaluate restorative justice – and here again my point of departure is the Hebrew Bible, which remains one of the most reflective of texts on crime and the moral order. There is not one track in the Hebrew Bible, but two. They are different and they co-exist. One I have already spoken about. It is dominated by the word *justice*, meaning reciprocity.

The other is defined by a cluster of concepts, including remorse, repentance, atonement, forgiveness and mercy. The reason why there are two tracks is that at the heart of the moral universe as understood by Judaism and Christianity, there is not just an impersonal set of rules but also an intensely personal Presence, the Supreme Judge, God Himself, who not only judges but also forgives. That is why the holiest day of the Jewish year is Yom Kippur, the Day of Atonement. Nowadays we might call it the day of restorative justice.

The distinction between justice and atonement is that justice deals with *objective harm*, property damaged, a person injured, a face scarred, a life taken. Atonement deals not with objective but with *subjective harm*: the loss, trauma and grief caused to the victim or in some cases the family of the victim. Retributive justice seeks to restore the objective moral order. Restorative justice seeks to restore the subjective order, the *relationships* damaged by crime. They can only be healed by a direct personal encounter between offender and victim (and in some cases, wider circles such as family or community). That is restorative justice.

There is a fundamental principle in Jewish law, that the Day of Atonement only atones for sins between us and God. If we have harmed or offended other people we are only forgiven if we make restitution, show contrition and apologise, and they accept our apology. The reason is that even God cannot do the logically impossible, which is *to forgive on someone else's behalf*. He forgives us for offences against Him, but if we seek forgiveness for an offence against X, we first have to be forgiven by X. It cannot be done vicariously, and the force of 'cannot' is logical. Only the victim or *in extremis* the family of the victim can forgive, which is why restorative justice requires an I–Thou encounter between criminal and victim.

It therefore follows that there is a place for restorative justice, but only as an accompaniment to, never an alternative to, judicial sentencing and punishment. The very essence of criminal law as opposed to its ancient precursors (retaliation and revenge, and their opposites, forgiveness and atonement) is that *law is impersonal*. The judge does not sit in court in place of the victim. If he or she did, we would have a system of revenge, not a system of justice. Therefore, *a judge cannot forgive* – despite the fact that he or she may and should take into account remorse, contrition, the personal circumstances of the offender and the likelihood of re-offence as mitigating factors when passing sentence. Restorative justice is therefore valuable, but it is a misnomer to call it *justice*. Justice is precisely what it is not. It is a form of atonement – or as we might call it today, mediation, conflict resolution, therapy or catharsis. That is its virtue, *not* that it is a form of justice.

Why do I see restorative justice as valuable? Because it addresses one of the main failings in social thought from the eighteenth century onward, namely the attempt to see humanity, morality and society in terms drawn from the natural sciences. When you try to analyse a problem scientifically you usually begin by analysing phenomena into their smallest constituents, their 'atoms'.

This is what Thomas Hobbes did in one of the key texts of modernity, *Leviathan*.* He saw people as atoms, as did the French revolutionaries in 1789, and as indeed has the whole tendency of abstract political and legal thought that Harvard jurist Mary-Ann

* Thomas Hobbes, *Leviathan* (London: Penguin Classics, 2017).

Glendon calls 'rights talk'. The most distinguished critic of this tendency was Edmund Burke, who spoke instead of the 'little platoons' that link individuals to groups. Rights-talk theorists tend to see individuals in the abstract, shorn of any constitutive attachments to family, community, society, history and tradition.

That may make sense theoretically but not humanly, because we are *not* atoms. We are children of these parents, members of that community, bearers of this history, friends of these neighbours – and these attachments are fundamental to who we are and what we become. Several centuries of social thought, however, has tended to ignore them. The result is that family, community and other social and socialising bonds have become fragile and attenuated in today's world.

Some years ago, I spent a day in Sherborne House, the centre for young offenders that was the subject of Roger Graef's television documentary and book, *Living Dangerously*. It is a centre for young offenders, mostly around eighteen years old, who have been in a life of crime for eight to ten years. It is their last chance before a custodial sentence. I was making a television documentary and there were two moments I found heart-stopping.

The first came when I asked the young offenders, 'When you have children what kind of father would you like to be?' To my amazement, several of them started crying. They knew exactly what they wanted to be – someone who was always there for his children: firm, strong and consistent, but above all *there*. My question caught them unawares, and they suddenly became conscious of what they had lacked from their own fathers.

The second came when I asked the director of the centre what networks of support the young people would have when they left. The answer was, more or less, none – at least not from the local community or from their families. For the first time I sensed what it must be like to be a young offender without the supports I had always taken for granted. To break any behavioural habit is difficult. Without help, it can be impossible. I was reminded of the African saying, taken by Hillary Clinton as the title of a book: 'It takes a village to raise a child.' We are not social atoms.

What restorative justice restores is insight into the human context of crime. It does not address the act, the wrong or the harm. It addresses *persons*, the criminal and the victim, and takes them seriously as persons. It focuses on the whole network of relationships within which we have our being. At least some forms of crime flourish in anonymity, when you neither know the victim nor do you think it likely you will meet. Restorative justice restores the personal face of crime by confronting the criminal with his victim and vice versa. As such, it may begin a process of healing, whether through apology and restitution on the part of the perpetrator, or forgiveness (or at least understanding) on the part of the victim and community. This is not justice – classically it was called atonement – but it is a not unimportant *accompaniment* of justice. It is the human face of crime.

My argument has been simple. First, I sketched a chapter in the history of ideas, beginning with retaliation or revenge which belong to a world in which force prevails (tragically the international arena still seems mired in that model); moving to the revolution of monotheism in which human revenge is forbidden, its place taken by the impersonal processes of law. From there I spoke of the transformation of thought from the eighteenth century onwards, in which punishment came to be seen less in terms of the past, the actual crime, and more in terms of future consequences – a move away from justice toward social engineering. From there I moved to the recent interest in restorative justice with its attempt to re-personalise crime by confronting the criminal with the victim and (sometimes) the victim's family and community. I argued that this is not a form of justice, nor can it substitute for the impartial process of the court. It belongs to what was once called atonement, and now, mediation or conflict resolution. It is best seen not as an alternative to punishment-as-justice, but as a valuable accompaniment, allowing the victim to feel that his or her voice has been heard, the perpetrator to confront the human consequences of crime, and the community to assist in the re-integration of both.

Having spoken about restorative justice, I have hinted at a fundamental idea that must concern all of us as citizens. One of the great teachings of the Bible is that the creation of a law-governed society cannot be a task for courts alone. It is essentially a task of families and communities, and of education as conceived in the Bible – namely the *internalisation of law*, so that the more the law is engraved in our consciences (what Freud called the superego), the less oppressive is the need for police, surveillance and other mechanisms of enforcement. The concept of education-as-internalisation has begun to reappear in our national curriculum under the heading of Citizenship. The maintenance of law is a complex partnership in which we all share responsibility: parents, schools, neighbourhoods, communities, friends and publicly recognised role models. Law ends in court, but it begins elsewhere, in habits of law-abidingness to which we must all contribute.

Permit me to end with a simple tribute to your work. Twelve-and-a-half years ago, when I became Chief Rabbi, I was invited to a dinner to talk about my hopes for the Jewish community. Present was a very distinguished lawyer, sadly no longer in the land of the living – the late Sir Peter, later Lord Chief Justice Taylor. At the end of my talk, he turned to me and said, 'Chief Rabbi, I applaud your vision, but what will you do with a wicked old sinner like me?' I replied, 'Peter, how can I possibly allow you to speak of yourself in such language? Do you not recall the saying of the Jewish sages 2,000 years ago: "Any judge who delivers a true verdict becomes a partner with God in the work of creation"?' Sir Peter had the good grace to blush. In an age in which too many cruel jokes are made about lawyers, let me salute you as God's partners in the dual process of creating a just and gracious society – the love of law and the law of love.

On Freedom

On 16 June 2003, Rabbi Sacks delivered the Sir Isaiah Berlin Memorial Lecture at the Hampstead Synagogue in London.

I count it a great privilege to deliver this Sir Isaiah Berlin Memorial Lecture. It is my tribute to a man I hugely admired and whose thoughts very much influenced my own – all the more to do so in this synagogue of which he was a member for so many years, in the presence of Lady Aline whose graciousness gives an aura to this evening which no one else could give and in the company of his stepson, Peter Halban. Tonight we honour one who conferred immense honour on the Jewish community and on British academic and intellectual life.

Sadly, I came to know Sir Isaiah toward the end of his life. Only once, in Cambridge thirty-five years ago, did I attend a lecture of his, hearing that remarkable voice which was able to speak in a torrent of words with unparalleled erudition in labyrinthine sentences delivered at lightning speed – I could not listen as fast as he could talk. There was only one Sir Isaiah Berlin. I discovered this by chance in the early 1990s when I asked what had happened to the concept of wisdom in public life. I asked many people at random, Jewish and non-Jewish, to name a sage in Britain. They all gave the same answer. Instantly they replied, 'Sir Isaiah Berlin'. When I asked them for a second, they couldn't think of one. That is a measure of the esteem in which he was held and which he so richly deserved.

He had a wonderful self-deprecating humour. I love the story he once told, of the taxi driver who said to him, 'You're Isaiah Berlin, the philosopher, aren't you? I don't think much of philosophers. I had that Bertrand Russell in the back of my cab one day and I said, "Lord Russell, you're a philosopher. What's it all about then, Guv?" – and do you know, he couldn't tell me.' I think it was Isaiah who coined my favourite academic put-down: 'On the surface, he's profound, but deep down, he's superficial.'

I will never forget our last encounter and non-encounter. In 1997 I had published a book called *The Politics of Hope*,* in which I argued that Isaiah Berlin was right in 1958 – when he delivered his inaugural lecture as Chichele Professor of Social and Political Theory at Oxford, the famous 'Two Concepts of Liberty' – to see that the greatest threat to liberty at that time was totalitarianism. But almost forty years later, I wondered whether there might not be another threat, this time not external but internal, the collapse of our structures of solidarity, of families, communities, traditions and voluntary organisations that sustained liberal democracies in the past, giving them what de Tocqueville and later Robert Bellah called 'habits of the heart'. I discussed the idea briefly with Sir Isaiah, and he asked me to send him the book.

Some months passed and, not having heard from him, I phoned him at his home in Oxford. Lady Aline answered and said, 'Chief Rabbi, we have just been talking about you.' I asked, 'In what context?' She replied, 'Isaiah has just asked you to officiate at his funeral.' I said, 'pe pe pe' – not an Oxford degree like PPE, but an old Yiddish way of averting the evil eye – but Isaiah did die just a few days later. I did officiate at his funeral in Oxford and then later at that quite unique memorial service in the Hampstead Synagogue. Sometime later, his biographer, Michael Ignatieff, came to our home for a conversation about Isaiah and wondered why he had insisted on an orthodox Jewish funeral. I said (and wrote in *The Times*), that Sir Isaiah may not have been a believing Jew, but he was a loyal Jew – and that is no small thing.

Tonight, I go further and say that the word *emunah*, usually translated as 'belief', actually, in biblical (as opposed to medieval) Hebrew means, not 'faith' but 'faithfulness' or 'loyalty'. That was Sir Isaiah.

* Jonathan Sacks, *The Politics of Hope* (London: Jonathan Cape, 1997).

Tonight, therefore, we honour a faithful and loyal Jew who brought pride and honour to his people. What I want to do tonight – and what I was unable to do in his lifetime – is to ask in very broad terms what the relationship was between his philosophical concerns and those of Judaism itself, and then to focus on one detail in his work, perhaps the most important in his whole constellation of ideas – an idea on the face of it quite contrary to Jewish belief but which I will argue is not so. My question will be whether Sir Isaiah's work might not lead us to see something in Judaism that we may have overlooked. It might even be, and this will be my final suggestion, that it is this aspect of Judaism that we discover in and through Sir Isaiah's work that speaks most powerfully to the world as it presents itself to us in this tense and conflictual age. Is there something in Sir Isaiah's work that might guide us away from a clash of civilisations?

What were the dominant themes of his work? There were three. The first was his eloquent and impressive defence of freedom, in respect of which he will be ranked – along with two others who came to this country fleeing persecution, Sir Karl Popper and Friedrich Hayek – as one of the giants who made the case for liberty in the twentieth century more powerfully than any of their contemporaries. Sir Isaiah wrote an extraordinary chapter in the story of British liberty whose earlier contributors included John Milton, John Locke and John Stuart Mill.

Second was the theme chosen by his literary executor, Henry Hardy, as the title of one of the volumes of his collected essays, namely *The Power of Ideas*.* Isaiah believed that history is not simply the play of blind causes. It is not governed by causal necessity, as Spinoza thought, nor inexorable economic forces, as Marx

* Isaiah Berlin (ed. Henry Hardy), *The Power of Ideas* (London: Chatto & Windus, 2000).

argued, nor by biological or socio-biological imperatives, as Darwin's followers have maintained. Sir Isaiah was not a determinist. He believed that human action is not simply a response to a situation, but a response to how we perceive and interpret the situation – and that depends on the ideas we bring to bear on it. Hence the power of ideas is connected with the concept of human freedom and thus ultimately with a free society.

Third was his conviction that ideas have a history. I was talking recently to another philosopher, Jonathan Glover, now Professor of Medical Ethics at King's College, London, who had been a student of Sir Isaiah. He reminded me of the gust of fresh air that Sir Isaiah breathed into Oxford in the 1950s and 1960s. That was one of the most arid periods in British philosophy, dominated by linguistic philosophy in which it was argued that you could solve, or dissolve, philosophical problems simply by clarifying what words mean. This was philosophy almost without a sense of history. And here was Isaiah Berlin speaking with intimate knowledge of writers most of us had never heard of, let alone read: Belinski and Bakunin, Herder and Herzen, Ficino and Fourier. There is a line in [the Jewish prayer of] Hallel: 'I called to God from my confinement, and He answered me with expanses' (Psalm 118:5). That is what Isaiah gave Oxford philosophy in those days. He was the man who rescued British philosophy from its parochialism and showed that ideas are not timeless; they are set in time.

It seems to me that these three ideas are not accidentally connected with the Jewish values Sir Isaiah carried with him, consciously or unconsciously, despite the fact that he never explicitly related them to Jewish sources. Let us consider them in the reverse order.

The idea that history is a central category in understanding humanity mirrors his understanding of Jewish identity itself. He wrote: 'All Jews who are at all conscious of their identity as Jews are steeped in history. They have longer memories; they are aware of a longer continuity as a community than any other which has survived.'* He quotes a lovely line from Alexander Herzen to the effect that 'Slavs have no history, only geography.' The Jewish people, he said, suffer from the opposite affliction. We have all too much history and all too little geography. The historical dimension was what Isaiah most identified with as a Jew.

Second, the power of ideas: his whole work was a kind of commentary to the famous line from Zechariah, that we achieve the great human victories 'Not by might, nor by force but by My spirit, says God' (Zechariah 4:6). It is not too much to say that Jewish history is the supreme example of a people sustained by ideas – exile and redemption, covenant and destiny, justice and compassion. Indeed, Jews survived as a nation for almost 2,000 years without any of the normal attributes of a nation: shared territory, an overarching political order, a common culture or the same language of everyday life. Jewish history depended on the existence of a set of shared ideas, the hopes begotten by those ideas and the practices in which they were expressed.

As for freedom, if there was one ritual which Sir Isaiah cherished above others it was the Pesach seder, Passover evening with its narrative of freedom. Judaism is a faith which began and is sustained annually in the reminder of what the lack of freedom feels like: the bread of affliction and the bitter herbs of slavery. So, there is a strong degree of kinship, elective affinity, family resemblance between the work of Isaiah Berlin and the tradition of which he was a part.

That is my first observation. Now I want to focus on a specific detail of his work to which he himself attached great significance and in virtue of which Noel Annan said that Sir Isaiah 'seems to me to have written the truest and most moving of all interpretations of life that my own generation made'. It is this aspect which

* Isaiah Berlin, *Against the Current* (London: Pimlico, 1997), p. 252.

led John Gray, in his book *Isaiah Berlin*,* to write that 'Berlin's liberalism – which is, if I am not mistaken, the most profoundly deliberated and most powerfully defended in our time, or perhaps in any time – diverges radically from those that have dominated politically philosophy in the post-war world'. This is the idea to which Sir Isaiah gave the name pluralism and which he tells us he became aware of through his readings of Machiavelli, Vico, Herder and Herzen.

Now there are several ideas here that we have to disentangle. One is that not all values are compatible. This is a difficult idea to grasp, but he expressed it powerfully and clearly. We cherish equality. We value freedom. But you cannot maximise both at once. If you pursue equality, as in the case of Soviet Communism, you sacrifice much freedom. If you pursue freedom, through free market capitalism, you lose a large measure of equality. It was his great insight that the values to which we subscribe, do not exist in harmony. They are in conflict.

The second insight, following on from the first, was that this applies not only to values and individual ideals but also to systems of ideals, to cultures and civilisations. Sir Isaiah attributes this idea to Herder: 'Herder', he wrote, 'laid it down that every culture possesses its own centre of gravity; each culture has its own points of reference; there is no reason why these cultures should fight each other . . . but unification was destruction. Nothing was worse than imperialism. Rome, which crushed native civilisations in Asia Minor in order to produce one uniform Roman culture, committed a crime. The world was a great garden in which different flowers and plants grew, each in its own way, each with its own claims and rights and past and future. From which it followed that no matter what men had in common . . . there were no universally true answers as valid for one culture as for another.'

From this he concluded: 'What is clear is that values can clash – that is why civilisations are incompatible.' Sir Isaiah foresaw

* John Gray, *Isaiah Berlin* (Princeton: Princeton University Press, 1996).

and diagnosed the clash of civilisations long before that phrase entered our consciousness. He says: 'These collisions of values are of the essence of what they are and what we are. If we are told that these contradictions will be solved in some perfect world in which all good things can be harmonised in principle, then we must answer, to those who say this, that the meanings they attach to the names which for us denote the conflicting values, are not ours. We must say that the world in which what we see as incompatible values are not in conflict is a world altogether beyond our ken; that principles which are harmonised in this other world are not the principles with which, in our daily lives, we are acquainted; if they are transformed, it is into conceptions now known to us on Earth. But it is on Earth that we live, and it is here that we must believe and act.'

In other words, any attempt to impose a single vision of the good on the world, or even on a single society, is fundamentally untrue to the human condition and leads to massive and unacceptable loss of liberty. Now Isaiah Berlin saw this as a radical discovery because it suggested that all great monistic visions, whether philosophical like Plato's, or religious like the Christianity and Islam of the Middle Ages, or secular like fascism and Communism – all were false and dangerous. The best we could hope for is a modest kind of politics, one in which we do not seek to implement an ideal but in which we grant people maximum freedom to pursue the different and conflicting ideals that constitute the human situation.

What kind of politics would that be like? On this, one of his most important disciples, John Gray, wrote in another book, *The Two Faces of Liberalism,* 'Liberalism has always had two faces. From one side toleration is the pursuit of an ideal form of life. From the other it is the search for terms of peace amongst different ways of life. In the former view, liberal institutions are seen as applications of universal principles. In the latter, they are a means to peaceful co-existence. In the first, liberalism is a prescription for a universal regime. In the second, it is project of co-existence that can be pursued in many regimes.'* In recent times, the most famous exponent of the first view was John Rawls; of the second, Isaiah Berlin. Gray calls this second approach 'modus vivendi liberalism'.

What is the difference between Rawlsian liberalism and modus vivendi liberalism? Rawlsian liberalism says, in effect, that people may have different religious convictions, but they do not bring them into the public square. When you enter the political domain, you speak a common language that Rawls calls 'the language of public reason'. One of the best examples of this was the rule recommended by nineteenth-century German Jews, 'Be a man in the street and a Jew at home.' Religious commitments are private. In the public domain we all speak the same language, suppressing our differences. This can lead to quite contorted psychologies. I am reminded of the comment made by the late Rabbi Shlomo Carlebach who used to say about the American students he met: 'If someone says, I am a Catholic, I know he or she is a Catholic. If they say, I am Protestant, I know he is a Protestant. If someone says, I'm just a human being, I know he's a Jew.'

There is, however, another conception, an older one, namely that religious convictions or cultural commitments are not things you leave behind when you enter the public square. They are part of who and what we are, in the street, the polling booth, even in Parliament. If so, then the public square will be an arena of real and intractable conflict. Whether we speak of voluntary euthanasia, stem cell research, cloning, animal welfare, environmental ethics or any other of the myriad issues that concern us, public debate will disclose substantive conflicts for which there is no neutral decision procedure, and the best we can hope for is not that we will agree but that we will get along. We will establish not a consensus but a modus vivendi, a way of living peaceably together.

This was the kind of politics Sir Isaiah believed in. He was convinced that we could never create an ideal society in which

* John Gray, *The Two Faces of Liberalism* (Cambridge: Polity Press, 2000).

all our multiple visions of the good were simultaneously realised. His favourite quotation in this context was the sentence he attributed to Professor R. G. Collingwood's translation of a line by Immanuel Kant, 'Out of the crooked timber of humanity, no straight thing was ever made.' I add, as a footnote, that I suspect Kant himself was here quoting the Bible – 'That which is crooked cannot be made straight' (Ecclesiastes 1:15).

If this is indeed the case, it seems to call into question one of Judaism's greatest ideas, namely, of the Messianic Age. We do believe that one day there will be a perfect world; yet if Sir Isaiah is right, there cannot be. There are two ways of reconciling the apparent contradiction. One is to say that Sir Isaiah Berlin helped us understand why, in answer to the question, 'Has the Messiah yet arrived?' the Jewish answer is always 'Not yet'. The other is to say, like the third-century rabbinic sage Shmuel, that 'the only difference between our time and Messianic time is that the Jewish people will no longer be under the dominion of other nations', in other words, there will be no miraculous transformation of nature, but rather that Jews will return to their land and live at peace with their neighbours – about which we pray that this be possible and that it comes to pass speedily in our days.

It is here, however, that I want to make a fundamental point. It is well known that the prophets of ancient Israel were the first to conceive of peace as an ideal. That was a revolutionary proposition in an age of epic heroes, military virtues and glory won on the battlefield. As fate would have it, it was an earlier Isaiah, not the philosopher but the prophet, who gave voice to the great words engraved in imagination of the West:

> They shall beat their swords into ploughshares,
> Their spears into pruning hooks.
> Nation shall not lift up sword against nation,
> Neither shall they learn war any more.
> (Isaiah 2:4)

Isaiah's younger contemporary, the prophet Micah, quoted those words (Isaiah 2, Micah 4) and added some of his own, so prescient of Sir Isaiah's idea:

> They shall sit, every man under his vine and under his fig tree,
> And none shall make them afraid,
> For the mouth of the Lord of the Hosts has spoken.
> For all the peoples walk, each in the name of its God,
> But we will walk in the name of the Lord our God for ever.
> (Micah 4:4–5)

This is perhaps the earliest anticipation of pluralism in history (to be sure, Micah does not have in mind pluralism as we understand it today: Rashi and Radak interpret the verse to mean that the other nations were wrong. But his vision remains beatific). Let us call this the prophetic vision of peace. However, and this is my central argument this evening, what is fascinating is that Judaism pioneered not one concept of peace but two, and they are quite different. The first was prophetic. The second appeared much later, at around the first or second century CE, after the destruction of the Second Temple. The rabbis gave it the name *darkhei shalom*, 'the ways of peace'.

What in practice does this second doctrine require? The sages declared, 'We should provide sustenance for the poor of idolaters as well as the poor of Israel. We must visit the sick of the non-Jewish community as well as those of the Jewish community. Just as we have an obligation to see to the burial of a Jew, so must we do likewise for a non-Jew. We pay obituary tributes to one, not of our faith, who has died as we do for one of our own faith who has died. We must allow members of the idolatrous cultures among whom we live to gather food set aside for the poor, namely, the corner of the field, the forgotten sheaf and so on.' All of these rules were ordained because of 'the ways of peace'.

It is important to understand precisely what the rabbis were referring to. They were addressing the situation in which Jews found themselves as a minority in a predominantly non-Jewish society. They were not speaking about what the Bible refers to as a *ger toshav*, 'a resident alien', a non-Jew who lives within a Jewish state. To fall within this category, an individual was required to keep the seven Noahide Laws, one of which is a prohibition against idolatry. The 'ways of peace' belong to a post-biblical environment, but their strength lies in their inclusivity. They are not restricted to non-Jews with whom we agree on basic principles of morality; still less do they refer to Christians and Muslims (Maimonides regarded Islam as a pure monotheism; Jacob Emden held the same view about Christianity). The 'ways of peace' apply even to idolaters, in other words those opposed to everything we believe. Nonetheless, we have welfare responsibilities to them. We have to provide them with food when they are hungry, support them when they are poor, visit them when they are sick, and comfort them when they are bereaved.

What we find in these rabbinic texts of the second century is a strong form of modus vivendi liberalism, a set of principles of how to live graciously with people whose beliefs and way of life are incompatible with ours. Despite these profound differences, we must engage in common citizenship, contributing to their, as well as our own, common good. Hence the momentous difference between the prophetic and the rabbinic concept of peace. The prophetic vision is a utopian peace, one that will come about at the end of days (what Fukuyama, following Hegel, called the 'end of history'). The rabbinic vision is non-utopian. It is peace for an unredeemed world, one tailored to fit the crooked timber of humanity.

Where does this idea come from? The rabbis derived it from the verse, 'Its ways are ways of pleasantness, and all its paths are peace' (Proverbs 3:17). That is its textual warrant. Historically, however, it was born in the painful experience of exile. It emerged because Jews, having in the biblical era lived in their own land, were now dispersed minorities in pagan cultures. Definitive in this context was the letter written 2,600 years ago by the prophet

Jeremiah to the exiles in Babylon and Egypt: 'Build houses and settle down, plant vineyards and gardens and eat their fruit. Take wives and have children . . . Seek the peace of the city to which you have been exiled. Pray to God on its behalf, for in its peace, you will find peace; in its prosperity, you will find prosperity' (Jeremiah 29:5–7).

There is one other phenomenon of which the rabbis were acutely aware, namely the conflict of values. To take only the simplest example, there is often a conflict between peace and truth. When angels come to visit Abraham and Sarah and they tell Sarah (who was 89 at the time) that she would have a child, she laughs and says, 'Now that I am withered, shall I have the joy of motherhood? Besides which, my husband is old' (Genesis 18:12). When God reports this to Abraham, He says, 'Why did Sarah laugh?', saying, 'How can I have children when I am so old?' (Genesis 18:13) – discreetly omitting the second half of the sentence where she complains that Abraham is old. From this and other sources, the rabbis concluded that there are times when peace takes precedence over truth.

At the Memorial Service for Sir Isaiah, I quoted the remarkable *midrash* about how, when God was about to create mankind, the angels disagreed as to whether this was wise or not. The angel of kindness said, 'Create humanity because human beings do kind deeds.' The angel of truth said, 'Do not create humanity, because human beings tell lies.' The angel of generosity said, 'Create, because human beings are often generous.' The angel of peace said, 'Do not create, because they are full of strife.' What did God do? He took truth and threw it to the ground. There are times when (absolute) truth must be sacrificed for the sake of peace. This is a *midrash* on precisely Sir Isaiah's philosophical theme. On Earth, values conflict; and if man is to be created, it must be on Earth, within its parameters and possibilities.

The rabbis understood this very clearly. Our world and its history thus far are non-utopian. There are values that are intellectually incommensurable and practically incompatible. We must therefore, at times, make a painful choice, deciding which of two values takes priority. The sages quite clearly chose peace over truth, even though they loved truth with every fibre of their being. Without peace, there can be no society; and without society, there can be no human pursuit of truth for we are (on this, Judaism concurs with Aristotle) essentially social animals.

Let me quote in this context a much later – nineteenth century – sage: this time, not another Isaiah but another Berlin, Rabbi Naftali Zvi Yehudah Berlin, known as the Netziv (1817–93), head of the famous *yeshiva* in Volozhyn. The Netziv's comment is directed to the episode in which Moses' father-in-law Jethro sees him judging the people alone and tells him that what he is doing is 'not good'. He should establish a hierarchy of delegated authority – heads of thousands, hundreds, fifties and tens – so that 'you will be able to stand the strain and all the people will come to their place in peace' (Exodus 18:23). The Netziv's question is simple. Delegation would clearly help Moses to bear the strain, but how would it create 'peace' for the people?

His answer is fascinating. In Jewish law, a judge may propose mediation instead of a strict judicial hearing. The difference is that in a judicial hearing, one of the parties wins and the other loses, whereas a mediated settlement allows both parties to feel that they have achieved a satisfactory outcome (the discussion can be found in Babylonian Talmud Sanhedrin 6b). The strict application of law aims at truth; a mediated settlement aims at peace. A judge, however, can only opt for mediation if he does not yet know the full facts of the case and has not yet reached a verdict. Moses, the supreme prophet, instantly knew who was in the right and who in the wrong and could therefore never propose mediation. Delegating most of the cases to lesser mortals, he was thus enabling more mediated settlements and thus bringing peace to the people. Here too, truth and peace are seen as sometimes incompatible values, between which the Jewish preference is for peace.

The second comment of the Netziv is closer still to Sir Isaiah's concerns. It occurs in the context of the Tower of Babel

(Genesis 11). That narrative begins, 'Now the whole world had one language and shared words' (Genesis 11:1). What, asked the Netziv, is wrong with that? To the contrary, the passage seems to emphasise the unity of the builders, and unity is surely a good thing. The Netziv's answer is original and insightful. Babel, he intimated, was the first totalitarian state. There was nothing wrong with its builders sharing a language. But the phrase 'shared words' implies an imposed uniformity of belief. In a manner reminiscent of Aristotle's critique of Plato's *Republic*, he argues that the suppression of diversity of viewpoints is not the making, but the destruction, of society.

Finally, let me cite his most striking observation. It is made in the introduction to his commentary to the Book of Genesis. In the course of his remarks the Netziv notes the difference between the First and Second Temples, both of which were destroyed. At the time of the First Temple, says Netziv, the Israelites were guilty of grave sins. At the time of the Second, they were 'righteous and pious people who laboured in the study of the Torah'. What then brought about its destruction? The answer he gives is that 'They suspected anyone they saw worshipping God in a way different to theirs, of being a heretic and a sectarian.' They were not able to tolerate diversity in the service of God. It is an observation that would have delighted Sir Isaiah. Religious intolerance is something neither Berlin, in their different ways, could endorse.

So, to summarise, there are two concepts of peace in Judaism. The prophet Isaiah envisioned a utopian peace, when the wolf will live with the lamb. But there is also a more modest, non-utopian peace to which rabbinic Judaism gave expression, one based on good citizenship, neighbourly relations and the attempt to create a society and a common good together with people who believe everything that you hold false or mistaken. That is modus vivendi liberalism, what the sages called *darkhei shalom*, the liberalism of an irreducibly plural society. I hope therefore that I have shown how the thought of Sir Isaiah Berlin was part of a long-standing Jewish tradition, one of whose great voices was the prophet Isaiah, and another was a Rabbi Berlin. To be a member of the Jewish people is to be part of a faith of great internal diversity: of Hillel and Shammai, Abaye and Rava, Rashi and Maimonides, the Vilna Gaon and the Baal Shem Tov, and what the sages called 'arguments for the sake of heaven'. It is also to be part of a people accustomed to living with external diversity, between Jews and non-Jews, monotheists and non-monotheists, and yet striving, nonetheless, to create a state of civil peace through modus vivendi liberalism. These were values about which Sir Isaiah cared passionately and which he expounded with such eloquence.

Sir Isaiah himself was very careful to distinguish between two words, monotheism and monism. He opposed the second, not the first – and it is monism (what in another context I have called 'the attempt to impose a single answer on a plural world'), not monotheism, that is dangerous. Judaism is not monist. We do not hold that there is only one way to reach God, despite the fact that we believe that there is only one God. My argument has been that the rabbinic idea of *darkhei shalom* is a genuine and thus far unexplored resource as to how, in practice, we might enact a form of modus vivendi liberalism, and how we might construct a free and gracious social order amongst people of profoundly differing beliefs, as well as a peaceful world order despite the danger of a clash of civilisations.

To quote Sir Isaiah himself, towards the end of his essay, 'The Pursuit of the Ideal': 'Of course, social and political conditions will take place; the mere conflict of positive values alone makes this unavoidable. Yet they can, I believe, be minimised by promoting and preserving an uneasy equilibrium which is constantly threatened and in constant need of repair – that alone, I repeat is the precondition for decent societies and morally acceptable behaviour, otherwise we are bound to lose our way.' That is the case I have argued, tonight and in several of my books, as my tribute to Sir Isaiah Berlin.

Let me end with another quotation, this time from his 1952 radio lectures, republished recently as the book *Freedom and Its*

Betrayal: 'The essence of liberty has always lain in the ability to choose as you wish to choose, because you wish so to choose, uncoerced, unbullied, not swallowed up in some vast system; and in the right to resist, to be unpopular, to stand up for your convictions merely because they are your convictions. That is true freedom, and without it there is neither freedom of any kind, nor even the illusion of it.'*

That is the freedom for which he became the great spokesman. It is also the freedom for which Jews throughout the ages fought, and not a few died: the freedom to be different, to be iconoclasts, challenging the idols of the age, whatever the idols and whatever the age; the freedom to be a counter-voice in the conversation of mankind. To that great story, Sir Isaiah Berlin added an illustrious chapter. May his memory be a blessing.

* Isaiah Berlin, *Freedom and Its Betrayal* (London: Pimlico, 2003).

Faith and Fate

On 28 July 2008, Rabbi Sacks was invited by the then-Archbishop of Canterbury, Dr Rowan Williams, to address the plenary session of the decennial gathering of Anglican bishops from around the world at the Lambeth Conference in Canterbury.

Friends – this is for me a profoundly moving moment. You have invited me, a Jew, to join your deliberations, and I thank you for that, and for all it implies. There is a lot of history between our faiths, and for me to stand here, counting as I do the Archbishop of Canterbury [Dr Rowan Williams] and the Archbishop of York [John Sentamu] as beloved colleagues, is a signal of hope for our children and the world they will inherit.

Many centuries ago, the Jewish sages asked, who is a hero of heroes? They answered, not one who defeats his enemy but one who turns an enemy into a friend. That is what has happened between Jews and Christians: strangers have become friends. And on this, I think the first occasion a rabbi has addressed a plenary session of the Lambeth Conference, I want to thank God in the words of the ancient Jewish blessing, *Shehecheyanu vekiyemanu vehigiyanu lazman hazeh*. Thank You, God, for bringing us to this time.

You have asked me to speak about covenant, and that is what I am going to do. We will discover not only a transformative idea, one that changes us as we think of it; not only a way forward for faith in the twenty-first century. We will also find ourselves better able to answer the question of what the role of religion in society is, even in a secular society like Britain.

And let's begin our journey at the place we passed on our march last Thursday, in Westminster [to demand urgent action on global poverty]. It was such a lovely day that I imagine meeting up with my granddaughter on the way back and taking her to see some of the sights of London.

We'd begin where we were, outside Parliament, and I imagine her asking what happens there, and I'd say, politics. And she'd ask, what's politics about, and I'd say: it's about the creation and distribution of power.

And then we'd go to the city, and see the Bank of England, and she'd ask what happens there and I'd say: economics. And she'd say: what's economics about, and I'd say: it's about the creation and distribution of wealth.

And then on our way back we'd pass St Paul's Cathedral, and she'd ask, what happens there, and I'd say: worship. And she'd ask: what's worship about? What does it create and distribute? And that's a good question, because for the past fifty years our lives have been dominated by the other two institutions: politics and economics, the state and the market, the logic of power and the logic of wealth. The state is us in our collective capacity. The market is us as individuals. And the debate has been: which is more effective? The left tends to favour the state. The right tends to favour the market. And there are endless shadings in between.

But what this leaves out of the equation is a third phenomenon of the utmost importance, and I want to explain why. The state is about power. The market is about wealth. And they are two ways of getting people to act in the way we want. Either we force them to – the way of power. Or we pay them to – the way of wealth.

But there is a third way, and to see this let's perform a simple thought experiment. Imagine you have total power, and then you decide to share it with nine others. How much do you have left? One-tenth of what you had when you began. Suppose you have a thousand pounds, and you decide to share it with nine others.

How much do you have left? One-tenth of what you had when you began.

But now suppose that you decide to share, not power or wealth, but love, or friendship, or influence, or even knowledge, with nine others. How much do I have left? Do I have less? No, I have more; perhaps even ten times as much. Why? Because love, friendship and influence are things that only exist by virtue of sharing. I call these covenantal goods – the goods that, the more I share, the more I have.

In the short term at least, wealth and power are zero-sum games. If I win, you lose. If you win, I lose. Covenantal goods are non-zero-sum games, meaning, if I win, you also win. And that has huge consequences. Wealth and power, economic and politics, the market and the state, are arenas of *competition*, whereas covenantal goods are arenas of *co-operation.*

Where do we find covenantal goods like love, friendship, influence and trust? They are born, not in the state, and not in the market, but in marriages, families, congregations, fellowships and communities – even in society, if we are clear in our minds that society is something different from the state. One way of seeing what's at stake is to understand the difference between two things that look and sound alike but actually are not, namely *contracts* and *covenants.*

In a contract, two or more individuals, each pursuing their own interest, come together to make an exchange for mutual benefit. So, there is the commercial contract that creates the market, and the social contract that creates the state.

A covenant is something different. In a covenant, two or more individuals, each respecting the dignity and integrity of the other, come together in a bond of love and trust, to share their interests, sometimes even to share their lives, by pledging their faithfulness to one another, to do together what neither can achieve alone.

A contract is a *transaction.* A covenant is a *relationship.* Or to put it slightly differently: a contract is about interests. A covenant is about identity. It is about you and me coming together to form an 'Us'. That is why contracts *benefit*, but covenants *transform.*

So, economics and politics, the market and the state, are about the logic of competition. Covenant is about the logic of co-operation.

Now I want to ask, why is it that societies cannot exist without co-operation? Why is it that state and market alone cannot sustain a society? The answer to that is an absolutely fascinating story, and it begins with Charles Darwin.

Darwin hit a problem he could not solve. I understand from Darwin that all life evolves by natural selection, which means, by the way of competition for scarce resources: food, shelter and the like.

If so, you would expect that all societies would value the most competitive, even the most ruthless individuals. But Darwin noticed that it isn't so. In fact, in every society of which he knew, it was the most altruistic individuals who were the most valued and admired, not the most competitive. Or, if I can put it in the language of Richard Dawkins: a bundle of selfish genes get together and produce selfless people. That was Darwin's paradox, and it lay unsolved until the late 1970s.

It was then that three very different disciplines converged: sociobiology, a branch of mathematics called games theory and high-speed computer simulation. Together they produced something called the iterated prisoner's dilemma.

To cut a long story short, what they discovered was that though natural selection works through the genes of individuals, individuals – certainly in the higher life-forms – survive only because they are members of groups. And groups survive only on the basis of reciprocity and trust, on what I have called covenant, or the logic of co-operation. One human versus one lion, the lion wins. Ten humans versus one lion, the humans are in with a chance.

It turns out that the very things that make *Homo sapiens* different – the use of language, the size of the brain, even the moral sense itself – have to do with the ability to form and sustain groups: the larger the brain, the larger the group.

Neo-Darwinians call this reciprocal altruism. Sociologists call it trust. Economists call it social capital. And it is one of the great intellectual discoveries of our time. Individuals need groups. Groups need co-operation. And co-operation needs covenant, bonds of reciprocity and trust.

Traditionally, that was the work of religion. After all, the word 'religion' itself comes from a Latin root meaning 'to bind'. And whether we take a conservative thinker like Edmund Burke, or a radical like Thomas Paine, or a social scientist like Émile Durkheim, or an outside observer like Alexis de Tocqueville, they all saw this, and explained it, each in their own way. And now it has been scientifically demonstrated. If there is only competition and not co-operation, if there is only the state and the market and no covenantal relationships, society will not survive.

What then happens to a society when religion wanes and there is nothing covenantal to take its place? Relationships break down. Marriage grows weak. Families become fragile. Communities atrophy. And the result is that people feel vulnerable and alone. If they turn those feelings outward, the result is often anger turning to violence. If they turn them inward, the result is depression, stress-related syndromes, eating disorders, drug and alcohol abuse. Either way, there is spiritual poverty in the midst of material affluence.

It doesn't happen all at once, but slowly, gradually and inexorably. Societies without covenants and the institutions needed to inspire and sustain them, disintegrate. Initially, the result is a loss of graciousness in our shared and collective lives. Ultimately, it is a loss of freedom itself.

That is where we are. And now let's go back to where it all began.

In the ancient Near East, covenants existed in the form of treaties between tribes or states. They had little to do with religion.

To the contrary, in the ancient world, religion was about politics and economics, power and wealth. The gods were the supreme powers. They were also the controllers of wealth, in the form of rain, the Earth's fertility and its harvests. So, if you wanted power or wealth, you had to placate the gods.

The idea that there could be a covenant between God and humanity must have seemed absurd. If you had told people there could be, between the Infinite and the finite, between the eternal and the ephemeral, a bond of love and trust, I think they would have said: 'Go and lie down until the mood passes.'

If you had added that God loves, not the wealthy and the powerful, but the poor and the powerless, they would have thought you were mad. But that was the idea that transformed the world.

Covenant is a key word of Tanach, the Hebrew Bible, where it occurs more than 250 times. No one put it more simply than the prophet Hosea, in words we say every weekday morning at the start of our prayers:

> I will betroth you to me for ever;
> I will betroth you to me in righteousness and justice, love and compassion.
> I will betroth you in faithfulness,
> and you will know the Lord.
> (Hosea 2:21–22)

A covenant is a betrothal, a bond of love and trust. And it was the prophet Jeremiah who in the name of God so beautifully spelled out the result:

> I remember the devotion of your youth,
> the love of your betrothal,
> how you were willing to follow me into the desert,
> through an unknown, unsown land.
> (Jeremiah 2:2)

Covenant is what allows us to face the future without fear, because we know we are not alone. 'Though I walk through the valley of the shadow of death, I will fear no evil for You are with me' (Psalm 23:4). Covenant is the redemption of solitude.

There are three covenants set out in the Bible's opening books of Genesis and Exodus. The first, in Genesis 9, is the covenant with Noah and through him with all humanity. The second, in Genesis 17, is the covenant with Abraham. The third, in Exodus 19 – 24, is the covenant with the Israelites in the days of Moses. None supersedes or replaces the others. And without going into details, I want to look at one significant distinction between two types of covenant.

For this insight we are indebted to the individual I regard as the greatest Jewish thinker of the twentieth century, a man whose name may not be familiar to you, Rabbi Joseph Soloveitchik. Perhaps the simplest way of approaching the idea is to ask: when did the Israelites become a nation? The Mosaic books give us two apparently contradictory answers. The first is: in Egypt. We read in Deuteronomy 26: 'our ancestors went down to Egypt and there they became a nation' (Deuteronomy 26:5). The second answer is, only when the Israelites *left* Egypt and stood at the foot of Mount Sinai, where they became, in the words of Exodus 19, 'a kingdom of priests and a holy nation' (Exodus 19:6). Now these two answers can't both be true – or can they?

Rabbi Soloveitchik's answer is that both are true, but they involve two different kinds of covenant. There is, he said, a covenant of *fate* and a covenant of *faith*, and they are very different things.

A group can be bound in the covenant of fate when they suffer together, when they face a common enemy. They have shared tears, shared fears, shared responsibility. They huddle together for comfort and mutual protection. That is a covenant of fate.

A covenant of faith is quite different. That is made by a people who share dreams, aspirations and ideals. They don't need a common enemy, because they have a common hope. They come together to create something new. They are defined not by what happens to them but by what they commit themselves to do. That is a covenant of faith.

Now we understand how it was that the Israelites had two foundational moments, the first in Egypt and the second at Sinai. In Egypt they became a nation bound by a covenant of fate – a fate of slavery and suffering. At Sinai they became a nation bound by a covenant of faith, defined by the Torah and by God's commands. That distinction is vital to what I have to say today.

Why is it that no one made this distinction before Rabbi Soloveitchik, in other words, before the second half of the twentieth century? The answer lies in one word: Holocaust.

At the level of faith, Jews in the nineteenth and twentieth centuries were deeply divided. But during the Holocaust they shared the same fate, whether they were Orthodox or non-Orthodox, religious or secular, identifying or totally assimilated. What Rabbi Soloveitchik was doing, within a deeply fragmented Jewish world, was to rescue a sense of solidarity with the victims. Hence his concept, always implicit within the tradition but never spelled out so explicitly before, of a covenant of fate even in the absence of a covenant of faith.

Now that we have made this distinction, we can state a proposition of the utmost importance. When we read Genesis and Exodus superficially, it seems as if the covenants of Noah, Abraham and Sinai are the same sort of thing. But now we can see that they are not the same kind of thing at all.

The covenants of Abraham and Sinai are covenants of faith. But the covenant of Noah says nothing about faith. The world had been almost destroyed by a flood. All mankind, all life, with the exception of Noah's Ark, had shared the same fate. Humanity after the

Flood was like the Jewish people after the Holocaust. The covenant of Noah is not a covenant of faith but a covenant of fate.

God says: 'Never again will I destroy the world. But I cannot promise that *you* will never destroy the world – because I have given you free will. All I can do is teach you how not to destroy the world.' How?

The covenant of Noah has three dimensions. First: 'He who sheds the blood of man, by man shall his blood be shed, for in the image of God, He created man' (Genesis 9:6). The first element is *the sanctity of human life*.

The second: read Genesis 9 carefully and you will see that *five times* God insists that the covenant of Noah is not merely with humanity, but with all life on Earth. So, the second element is *the integrity of the created world*.

The third lies in the symbol of the covenant, the rainbow, in which the white light of God is refracted into all the colours of the spectrum. The rainbow symbolises what I have called *the dignity of difference*. The miracle at the heart of monotheism is that unity up there creates diversity down here. These three dimensions define the covenant of fate.

There is a famous prophecy in Isaiah 11, that one day the wolf will lie down with the lamb. It hasn't happened yet (though there is the apocryphal story of a zoo in which, in a single cage, a lion did lie down with a lamb. 'How do you do that?' a visitor asked. The zookeeper replied: 'Simple – you just need a new lamb every day').

There was, however, one time when the wolf *did* lie down with the lamb. When? In Noah's Ark. Why? Not because they were friends, but because otherwise they would have drowned. That is the covenant of fate.

Note that the covenant of fate *precedes* the covenant of faith, because faith is particular, but fate is universal. That, then, is Genesis 9: the global covenant of human solidarity.

And with that, I come to the present. We are living through one of the most fateful ages of change since *Homo sapiens* first set foot on Earth. Globalisation and the new information technologies are doing two things simultaneously. First, they are fragmenting our world. Narrowcasting is taking the place of broadcasting. National cultures are growing weaker. We are splitting into ever smaller sects of the like-minded.

But globalisation is also thrusting us together as never before. The destruction of a rainforest adds to global warming everywhere. Political conflict in one place can create a terrorist incident in another, thousands of miles away. Poverty there moves consciences here. At the very moment that covenants of faith are splitting apart, the covenant of fate is forcing us together – *and we have not yet proved equal to it.*

All three elements of the global covenant are in danger. The sanctity of human life is being desecrated by terror. The integrity of creation is threatened by environmental catastrophe. Respect for diversity is imperilled by what one writer has called the clash of civilisations. And to repeat – the covenant of fate precedes the covenant of faith. Before we can live *any* faith, we have to live. And we must honour our covenant with future generations that they will inherit a world in which it is possible to live. That is the call of God in our time.

Friends, I stand before you as a Jew, which means not just as an individual, but as a representative of my people. And as I prepared this lecture, within my soul were the tears of my ancestors. We may have forgotten this, but for a thousand years, between the First Crusade and the Holocaust, the word 'Christian' struck fear into Jewish hearts. Think only of the words the Jewish encounter with Christianity added to the vocabulary of human pain: Blood Libel, book burnings, disputations, forced conversions, inquisition, auto-da-fé, expulsion, ghetto and pogrom. I could not stand here today in total openness, and not mention that book of Jewish tears.

And I have asked myself, what would our ancestors want of us today?

And the answer to that lies in the scene that brings the Book of Genesis to a climax and a closure. You remember: after the death of Jacob, the brothers fear that Joseph will take revenge. After all, they had sold him into slavery in Egypt.

Instead, Joseph forgives – but he does more than forgive. Listen carefully to his words:

> You intended to harm me,
> but God intended it for good,
> to do what is now being done,
> to save many lives.
> (Genesis 50:20)

Joseph does more than forgive. He says, out of bad has come good. Because of what you did to me, I have been able to save many lives. Which lives? Not just those of his brothers, but the lives of the Egyptians, the lives of strangers. I have been able to feed the hungry. I have been able to honour the covenant of fate – and by honouring the covenant of fate between him and strangers, Joseph is able to mend the broken covenant of faith between him and his brothers.

In effect, Joseph says to his brothers: we cannot *unwrite* the past, but we can *redeem* that past – if we take our tears and use them to sensitise us to the tears of others.

And now we see a remarkable thing. Although Genesis is about the covenant of faith between God and Abraham, it begins and ends with the covenant of fate: first in the days of Noah, and later in the time of Joseph.

Both involve water: in the case of Noah, there is too much, a flood; in the case of Joseph, too little, a drought.

Both involve saving human life. But Noah saves only his family. Joseph saves an entire nation of strangers.

Both involve forgiveness. In the case of Noah, God forgives. In the case of Joseph, it is a human being who forgives.

And both involve a relationship with the past. In the case of Noah, the past is obliterated. In the case of Joseph, the past is redeemed.

And today, between Jews and Christians, that past is being redeemed. In 1942, in the midst of humanity's darkest night, a great Archbishop of Canterbury, William Temple, and a great Chief Rabbi, Joseph Hertz, came together in a momentous covenant of fate, called the Council of Christians and Jews. And since then, Jews and Christians have done more to mend their relationship than any other two religions on Earth, so that today we meet as beloved friends.

And now we must extend that friendship more widely. We must renew the global covenant of fate, the covenant that began with Noah and reached a climax in the work of Joseph, the work of saving many lives.

And that is what we began to do last Thursday when we walked side-by-side: Christians, Jews, Sikhs, Muslims, Hindus, Buddhists, Jains, Zoroastrians and Baha'i. Because though we do not share a faith, we surely share a fate. Whatever our faith or lack of faith, hunger still hurts, disease still strikes, poverty still disfigures, and hate still kills. Few put it better than that great Christian poet, John Donne: 'Every man's death diminishes me, for I am involved in mankind.'

Friends, if we look at Genesis 50, we will see that just before Joseph says his great words of reconciliation, the text says: 'Joseph wept.' Why did Joseph weep? He wept for all the needless pain the brothers had caused one another. And shall we not weep when we see the immense challenges with which humanity is faced in the twenty-first century – poverty, hunger, disease, environmental catastrophe. And what is the face religion all too often shows to the world? Conflict – between faiths, and sometimes within faiths.

And we, Jews and Christians, who have worked so hard and so effectively at reconciliation, must show the world another way: honouring humanity as God's image, protecting the environment as God's work, respecting diversity as God's will, and keeping the covenant as God's word.

Too long we have dwelt in the valley of tears. Let us walk together towards the mountain of the Lord, side-by-side, hand in hand, bound by a covenant of fate that turns strangers into friends. In an age of fear, let us be agents of hope. Together let us be a blessing to the world.

A Gathering of Many Faiths

On 17 September 2010, Pope Benedict XVI joined the leaders of other religions in the Waldegrave Drawing Room at St Mary's University in Twickenham where Rabbi Sacks addressed the gathering on behalf of the faith communities of Britain.

Your Holiness, we welcome you, leader of a great faith, to this gathering of many faiths, in a land where once battles were fought in the name of faith, and where now we share friendship across faith. That is a climate change worth celebrating. And we recognise the immense role the Vatican has played and continues to play in bringing it about. It was *Nostra Aetate* forty-five years ago that brought about the single greatest transformation in interfaith relations in recent history. And we recognise your visit here today as a new chapter in that story and a vital one. The secularisation of Europe that began in the seventeenth century did not happen because people lost faith in God. Newton and Descartes, the heroes of the Enlightenment, believed in God very much indeed. What led to secularisation was that people lost faith in the ability of people of faith to live peaceably together. And we must never go down that road again.

We remember the fine words of John Henry Cardinal Newman, 'We should ever conduct ourselves towards our enemy as if he will one day to be our friend,' as well as Your Holiness's own words in *Caritas in veritate*, that the development of peoples depends on a recognition that the human race is a single family working together in true communion, not simply a group of subjects who happen to live side by side. We celebrate both our commonalities and our differences, because if we had nothing in common, we couldn't communicate. And if we had everything in common, we'd have nothing to say.

You, Your Holiness, have spoken of the Catholic Church as 'a creative minority', and perhaps that's what we should all aspire to be: creative minorities inspiring one another and bringing our different gifts to the common good. Britain has been so enriched by its minorities, by every single group represented here today and the intricate harmonies of our several voices.

And one of our commonalities is that we surely believe that faith has a major role in strengthening civil society. In the face of a deeply individualistic culture, we offer community. Against consumerism, we talk about things that have value, but not a price. Against cynicism, we dare to admire and respect. In the face of fragmenting families, we believe in consecrating relationships. We believe in marriage as a commitment, parenthood as a responsibility and the poetry of everyday life when it is etched in homes and schools with the charisma of holiness and grace.

In our communities, we value people not for what they earn or what they buy or even how they vote, but for what they are. Every one of them, a fragment of the Divine presence. We hold life holy. And each of us is lifted by the knowledge that we are part of something greater than all of us that created us in forgiveness and love, and that asks us to create in forgiveness and love. Each of us in our own way is a guardian of values that are in danger of being lost in our short attention span, hyper-active, information-saturated, wisdom-starved age. And our faiths are profoundly different, yet we recognise in one another the presence of faith itself, that habit of the heart that listens to the music beneath the noise, that knows that God is the point at which soul touches soul and is enlarged by the presence of Otherness.

Your Holiness, you have honoured us with your presence, and we honour you. May you continue to lead with wisdom and generosity of spirit and may all our efforts combine to become a blessing to humanity and to God.

A New Chief Rabbi

Rabbi Sacks delivered remarks in the presence of HRH The Prince of Wales at the induction of Rabbi Ephraim Mirvis as the seventh Chief Rabbi of the United Hebrew Congregations of the Commonwealth on 1 September 2013 in St John's Wood Synagogue in London.

Your Royal Highness, Deputy Prime Minister, Leader of the Opposition, Your Graces, Your Excellencies, Dayanim, Rabbanim, President of the United Synagogue, President of the Board of Deputies, distinguished guests.

First on behalf of all of us, I want to thank Your Royal Highness for the honour of your presence here with us today. Never before has the induction of the Chief Rabbi been graced with so royal a presence, and it testifies to the generosity of spirit and the greatness of heart you have shown to all the faiths, while remaining steadfast and exemplary in your own. May God bless you and may you, through all you do, continue to bless us.

Chief Rabbi Mirvis. How fitting that phrase sounds.

This is not the first time I have inducted you as my successor. I did so as the Rabbi of the Western Marble Arch synagogue.

Nor is this the first time you have been inducted as Chief Rabbi. I was blessed to have both a predecessor and a successor who had both previously been Chief Rabbis of Ireland. But it is the first time that I do so with such emotion.

We are just a few yards from Abbey Road where The Beatles recorded almost all of their hits. And to paraphrase the words of one of their best songs: 'You say hello, and I say goodbye.'

I cannot tell you how delighted I am for you and Chief Rebbetzen Valerie. This is one of the great positions of rabbinic leadership in the Jewish world, one of the most respected, one of the most influential, as well as one of the most challenging.

For almost every day of twenty-two years Elaine and I have felt it an overwhelming privilege to be able to serve so great a community of communities, of wonderful people who give so much to Jewish life and to the life of this great country. And now we hand this office to you, knowing that you will serve it with distinction, wisdom and grace, as you have done throughout your rabbinic career until now. You are the right man in the right job at the right time. May God be always with you in the years ahead.

Since Rosh Hashanah begins in just four days' time, earlier than it has since 1899, then let me take my blessings to you in terms of the three great festivals of [the Jewish month of] Tishri, each of which represents a different aspect of Jewish leadership.

First, Rosh Hashanah, whose unique *mitzvah* is the blowing of the shofar [the ram's horn]. And it was Isaiah to whom God said: *kashofar Harem kolecha*. 'Lift up your voice like a shofar' (Isaiah 58:1).

A leader is like a shofar. It is the sound of the shofar that defines the mood of the community. Sometimes it is a *tekiah*, a clarion call summoning people to a collective task. Sometimes it is a *shevarim* or a *teruah*, a sound of tears as we weep, whether for ourselves or others.

A shofar is always simple and plain. No great art went into its manufacture. No one, to my knowledge, has yet written a shofar concerto. A shofar moves us simply because it is our cry to God. At Mount Sinai where the people heard *kol shofar chazak meod*, it was God's cry to us.

Rabbi Mirvis, let your voice be clear and simple, calling us to the greatest vocation with which a people was ever charged, to be God's witnesses in an often wayward world. And never forget those extraordinary words from the *Unetaneh tokef* prayer we will say in just a few days' time: *uveshofar gadol yitaka* ('the great shofar sounds'), *vekol demama daka yishama* ('and a still small voice heard'), *umalachim yechafezun* ('and that is where the angels tremble'). The prophet Elijah discovered that God was not in the whirlwind, the earthquake or the fire, but in the still, small voice of calm, that is gentle but clear. Let it guide us through the wilderness of these turbulent times. And may it move us all, as the shofar does move us all, to be a little better, humbler, and more spiritual than we were before.

Second, Yom Kippur. On Yom Kippur the High Priest placed his hands on the *seir hamishtaleach*, the scapegoat, and over it confessed the sins of the people. We used to have in our office a cartoon of the man who served as Chief Rabbi in early Victorian England, Solomon Hirschell. In those days people in Britain were not quite sure of what a Chief Rabbi was, so the caption underneath reads, 'Rabbi Solomon Hirschell, High Priest of the Jews'. There was a time when I used to say that since then, only one thing has changed. Now instead of being High Priest a Chief Rabbi is the scapegoat.

But there is one line in the Torah's description of the holiest task of the holiest man on the holiest day of the year that speaks to my experience, and I am sure it will be of yours, of being a Chief Rabbi: *kol adam lo yehiyeh b'ohel meod be'vo'oh l'chaper bakodesh* ('No one was with him in the tent of meeting when he went to secure atonement in the most holy place') (Leviticus 16:17).

Beneath all the public work of this most public of religious offices is the private communion you have with God, when you pray, when you learn, when you open yourself to heaven in the very depths of your soul. Those lonely moments are moments where you are honest, open and vulnerable. And that is where, in the privacy of your soul, you will hear the *Shekhinah*, the Divine presence, whispering to you, through the texts of our tradition and the wisdom of our Sages.

You will hear, Rabbi Mirvis, the call beneath the noise, summoning you, and through you, us, to our sacred task as *mamlechet cohanim vegoi kadosh*, a kingdom of priests and a holy nation. It is that private relationship with God – not newspaper headlines, not popularity not public acclaim – that defines what your leadership will be. May Hashem's presence never part from you, and through that private encounter may you lift all of us to the heights.

And lastly Sukkot, what in English we call Tabernacles, when we leave the comfort of our homes and for a week know what it feels like to live in a *dirat aray*, a temporary dwelling. I have a strong suspicion that when God gave us that command, He did not have England specifically in mind because that is when you open yourself to the wind, the rain and the cold with only leaves as our shelter. And I call Sukkot the festival of insecurity, the festival when we leave behind the security of home. And it is one of the most majestic, counter-intuitive gestures of Jewish tradition that we call Sukkot, the festival of insecurity, *zman simchatenu*, our festival of joy.

I have always believed, and acted on that belief, that Judaism is not just for Jews but for the world. So said Moses, so said Isaiah, and so said God to Jonah and Jeremiah. Our task is to be true to our faith and a blessing to others regardless of their faith, and the stronger we are in our Judaism the greater will be the blessings we bring to the world.

And if we were to ask, what is the greatest message we can bring to the world in this time of unprecedented change and of great danger, not just to Israel, not just to Jews, but to all of us, it would be the message of Sukkot, the one festival that according to the prophet Zechariah will one day be celebrated by all of humanity.

And what Sukkot is saying to us is this: you can live in the midst of great insecurity, exposed to all the winds of change, but if you sit *betzelah de-mehemnuta*, under the shadow of faith, you need feel no fear, for God is with us; and in the midst of that vulnerability, global and personal, you can still experience *zman simchatenu*, a time of joy.

Ours is an age of religious extremism, and religious extremism is always driven by fear: fear of change, fear of loss, fear of a world beyond our control. And it is our task as Jews to say:

'Faith is not fear. Faith is the antidote to fear.' *Lo ira ra ki ata imadi.* 'I will fear no evil for You are with me' (Psalm 23:4). Be a voice, Rabbi Mirvis, of tolerance, and gentleness and generosity of spirit.

The ancient world, the pagan world, believed that the gods were to be found in power and the elemental forces of nature. It was Abraham and his descendants who taught the world that God is to be found not in power but in love and forgiveness, two virtues all too rare today. Teach us all, to love and forgive, and you will be one of the great religious leaders of our time.

Rabbi Mirvis, you are now – or in thirty seconds – going to be Chief Rabbi Ephraim Mirvis; so your initials now read C.R.E.M, CREM. And I can safely say that for us you are the crème de la crème. May God bless you and Rebbetzen Valerie and your lovely family. May He give you wisdom and strength and confidence and courage. May you lead us all to hear God's call and inspire us all to do His will.

On Creative Minorities

Rabbi Sacks delivered the twenty-sixth Erasmus Lecture, hosted by First Things, America's most influential journal of religion and public life, in New York on 21 October 2013.

Almost exactly twenty-six centuries ago, a man not otherwise known for his positive psychology sat down to write a letter to his coreligionists in a foreign land. The man was Jeremiah. The people to whom he wrote were the Jews who had been taken captive to Babylon after their defeat at its hands, a defeat that included the destruction of Solomon's Temple, the central symbol of their nation and the sign that God was in their midst.

We know exactly what the feeling of those exiles was. A psalm has recorded it in the most powerful way: 'By the rivers of Babylon we sat and wept when we remembered Zion . . . How can we sing the songs of the Lord in a foreign land?' (Psalm 137:1, 4)

This was, of course, what Jeremiah had predicted. But there is no air of triumphalism in his letter, no 'I told you so.' What he wrote was massively counter-intuitive. Yet it would be no exaggeration to say that it changed the course of Jewish history, perhaps even, in an indirect way, that of Western civilisation as a whole. This is what he wrote:

> Build houses and settle down; plant gardens and eat what they produce. Marry and have sons and daughters; find wives for your sons and give your daughters in marriage, so that they too may have sons and daughters. Increase in number there; do not decrease. Also, seek the peace and prosperity of the city to which

> I have carried you into exile. Pray to the Lord for it, because if it prospers, you too will prosper.
> (Jeremiah 29:5–7)

What Jeremiah was saying was that it is possible to survive in exile with your identity intact, your appetite for life undiminished, while contributing to the wider society and praying to God on its behalf. Jeremiah was introducing into history a highly consequential idea: the idea of a creative minority.

At this distance of time, it can be hard for us to realise how revolutionary this was. Religions until then were inextricably linked to geographically, politically, culturally and linguistically defined spaces. That is what the exiles meant when they said, 'How can we sing the Lord's song in a foreign land?' If your nation was defeated, it meant your god had been defeated, and you accepted that defeat, graciously or otherwise. If you went into exile, as the Northern Kingdom had done a century and a half earlier, then you assimilated into the majority culture and became one – or, in that case, ten – of history's lost tribes.

Only a unique configuration of ideas made Jeremiah's vision possible. The first idea was monotheism. If God was everywhere, then he could be accessed anywhere, even by the waters of Babylon.

The second was belief in the sovereignty of the God of history over all other powers. Until then, if a people were conquered, it meant the defeat of a nation and its god. For the first time, in Jeremiah's telling of the Babylonian conquest of Israel, the defeat of a nation is understood as being accomplished by its God. God was still supreme. Babylon was merely the instrument of His wrath. A people could suffer defeat and keep its faith intact.

The third was the belief that God kept His faith intact. He would not break His word, His covenant with Israel, however many times Israel broke its covenant with God. He could be relied on to honour His promise, just as He had when the Israelites were slaves in Egypt. In the future, as in the past, He would bring his people back to their land.

So Jeremiah, like all the prophets, was ultimately a voice of hope. The prophetic message is always: if the people return to God, then God will return to the people, and the people will return to their land. Only hope can sustain a minority in exile, and only a transcendent God, above all principalities and powers, can guarantee that hope, even if it takes centuries or millennia to be fulfilled.

Jeremiah's letter became the basis of Jewish hope for survival in the Diaspora for twenty-six centuries until today – a fraught, risk-laden, and tenuous survival, to be sure, but a remarkable one nonetheless.

Jews were creative in three distinct ways. The first was internal. It was in Babylon, for example, that the Torah was renewed as the heart of Jewish life. We see this clearly in the pioneering work of national education undertaken by Ezra and Nehemiah when they returned to Israel. And it was in Babylon again, a thousand years later, that the masterwork of rabbinical Judaism, the Babylonian Talmud, was compiled. The encounter with Christianity in the Middle Ages led to the flowering of Jewish Bible commentary. The meeting with medieval Islam begat Jewish philosophy. Every exile led to some new form of religious expression.

Second, Jews were cultural mediators between their host society and other civilisations. Through trade, for example, they brought to the West many of the inventions of China during the Middle Ages. Maimonides occupied an important role in bringing the Islamic rediscovery of Plato and Aristotle to the Christian world, becoming the bridge between Averroes and Aquinas.

Third, when in the modern age Jews were admitted for the first time to the cultural mainstream of the West, they gave rise to a remarkable number of architects of the modern mind. Among those of Jewish descent, if not of religious affiliation, were Spinoza, Marx, Freud, Einstein, Wittgenstein, Durkheim, Lévi-Strauss, and many others.

So, you can be a minority, living in a country whose religion, culture, and legal system are not your own, and yet sustain your identity, live your faith, and contribute to the common good, exactly as Jeremiah said. It isn't easy. It demands a complex finessing of identities. It involves a willingness to live in a state of cognitive dissonance. It isn't for the faint-hearted. But it is creative.

Fast forward twenty-six centuries from Jeremiah to 13 May 2004, to a lecture on the Christian roots of Europe by Cardinal Joseph Ratzinger, later to become Pope Benedict XVI. There he confronted the phenomenon of a deeply secularised Europe, more so perhaps than at any time since the conversion of Constantine in the third century.

That loss of faith, Ratzinger argued, had brought with it three other kinds of loss: a loss of European identity, a loss of moral foundations and a loss of faith in posterity, evident in the falling birth rates that he described as 'a strange lack of desire for the future'. The closest analogue to today's Europe, he said, was the Roman Empire on the brink of its decline and fall. Though he did not use these words, he implied that when a civilisation loses faith in God, it ultimately loses faith in itself.

Is this inevitable? Or reversible? Can a civilisation that has begun to decline recover and revive? The Cardinal suggested that this was the issue at stake between two historians, Oswald Spengler and Arnold Toynbee. For Spengler, civilisations are like organisms. They are born, they grow, they reach maturity, and then they age and decline and die. There are no exceptions.

For Toynbee, there is a difference between the material and spiritual dimensions of a civilisation. Precisely because they have a spiritual dimension, they are open to the human ability to recover. That gift, said Toynbee, belonged to what he called creative minorities, history's great problem-solvers. Therefore, concluded Ratzinger, 'Christian believers should look upon themselves as just such a creative minority, and help Europe to reclaim what is best in its heritage and to therefore place itself at the service of all humankind.'

This too was an unexpected response. For the Catholic Church, numbering 1.2 billion adherents, to define itself as a minority, especially in Europe, is a surprising proposition. Nor is this the only way a group can respond to the discovery that it has become a minority. There are three other ways. First, it can accommodate to secularisation: the way of religious liberalism. Second, it can resist it, sometimes violently, as religiously extremist groups are doing in many parts of the world today. Third, it can withdraw into protected enclaves, much as we see happening in certain groups within Ultra-Orthodox Judaism. This is a powerful strategy, and it has strengthened Jewish Orthodoxy immensely, but at the price of segregation from – and thus loss of influence on – the world outside.

The fourth possibility, to become a creative minority, is not easy, because it involves maintaining strong links with the outside world while staying true to your faith, seeking not merely to keep the sacred flame burning but also to transform the larger society of which you are a part. This is, as Jews can testify, a demanding and risk-laden choice.

Yet the future Pope was speaking at a challenging moment in the history of the West. There had been a time, only fifteen years before the lecture, when the West seemed to be triumphant. The Soviet Union had collapsed, the Berlin Wall had fallen, the Cold War was at an end, and it seemed as if liberal democracy and the market economy – two of the West's greatest achievements – were about to sweep the world.

Since then, however, we have seen two great civilisations, India and China, revive and begin to challenge the economic supremacy of the West. A third, Islam, is undergoing great turbulence. Meanwhile the financial collapse of 2008 revealed a whole series of economies, among them the United States and much of Europe, living beyond their means, borrowing more, manufacturing less, and sinking deep into personal and collective debt. From the inside, the West may look still strong, which technically and scientifically it is, but from the outside it has seemed to many to be already past its peak. So the Cardinal's comparison with the Roman Empire on the brink of its decline deserved to be taken seriously.

Civilisations do not last for ever. Not only did Spengler and Toynbee say so. So, in the fourteenth century, did the great Islamic sage Ibn Khaldun, and in the eighteenth Giambattista Vico. So indeed, has every student of long-term history. Perhaps the judgment that most resonates with where we are today is contained in the first volume of Will Durant's epic history series, *The Story of Civilization*. A 'certain tension between religion and society marks the higher stages of every civilisation,' Durant wrote. Religion begins 'fighting suicidally in the lost cause of the past' and 'priestly control of arts and letters is then felt as a galling shackle or hateful barrier, and intellectual history takes on the character of a "conflict between science and religion." '*

The intellectual classes abandon the ancient theology and – after some hesitation – the moral code allied with it; literature and philosophy become anticlerical. The movement of liberation rises to an exuberant worship of reason and falls to a paralysing disillusionment with every dogma and every idea. Conduct, deprived of its religious supports, deteriorates into epicurean chaos; and life itself, shorn of consoling faith, becomes a burden alike to conscious poverty and to weary wealth. In the end a society and its religion tend to fall together, like body and soul, in a harmonious death. Meanwhile among the oppressed another myth arises, gives new form to human hope, new courage to human effort, and after centuries of chaos builds another civilisation.

Can the decline of a civilisation be resisted? That was the issue raised, in their different ways, by Jeremiah in his day and Cardinal Ratzinger in ours. To understand what this might involve, it is worth revisiting the work of Toynbee's that brought the phrase 'creative minorities' into the conversation.

* Will Durant, *The Story of Civilization: Volume 1: Our Oriental Heritage* (New York: Fine Communications, 1997).

I had not read *A Study of History* until recently. I knew that it had upset many Jews because of its statement that Jews and Judaism were 'an extinct society which only survives as a fossil'.* They were even more upset by his later statement, in Volume 8, published in 1954, that Israel's treatment of the Arabs in 1948, when it was fighting for survival against the armies of five neighbouring states, was morally equivalent to the Nazi treatment of the Jews – a statement he did not retract but repeated in his 1961 debate with Israel's then-ambassador to Canada, the late Jacob Herzog.

What I did not fully appreciate was that the description of Judaism as a fossil is not a stray sentence in this twelve-volume work but close to the core of his argument. *A Study of History* is, as many have noted, less a study of history than applied theology of a distinctly supersessionist kind. For Toynbee, Western Christianity is not a development of Judaism but rather a continuation of Hellenistic society, emerging out of the disintegration first of Greece, then Rome. Judaism, for Toynbee, was not a fallen or defeated civilisation. It had never become a civilisation at all. Its very existence is an anomaly and an anachronism.

Reading these volumes, the first of which was published in 1934, I felt a great chill as I read a distinguished historian repeating a sentiment that had been responsible for so many persecutions over the centuries and was about to reach its tragic denouement in the Holocaust. When I realised that afterward he was prepared to consign even the State of Israel to the trash heap of history, I realised how deeply a certain attitude is embedded in the Western mind, and I want to challenge it, not because of the past but for the sake of the future, and not just because of Christian–Jewish relations but for the sake of those between the West and the world.

There is a failure of imagination at the heart of Toynbee's study of history, and it shapes not only his attitude toward Jews and Israel but much else besides.

* Arnold Toynbee, *A Study of History* (Oxford: Oxford University Press 1934-61, 12 volumes).

His argument in brief is this: civilisations are provoked by challenge. They never emerge automatically as a result of biology or geography. What happens is that a group or nation faces a problem – economic, military or climatic – that threatens its continued existence. An individual or small group then comes up with an innovative solution, the inspiration or discovery that opens the way to prosperity or victory. This is the birth of the creative minority.

The majority, recognising that the minority has opened the gate to success, proceeds to imitate it. The nation, now at an advantage relative to others, flourishes, eventually expanding to become an empire, or what Toynbee calls a 'universal state'. But this never lasts for ever.

Eventually the minority, having enjoyed success and power, ceases to be creative. It then becomes a dominant minority in power not because of what it is doing now but because of what it did in the past. At this point, social breakdown begins. Since the minority can no longer justify its position, it alienates the majority, or what Toynbee calls the proletariat. There is schism. The internal majority may then find solace in religion by creating a universal church. The external proletariat, outsiders who were once in awe of the established power, now lose their fear of it and engage in acts of violence and terror, giving rise, in Toynbee's phrase, to 'a bevy of barbarian war-bands'. Time, says Toynbee, 'works on the side of the barbarians'. When this happens, breakdown has become disintegration.

And so it goes. In Toynbee's judgment, 'of the twenty-one civilisations that have been born alive and have proceeded to grow, thirteen are dead and buried; . . . seven of the remaining eight are apparently in decline; and . . . the eighth, which is our own, may also have passed its zenith'.

There is, however, one possibility Toynbee does not consider. What if at least one creative minority had long ago seen what Toynbee and other historians would eventually realise? What if they had witnessed the decline and fall of the first great civilisations: Mesopotamia, Egypt, Assyria? What if they had seen how dominant minorities treat the masses, the proletariat, turning them into forced labour and conscripted armies so that rulers could be heroes in expansionist wars, immortalised in monumental buildings? What if they saw all of this as a profound insult to human dignity and a betrayal of the human condition?

What if they saw religion time and again enlisted to give heavenly sanction to purely human hierarchies? What if they knew that truth and power have nothing to do with one another and that you do not need to rule the world to bring truth into the world? What if they had realised that once you seek to create a universal state you have already begun down a road from which there is no escape, a process that ends in disintegration and decline? What if they were convinced that in the long run, the real battle is spiritual, not political or military, and that in this battle influence matters more than power?

What if they believed they had heard God calling on them to be a creative minority that never sought to become a dominant minority, that never sought to become a universal state, nor even in the conventional sense a universal church? What if they believed that God is universal but that love – all love, even God's love – is irreducibly particular? What if they were convinced that the God who created biodiversity cares for human diversity? What if they had seen the great empires conquer smaller nations, and impose their culture on them, and had been profoundly disturbed by this, as we today are disturbed when an animal species is driven to extinction by human exploitation and carelessness?

What if these insights led a figure like Jeremiah to reconceptualise the entire phenomenon of defeat and exile? The Israelites had betrayed their mission by becoming obsessed with politics at the cost of moral and spiritual integrity. So taught all the prophets from Moses to Malachi. Every time you try to be like your neighbours, they said, you will be defeated by your neighbours. Every time you worship power, you will be defeated by power. Every time you seek to dominate, you will be dominated.

For you, says God, are my witnesses to the world that there is nothing sacred about power or holy about empires and imperialism.

A nation will always need power to survive, but only as a means, not an end. In its land, Israel was, is, and will be a tiny nation surrounded by great empires that seek its destruction. Its very survival will always be testimony to something profound: the ability of a small people to outlast great powers by the sheer force of its commitment to justice, compassion, and human dignity. Whether as a nation in the Middle East or as a dispersed people in exile, it will always be a creative minority that declines the invitation to become a dominant minority. It will manifest by its very being the difficult, counter-intuitive truth that it is possible to worship the universal God without attempting to found a universal state or a universal church.

Such has been the mission of Jews throughout the ages. So, it is no accident that Toynbee cannot understand them except as an anomaly and an anachronism, because they stand outside his structure and fail to fit his categories. Indeed, they challenge those very categories. So, there is all the difference in the world between Jeremiah's concept of a creative minority and Toynbee's. Jeremiah calls on his minority to pray for the city and work for its prosperity. He does not ask them to convert the city by persuading its inhabitants to become Jewish any more than God asks Jonah to convert the people of Nineveh. He wants them to repent, not convert.

Within any great religious tradition, there is more than one voice. In Judaism there are the distinctive voices of the priest, the prophet and the sage, and they generate different kinds of literature. Within Christianity likewise, because of the circumstances of its early history, there is a Hellenistic voice and a Hebraic one. The Hellenistic voice speaks about universal truths. The Hebraic voice speaks about the particularity of love and forgiveness and about the differences that make each of us unique and that make human life itself holy.

The Hellenistic strand, of which Arnold Toynbee was an extreme example, leads in the direction of a universal church and a universal state. After all, Hellenism had already before the birth of Christianity given rise to two of the greatest empires the world has ever known. The Hebraic strand leads to the recognition that a small nation can play the role of a creative minority within the human arena, seeking influence, not power, hoping to inspire but not to conquer or convert.

Despite its claim to tolerance, Hellenism largely dismissed the non-Hellenistic world as barbarian and could not begin to understand why Jews might want to stay loyal to their seemingly parochial identity. The only explanation Hellenistic writers could give was that Jews were misanthropes who hated humankind. Under both the Seleucids and the Romans, there were attempts to suppress Judaism altogether, with tragic consequences. Any attempt to found a universal state or a universal church will always collide with Judaism's principled particularity, and that, more than any other factor, explains the persistence of antisemitism throughout the ages. Jews lived and sometimes died for the right to be different, and for the belief that unity in heaven creates diversity on Earth.

There are moments in history, and we are living through one now, when something new is taking shape but we do not know precisely what, when we are caught, in Matthew Arnold's words, 'Wandering between two worlds, one dead, / the other powerless to be born'. There have been many warning voices, from Alasdair MacIntyre to Niall Ferguson, suggesting that the West that dominated the world from the sixteenth to the twentieth centuries is in decline. Certainly, it no longer commands the respect it once did. It no longer even respects itself as it once did. In his lecture Cardinal Ratzinger referred sharply to what he called Europe's 'pathological self-hatred'.

What has come to be called the Judeo-Christian ethic is under sustained assault from two quite different directions: from those who would eliminate religion altogether, and from those who seek to create a universal theocratic state that is neither Christian nor Jewish.

Three phenomena cry out for attention. First is the religious equivalent of ethnic cleansing currently being carried out against Christians throughout much of the Middle East and parts of Africa. I think of the Christians who have fled Syria, and of the eight million Copts in Egypt who live in fear; of the destruction of the last church in Afghanistan and of the million Christians who have left Iraq since the 1990s. Until recently, Christians represented 20 per cent of the population of the Middle East; today, this figure is 4 per cent. This is one of the great crimes of our time, but it has gone almost unreported and unprotested.

Second is the return of antisemitism to many parts of the world today, a complex antisemitism that includes Holocaust denial, the demonisation of Jews, the return in modern guises of the Blood Libel and The Protocols of the Elders of Zion, the attempt in Europe to ban circumcision and *shechitah* [the religious slaughter of animals], in effect making the practice of Judaism impossible – not to mention the anti-Zionism that leads otherwise good and decent people to call into question Israel's right to exist, much as Toynbee did in his day. That this should have happened within living memory of the Holocaust is almost unbelievable.

The third concerns the West itself, which has already gone far down the road of abandoning the Judeo-Christian principles of the sanctity of life and the sacred covenant of marriage. Instead, it places its faith in a series of institutions, none of which can bear the weight of moral guidance: science, technology, the state, the market and evolutionary biology. Science tells us what is, not what ought to be. Technology gives us power but cannot tell us how to use that power. The liberal democratic state, as a matter of principle, does not make moral judgments. The market gives us choices but does not tell us which choices to make. Evolutionary biology tells us why we have certain desires, but not which desires we should seek to satisfy and which not. It does not explain the unique human ability to make second-order evaluations.

The results lie all around us: the collapse of marriage, the fracturing of the family, the fraying of the social bond, the partisanship of politics at a time when national interest demands something larger, the loss of trust in public institutions, the build-up of debt whose burden will fall on future generations and the failure of a shared morality to lift us out of the morass of individualism, hedonism, consumerism and relativism. We know these things, yet we seem collectively powerless to move beyond them. We have reached the stage described by Livy, in his description of ancient Rome, where we can bear neither our vices nor their cure.

So, the fateful question returns. Can civilisational decline be arrested? To which the great prophetic answer is 'yes'. For the prophets taught us that after every exile there is a return, after every destruction the ruins can be rebuilt, after every crisis there can be a rebirth, if – if we have faith in God's faith in us.

But the Judeo-Christian ethic will not return until the fracture at its heart is healed, the fracture that is the long estrangement between Christians and Jews and that has caused so many persecutions and cost so many lives. I have hinted at the way this healing can happen – namely, if together we recover the Hebraic rather than the Hellenistic voice, Jeremiah's rather than Toynbee's view of a creative minority. This means a willingness to be true to our tradition without seeking to impose it on others or judging others harshly because their way is not ours; a loyalty combined with humility that allows us to stay true to our faith while being a blessing to others regardless of their faith. That is what it meant to seek the peace of the city and what it now means to seek the peace of the world.

European history has had three supreme Hellenistic moments: first Athens, then Rome and then the Italian Renaissance, and we are living through the fourth. These were moments of supreme creativity, but each ended in decline and fall. Through it all, despite many tragedies, Jews and Judaism survived. Somehow, in a way I still find mysterious, the Hebraic presence found a way of defeating the law of entropy that causes civilisations to break down and eventually disintegrate.

I believe Jews and Christians can and should work together to promote the values that we share and that we believe truly are universal: the sanctity of life as the gift of God, the dignity of the human person as the image of God, the covenantal virtues of *tzedek, umishpat, chessed, ve-rachamim*; fairness, justice, love and compassion. Let us stand together in defence of the ecology of human freedom: the loving, stable family uniting parents and children in a bond of loyalty and care and supportive communities built on the principle of *chessed*, or *caritas*.

The time has come for a new meeting of Christians and Jews, based simply on the fact that a church that sees itself as a creative minority in the Jeremiah sense has made space for the existence of Jews and Judaism in a way that was not fully articulated before.

One reason I feel empowered to say this is the courage the Catholic Church has shown in the wake of the Holocaust to seek a new way in Jewish–Christian relations, begun by Pope John XXIII, continued through Vatican II and particularly in *Nostra Aetate*, sustained by the healing visit of Pope John Paul II to Jerusalem and given new impetus by Pope Benedict XVI's use of the phrase 'creative minority'.

The second reason is Pope Francis, whom I have not yet met but whose words I have followed closely. I was in Buenos Aires on the day he was elected Pope, and I was struck by the high regard in which he was held by the Jewish community in Argentina, a community that has felt very vulnerable since the terrorist attacks it suffered in the 1990s. I was equally struck by the warmth of his dialogue – published as a book, *On Heaven and Earth** – with a local rabbi [Rabbi Abraham Skorka].

What moved me especially were the words he used in his open letter of 11 September 2013, to Eugenio Scalfari, editor of the Italian newspaper *La Repubblica*. There he wrote: 'God never abandoned His covenant with Israel, and notwithstanding their

* Jorge Mario Bergoglio and Abraham Skorka, *On Heaven and Earth* (New York: Image, 2013).

terrible suffering over the centuries, the Jewish people have kept their faith. For this, we will never be sufficiently grateful to them as a Church, but also as human beings.' This is language we have rarely heard from a Pope before, and it embodies a truth we all too often forget: that if you are deeply loyal to your faith, you can respect the loyalty with which others stay loyal to theirs.

If we read the Book of Genesis carefully, we see that the great threat to humanity is sibling rivalry and what René Girard calls 'mimesis', the desire to have what your brother has rather than rest content with your own. There are four such scenes in Genesis: Cain and Abel, Isaac and Ishmael, Jacob and Esau, and Joseph and his brothers. A superficial reading suggests that sibling rivalry is inevitable, part of the human condition. Biologists tell us it exists in other species as well. But a deeper reading emerges if we focus simply on the last scene in each story in which we see the brothers together. In the case of Cain and Abel, Abel lies dead. In the case of Isaac and Ishmael, they are standing together at their father's grave. In the case of Jacob and Esau, they meet, embrace and go their separate ways. In the case of Joseph there is forgiveness and reconciliation, the first recorded instance of forgiveness in literature.

That last scene was memorably evoked by Pope John XXIII at the very beginning of this new chapter in Jewish–Catholic relations. Meeting a delegation of Jews in 1960, he said, in the words of the Bible itself, 'I am Joseph your brother' (Genesis 45:4). That, both in the biblical original and its recent re-enactment, was an extraordinary scene of reconciliation. But there is in the Bible a second scene, several years later, when Joseph goes further and says to his brothers 'You intended to harm me, but God intended it for good, to accomplish what is now being done, the saving of many lives' (Genesis 50:20). What Joseph means is that by our acts in the present we can redeem the past. We can rescue fragments of light from deep darkness when we take our pain and use it to sensitise us to the pain of others – when we 'save many lives'.

That second reconciliation between Joseph and his brothers was the essential prelude to the drama of redemption that took place in the Book of Exodus and for ever changed the history of the world. Might it not be that Jews and Catholics are being called to their own second reconciliation as they stand side by side, two creative minorities, seeking to save many lives, including those who, like the Egyptians in Joseph's day and the Babylonians in Jeremiah's, are not of our faith but are nonetheless made in the image of our God? Such a reconciliation might give new form to human hope, new courage to human effort, bringing us a little closer to Isaiah's vision of a world in which 'they will neither harm nor destroy on all my holy mountain, for the Earth will be filled with the knowledge of the Lord as the waters cover the sea' (Isaiah 11:9).

True creative minorities fight the battles of tomorrow, not those of yesterday. The Judeo-Christian ethic will, in my view, be reborn the moment there is a feeling that something new and momentous has occurred to heal the oldest injured relationship in the history of the West. When that day comes, Jews and Christians will stand together in their fight against the persecution of Christians in the Middle East; in defence of the legitimacy of the State of Israel as the place where the Jewish nation was born in ancient times, and reborn in ours; and as joint witnesses to the power of an ethic of love, forgiveness and the sanctity of human life, to offer a more compelling ground of human hope than the new barbarisms, secular and religious. Nothing less than the future of the West is at stake.

The Love That Brings New Life into the World

Rabbi Sacks delivered an address at an International Colloquium on 'The Complementarity of Man and Woman' hosted by Humanum at The Vatican under the auspices of Pope Francis on 17 November 2014.

I want this morning to begin our conversation by telling the story of the most beautiful idea in the history of civilisation: the idea of the love that brings new life into the world. There are of course many ways of telling the story, and this is just one. But to me it is a story of seven key moments, each of them surprising and unexpected.

The first, according to a report in the press on 20 October of this year, took place in a lake in Scotland 385 million years ago. It was then, according to this new discovery, that two fish came together to perform the first instance of sexual reproduction known to science. Until then all life had propagated itself asexually, by cell division, budding, fragmentation or parthenogenesis, all of which are far simpler and more economical than the division of life into male and female, each with a different role in creating and sustaining life.

When we consider, even in the animal kingdom, how much effort and energy the coming together of male and female takes in terms of displays, courtship rituals, rivalries and violence, it is astonishing that sexual reproduction ever happened at all. Biologists are still not quite sure why it did. Some say to offer protection against parasites, or immunities against disease. Others say it's simply that the meeting of opposites generates diversity. But one way or another, the fish in Scotland discovered something new and beautiful that's been copied ever since by virtually all advanced forms of life. Life begins when male and female meet and embrace.

The second unexpected development was the unique challenge posed to *Homo sapiens* by two factors: we stood upright, which constricted the female pelvis, and we had bigger brains – a 300 per cent increase – which meant larger heads. The result was that human babies had to be born more prematurely than any other species, and so needed parental protection for much longer. This made parenting more demanding among humans than any other species, the work of two people rather than one.

Hence the very rare phenomenon among mammals of pair bonding, unlike other species where the male contribution tends to end with the act of impregnation. Among most primates, fathers don't even recognise their children, let alone care for them. Elsewhere in the animal kingdom motherhood is almost universal but fatherhood is rare. So, what emerged along with the human person was the union of the biological mother and father to care for their child. Thus far nature, but then came culture, and the third surprise.

It seems that among hunter-gatherers, pair bonding was the norm. Then came agriculture, economic surplus, and cities and civilisation, and for the first time sharp inequalities began to emerge between rich and poor, powerful and powerless. The great ziggurats of Mesopotamia and pyramids of ancient Egypt, with their broad base and narrow top, were monumental statements in stone of a hierarchical society in which the few had power over the many. And the most obvious expression of power among alpha males, whether human or primate, is to dominate access to fertile women and thus maximise the handing on of your genes to the next generation. Hence polygamy, which exists in 95 per cent of mammal species and 75 per cent of cultures known to anthropology. Polygamy is the ultimate expression of inequality because it means that many males never get the chance to have a wife and child. And sexual envy has been, throughout history, among animals as well as humans, a prime driver of violence.

That is what makes the first chapter of Genesis so revolutionary with its statement that every human being, regardless of class, colour, culture or creed, is in the image and likeness of God Himself. We know that in the ancient world it was rulers, kings, emperors and pharaohs who were held to be in the image of God. So what Genesis was saying was that we are all royalty. We each have equal dignity in the kingdom of faith under the sovereignty of God.

From this it follows that we each have an equal right to form a marriage and have children, which is why, regardless of how we read the story of Adam and Eve – and there are differences between Jewish and Christian readings – the norm presupposed by that story is: one woman, one man. Or as the Bible itself says: 'That is why a man leaves his father and mother and is united to his wife, and they become one flesh' (Genesis 2:24).

Monogamy did not immediately become the norm, even within the world of the Bible. But many of its most famous stories, about the tension between Sarah and Hagar, or Leah and Rachel and their children, or David and Bathsheba, or Solomon's many wives, are all critiques that point the way to monogamy.

And there is a deep connection between monotheism and monogamy, just as there is, in the opposite direction, between idolatry and adultery. Monotheism and monogamy are about the all-embracing relationship between I and Thou, myself and one other, be it a human, or the divine Other.

What makes the emergence of monogamy unusual is that it is normally the case that the values of a society are those imposed on it by the ruling class. And the ruling class in any hierarchical society stands to gain from promiscuity and polygamy, both of which multiply the chances of my genes being handed on to the next generation. From monogamy, the rich and powerful lose and the poor and powerless gain. So the return of monogamy goes against the normal grain of social change and was a real triumph for the equal dignity of all. Every bride and every groom are royalty; every home a palace when furnished with love.

The fourth remarkable development was the way this transformed the moral life. We've all become familiar with the work of evolutionary biologists using computer simulations and the iterated prisoners' dilemma to explain why reciprocal altruism exists among all social animals. We behave to others as we would wish them to behave to us, and we respond to them as they respond to us. As C. S. Lewis pointed out in his book *The Abolition of Man*,* reciprocity is the Golden Rule shared by all the great civilisations.

What was new and remarkable in the Hebrew Bible was the idea that *love*, not just fairness, is the driving principle of the moral life. Three loves. 'Love the Lord your God with all your heart, all your soul and all your might' (Deuteronomy 6:5). 'Love your neighbour as yourself' (Leviticus 19:18). And, repeated no less than thirty-six times in the Mosaic books, 'Love the stranger because you know what it feels like to be a stranger' (Exodus 22:20). Or to put it another way: just as God created the natural world in love and forgiveness, so we are charged with creating the social world in love and forgiveness. And that love is a flame lit in marriage and the family. Morality is the love between husband and wife, parent and child, extended outward to the world.

The fifth development shaped the entire structure of Jewish experience. In ancient Israel an originally secular form of agreement, called a covenant, was taken and transformed into a new way of thinking about the relationship between God and humanity, in the case of Noah, and between God and a people in the case of Abraham and later the Israelites at Mount Sinai. A covenant is like a marriage. It is a mutual pledge of loyalty and trust between two or more people, each respecting the dignity and integrity of the other, to work together to achieve together what neither can achieve alone. And there is one thing even God cannot achieve alone, which is to live within the human heart. That needs us.

So the Hebrew word *emunah*, wrongly translated as 'faith', really means faithfulness, fidelity, loyalty, steadfastness, not walking away even when the going gets tough, trusting the other and honouring the other's trust in us. What covenant did, and we see

* C. S. Lewis, *The Abolition of Man* (London: HarperCollins, 2011).

this in almost all the prophets, was to understand the relationship between us and God in terms of the relationship between bride and groom, wife and husband. Love thus became not only the basis of morality but also of theology. In Judaism faith is a marriage. Rarely was this more beautifully stated than by Hosea when he said in the name of God:

> I will betroth you to me for ever;
> I will betroth you in righteousness and justice, love and
> compassion.
> I will betroth you in faithfulness, and you will know the Lord.
> (Hosea 2:21–22)

Jewish men say those words every weekday morning as we wind the strap of our *tefillin* [phylacteries] around our finger like a wedding ring. Each morning we renew our marriage with God.

This led to a sixth and quite subtle idea that truth, beauty, goodness, and life itself, do not exist in any one person or entity but in the 'between', what Martin Buber called *das Zwischenmenschliche*, the interpersonal, the counterpoint of speaking and listening, giving and receiving. Throughout the Hebrew Bible and the rabbinic literature, the vehicle of truth is conversation. In revelation God speaks and asks us to listen. In prayer we speak and ask God to listen. There is never only one voice. In the Bible the prophets argue with God. In the Talmud rabbis argue with one another. In fact, I sometimes think the reason God chose the Jewish people was because He loves a good argument. Judaism is a conversation scored for many voices, never more passionately than in the Song of Songs, a duet between a woman and a man, the beloved and her lover, that Rabbi Akiva called the holy of holies of religious literature.

The prophet Malachi calls the male priest the guardian of the law of truth. The book of Proverbs says of the woman of worth that 'the law of loving-kindness is on her tongue' (Proverbs 31:26). It is that conversation between male and female voices, between truth and love, justice and mercy, law and forgiveness, that frames the spiritual life. In biblical times each Jew had to give a half shekel to the Temple to remind us that we are only half. There are some cultures that teach that we are nothing. There are others that teach that we are everything. The Jewish view is that we are half, and we need to open ourselves to another if we are to become whole.

All this led to the seventh outcome, that in Judaism the home and the family became the central setting of the life of faith. In the only verse in the Hebrew Bible to explain why God chose Abraham, He says: 'I have known him so that he will instruct his children and his household after him to keep the way of the Lord by doing what is right and just' (Genesis 18:19). Abraham was chosen not to rule an empire, command an army, perform miracles or deliver prophecies, but simply to be a parent.

In one of the most famous lines in Judaism, which we say every day and night, Moses commands, 'You shall teach these things repeatedly to your children, speaking of them when you sit in your house or when you walk on the way, when you lie down and when you rise up' (Deuteronomy 6:7). Parents are to be educators, education is the conversation between the generations, and the first school is the home.

So, Jews became an intensely family-oriented people, and it was this that saved us from tragedy. After the destruction of the Second Temple in the year 70 CE, Jews were scattered throughout the world, everywhere a minority, everywhere without rights, suffering some of the worst persecutions ever known by a people, and yet Jews survived because they never lost three things: their sense of family, their sense of community and their faith. And they were renewed every week especially on Shabbat, the day of rest when we give our marriages and families what they most need and are most starved of in the contemporary world, namely time.

I once produced a television documentary for the BBC on the state of family life in Britain, and I took the person who was then Britain's leading expert on childcare, Penelope Leach, to a Jewish primary school on a Friday morning. There she saw the children enacting in advance what they would see that evening around the family table. There were the five-year-old mother and father blessing the five-year-old children with the five-year-old grandparents looking on. She was fascinated by this whole institution, and she asked the children what they most enjoyed about the Sabbath. One five-year-old boy turned to her and said, 'It's the only night of the week when Daddy doesn't have to rush off.' As we walked away from the school when the filming was over, she turned to me and said, 'Chief Rabbi, that Sabbath of yours is saving their parents' marriages.'

So that is one way of telling the story, a Jewish way, beginning with the birth of sexual reproduction, then the unique demands of human parenting, then the eventual triumph of monogamy as a fundamental statement of human equality, followed by the way marriage shaped our vision of the moral and religious life as based on love and covenant and faithfulness, even to the point of thinking of truth as a conversation between lover and beloved. Marriage and the family are where faith finds its home and where the Divine presence lives in the love between husband and wife, parent and child.

What then has changed? Here's one way of putting it. I wrote a book a few years ago [called *The Great Partnership**] about religion and science and I summarised the difference between them in two sentences. 'Science takes things apart to see how they work. Religion puts things together to see what they mean.' And that's a way of thinking about culture also. Does it put things together or does it take things apart?

What made the traditional family remarkable, a work of high religious art, is what it brought together: sexual drive, physical desire, friendship, companionship, emotional kinship and love, the begetting of children and their protection and care, their early

* Jonathan Sacks, *The Great Partnership* (London: Hodder & Stoughton, 2011).

education and induction into an identity and a history. Seldom has any institution woven together so many different drives and desires, roles and responsibilities. It made sense of the world and gave it a human face, the face of love.

For a whole variety of reasons, some to do with medical developments such as birth control, in vitro fertilisation and other genetic interventions, some to do with moral change such as the idea that we are free to do whatever we like so long as it does not harm others, some to do with a transfer of responsibilities from the individual to the state, and other and more profound changes in the culture of the West, almost everything that marriage once brought together has now been split apart. Sex has been divorced from love, love from commitment, marriage from having children and having children from responsibility for their care.

The result is that in Britain in 2012, 47.5 per cent of children were born outside marriage, expected to become a majority in 2016. Fewer people are marrying, those who are, are marrying later, and 42 per cent of marriages end in divorce. Nor is cohabitation a substitute for marriage. The average length of cohabitation in Britain and the United States is less than two years. The result is a sharp increase among young people of eating disorders, drug and alcohol abuse, stress-related syndromes, depression and actual and attempted suicides. The collapse of marriage has created a new form of poverty concentrated among single parent families, and of these, the main burden is borne by women, who in 2011 headed 92 per cent of single parent households. In Britain today more than a million children will grow up with no contact whatsoever with their fathers.

This is creating a divide within societies the like of which has not been seen since Disraeli spoke of 'two nations' a century and a half ago. Those who are privileged to grow up in stable loving association with the two people who brought them into being will, on average, be healthier physically and emotionally. They will do better at school and at work. They will have more successful relationships, be happier and live longer. And yes, there are many exceptions. But the injustice of it all cries out to heaven. It will go down in history as one of the tragic instances of what Friedrich Hayek called 'the fatal conceit', that somehow we know better than the wisdom of the ages and can defy the lessons of biology and history.

No one surely wants to go back to the narrow prejudices of the past. This week, in Britain, a new film [*The Imitation Game*] opens, telling the story of one of the great minds of the twentieth century, Alan Turing, the Cambridge mathematician who laid the philosophical foundations of computing and artificial intelligence and helped win the war by breaking the German naval code Enigma. After the war, Turing was arrested and tried for homosexual behaviour, underwent chemically induced castration and died at the age of 41 by cyanide poisoning, thought by many to have committed suicide. That is a world to which we should never return.

But our compassion for those who choose to live differently should not inhibit us from being advocates for the single most humanising institution in history. The family – man, woman, and child – is not one lifestyle choice among many. It is the best means we have yet discovered for nurturing future generations and enabling children to grow in a matrix of stability and love. It is where we learn the delicate choreography of relationship and how to handle the inevitable conflicts within any human group. It is where we first take the risk of giving and receiving love. It is where one generation passes on its values to the next, ensuring the continuity of a civilisation. For any society, the family is the crucible of its future, and for the sake of our children's future, we must be its defenders.

Since this is a religious gathering, let me, if I may, end with a piece of biblical exegesis. The story of the first family, the first man and woman in the garden of Eden, is not generally regarded as a success. Whether or not we believe in original sin, it did not end happily. After many years of studying the text, I want to suggest a different reading.

The story ends with three verses that seem to have no connection with one another. No sequence. No logic. In Genesis, God says to the man: 'By the sweat of your brow you will eat your food until you return to the ground, since from it you were taken; for dust you are and to dust you will return' (Genesis 3:19). Then in the next verse we read: 'The man named his wife Eve, because she was the mother of all life' (Genesis 3:20). And in the next, 'The Lord God made garments of skin for Adam and his wife and clothed them' (Genesis 3:21).

What is the connection here? Why did God telling the man that he was mortal lead him to give his wife a new name? And why did that act seem to change God's attitude to both of them, so that He performed an act of tenderness by making them clothes, almost as if He had partially forgiven them? Let me also add that the Hebrew word for 'skin' is almost indistinguishable from the Hebrew word for 'light', so that Rabbi Meir, the great sage of the early second century, read the text as saying that God made for them 'garments of light'. What did he mean?

If we read the text carefully, we see that until now the first man had given his wife a purely generic name. He called her *ishah*, woman. Recall what he said when he first saw her: 'This is now bone of my bones and flesh of my flesh; she shall be called "woman" for she was taken from man' (Genesis 2:23). For him she was a type, not a person. He gave her a noun, not a name. What is more he defines her as a derivative of himself: something taken from man. She is not yet for him someone other, a person in her own right. She is merely a kind of reflection of himself.

As long as the man thought he was immortal, he ultimately needed no one else. But now he knew he was mortal. He would one day die and return to dust. There was only one way in which something of him would live on after his death. That would be if he had a child. But he could not have a child on his own. For that he needed his wife. She alone could give birth. She alone could mitigate his mortality. And not because she was like him but precisely because she was unlike him. At that moment she ceased to be, for him, a type, and became a person in her own right. And a person has a proper name. That is what he gave her: the name *Chavah*, 'Eve', meaning, 'giver of life' (Genesis 3:20).

At that moment, as they were about to leave Eden and face the world as we know it, a place of darkness, Adam gave his wife the first gift of love, a personal name. And at that moment, God responded to them both in love, and made them garments to clothe their nakedness, or as Rabbi Meir put it, 'garments of light'.

And so it has been ever since, that when a man and woman turn to one another in a bond of faithfulness, God robes them in garments of light, and we come as close as we will ever get to God Himself, bringing new life into being, turning the prose of biology into the poetry of the human spirit, redeeming the darkness of the world by the radiance of love.

The Danger of Outsourcing Morality

On 26 May 2016, Rabbi Sacks delivered the following acceptance speech on receiving the John Templeton Foundation's prestigious Templeton Prize at the award ceremony in London.

The news that I had won this prize almost rendered me speechless, an event that would have been unprecedented in the history of the rabbinate. But it has left me moved, humbled, thankful and deeply motivated, because to me the award is not just about what has been done but also about how much there is still to do.

To me the prize is less about recognition of the past than about responsibility for the future, and it is to that future I turn tonight. This is a fateful moment in history. Wherever we look, politically, religiously, economically, environmentally, there is insecurity and instability. It is not too much to say that the future of the West and the unique form of freedom it has pioneered for the past four centuries is altogether at risk.

I want tonight to look at one phenomenon that has shaped the West, leading it at first to greatness, but now to crisis. It can be summed up in one word: *outsourcing*. On the face of it, nothing could be more innocent or productive. It's the basis of the modern economy. It's Adam Smith's division of labour and David Ricardo's theory of comparative advantage that says even if you are better than me at everything, still we both gain if you do what you're best at and I do what I'm best at and we trade. The question is: are there limits? Are there things we can't or shouldn't outsource?

The issue has arisen because of the new technologies and instantaneous global communication. So instead of outsourcing within an economy, we do it between economies. We've seen the outsourcing of production to low-wage countries. We've seen the outsourcing of services, so that you can be in one town in America, booking a hotel in another, unaware that your call is being taken in India. This seemed like a good idea at the time, as if the West was saying to the world: you do the producing and we'll do the consuming. But is that sustainable in the long run? Then banks began to outsource risk, lending far beyond their capacities in the belief that either property prices would go on rising for ever, or more significantly, if they crashed, it would be someone else's problem, not theirs.

There is, though, one form of outsourcing that tends to be little noticed: the outsourcing of *memory*. Our computers and smartphones have developed larger and larger memories, from kilobytes to megabytes to gigabytes, while our memories and those of our children have got smaller and smaller. In fact, why bother to remember anything these days if you can look it up in a microsecond on Google or Wikipedia?

But here, I think, we made a mistake. We confused *history* and *memory*, which are not the same thing at all. History is an answer to the question, 'What happened?' Memory is an answer to the question, 'Who am I?' History is about facts; memory is about identity. History is *his* story. It happened to someone else, not me. Memory is *my* story, the past that made me who I am, of whose legacy I am the guardian for the sake of generations yet to come. Without memory, there is no identity. And without identity, we are mere dust on the surface of infinity.

Lacking memory, we have forgotten one of the most important lessons to have emerged from the wars of religion in the sixteenth and seventeenth century and the new birth of freedom that followed. Even to say it sounds antiquarian, but it is this: *A free society is a moral achievement*. Without self-restraint, without the capacity to defer the gratification of instinct and without the habits of heart and deed that we call virtues, we will eventually lose our freedom.

That is what Locke meant when he contrasted *liberty*, the freedom to do what we ought, with *licence*, the freedom to do what we want. It's what Adam Smith signalled when, before he wrote *The Wealth of Nations*,* he wrote *The Theory of Moral Sentiments*.† It's what Washington meant when he said, 'Human rights can only be assured among a virtuous people.' And Benjamin Franklin, when he said, 'Only a virtuous people are capable of freedom.' And Jefferson, when he said, 'A nation as a society forms a moral person, and every member of it is personally responsible for his society.'

At some point the West abandoned this belief. When I went to Cambridge in the late 1960s, the philosophy course was then called Moral Sciences, meaning that just like the natural sciences, morality was objective, real, part of the external world. I soon discovered, though, that almost no one believed this any more. Morality was no more than the expression of emotion, or subjective feeling, or private intuition or autonomous choice. It was, within limits, whatever I chose it to be. In fact, there was nothing left to study but the meaning of words. To me this seemed less like civilisation than the breakdown of a civilisation.

It took me years to work out what had happened. Morality had been split in two and outsourced to other institutions. There were moral choices and there were the consequences of our moral choices. Morality itself was outsourced to the market. The market gives us choices, and morality itself is just a set of choices in which right or wrong have no meaning beyond the satisfaction or frustration of desire. The result is that we find it increasingly hard to understand why there might be things we want to do, can afford to do, and have a legal right to do, that nonetheless we should not do because they are unjust or dishonourable or disloyal or demeaning: in a word, unethical. Ethics was reduced to economics.

As for the consequences of our choices, these were outsourced to the state. Bad choices lead to bad outcomes: failed relationships, neglected children, depressive illness, wasted lives. But the

* Adam Smith, *The Wealth of Nations* (London: Penguin Classics, 1982).

† Adam Smith, *The Theory of Moral Sentiments* (London: Penguin Classics, 2010).

Government would deal with it. Forget about marriage as a sacred bond between husband and wife. Forget about the need of children for a loving and secure human environment. Forget about the need for communities to give us support in times of need. Welfare was outsourced to the state. As for conscience, that once played so large a part in the moral life, that could be outsourced to regulatory bodies. So having reduced moral choice to economics, we transferred the consequences of our choices to politics.

And it seemed to work, at least for a generation or two. But by now problems have arisen that can't be solved by the market or the state alone. To mention just a few: the structural unemployment that follows the outsourcing of production and services. The further unemployment that will come when artificial intelligence increasingly replaces human judgment and skill. Artificially low interest rates that encourage borrowing and debt and discourage saving and investment. Wildly inflated CEO pay. The lowering of living standards, first of the working class, then of the middle class. The insecurity of employment, even for graduates. The inability of young families to afford a home. The collapse of marriage, leading to intractable problems of child poverty and depression. The collapse of birth rates throughout Europe, leading to unprecedented levels of immigration that are now the only way the West can sustain its population, and the systemic failure to integrate some of these groups. The loss of family, community and identity that once gave us the strength to survive unstable times. And there are others.

Why have they proved insoluble? First, because they are global, and governments are only national. Second, because they are long term while the market and liberal democratic politics are short term. Third, because they depend on changing habits of behaviour, which neither the market nor the liberal democratic state are mandated to do. Above all, though, because they can't be solved by the market and the state alone.

You can't outsource conscience. You can't delegate moral responsibility away. When you do, you raise expectations that cannot be met. And when, inevitably, they are not met, society becomes freighted with disappointment, anger, fear, resentment and blame. People start to take refuge in magical thinking, which today takes one of four forms: the far right, the far left, religious extremism and aggressive secularism. The far right seeks a return to a golden past that never was. The far left seeks a utopian future that will never be. Religious extremists believe you can bring salvation by terror. Aggressive secularists believe that if you get rid of religion there will be peace. These are all fantasies and pursuing them will endanger the very foundations of freedom.

Yet we have seen, even in mainstream British and American politics, forms of ugliness and irrationality I never thought I would see in my lifetime. We have seen on university campuses in Britain and America the abandonment of academic freedom in the name of the right not to be offended by being confronted by views with which I disagree. This is *le trahison des clercs*, the intellectual betrayal, of our time, and it is very dangerous indeed. So, is there another way?

Two historical phenomena have long fascinated me. One is the strange fact that, having lagged behind China for a thousand years, the West overtook it in the seventeenth century, creating science, industry, technology, the free market and the free society.

The second is the no less strange fact that Jews and Judaism survived for 2,000 years after the destruction of the Second Temple, having lost everything on which their existence was predicated in the Bible: their land, their home, their freedom, their Temple, their kings, their prophets and priests.

The explanation in both cases, is the same. It is the precise opposite of outsourcing: namely the internalisation of what had once been external. Wherever in the world Jews prayed, there was the Temple. Every prayer was a sacrifice, every Jew a priest, and every community a fragment of Jerusalem. Something similar happened in those strands of Islam that interpreted *jihad* not as a physical war on the battlefield but as a spiritual struggle within the soul.

A parallel phenomenon occurred in Christianity after the Reformation, especially in the Calvinism that in the sixteenth and seventeenth centuries transformed Holland, Scotland, England of the Revolution and America of the Pilgrim Fathers. It was this to which Max Weber famously attributed the spirit of capitalism. The external authority of the Church was replaced by the internal voice of conscience. This made possible the widely distributed networks of trust on which the smooth functioning of the market depends. We are so used to contrasting the material and the spiritual that we sometimes forget that the word 'credit' comes from the Latin *credo*, 'I believe', and 'confidence', that requisite of investment and economic growth, comes from *fidentia*, meaning 'faith' or 'trust'.

What emerged in Judaism and post-Reformation Christianity was the rarest of character types: the inner-directed personality. Most societies, for most of history, have been either tradition-directed or other-directed. People do what they do, either because that is how they have always been done, or because that's what other people do.

Inner-directed types are different. They become the pioneers, the innovators and the survivors. They have an internalised satellite navigation system, so they aren't fazed by uncharted territory. They have a strong sense of duty to others. They try to have secure marriages. They hand on their values to their children. They belong to strong communities. They take daring but carefully calculated risks. When they fail, they have rapid recovery times.

They have discipline. They enjoy tough challenges and hard work. They play it long. They are more interested in sustainability than quick profits. They know they have to be responsible to customers, employees and shareholders, as well as to the wider public, because only thus will they survive in the long run. They don't do foolish things like creative accounting, subprime mortgages and falsified emissions data, because they know you can't fake it for ever. They don't consume the present at the cost of the future, because they have a sense of responsibility for the future. They have the capacity to defer the gratification of instinct. They do all this because they have an inner moral voice. Some call it conscience. Some call it the voice of God.

Cultures like that stay young. They defeat the entropy, the loss of energy, that has spelled the decline and fall of every other empire and superpower in history. But the West has, in the immortal words of Queen Elsa in *Frozen*, 'let it go'. It has externalised what it once internalised. It has outsourced responsibility. It's reduced ethics to economics and politics. Which means we are dependent on the market and the state, forces we can do little to control. And one day our descendants will look back and ask, 'How did the West lose what once made it great?'

Every observer of the grand sweep of history, from the prophets of Israel to the Islamic sage Ibn Khaldun, from Giambattista Vico to John Stuart Mill, and Bertrand Russell to Will Durant, has said essentially the same thing: that civilisations begin to die when they lose the moral passion that brought them into being in the first place. It happened to Greece and Rome, and it can happen to the West. The sure signs are these: a falling birth rate, moral decay, growing inequalities, a loss of trust in social institutions, self-indulgence on the part of the rich, hopelessness on the part of the poor, unintegrated minorities, a failure to make sacrifices in the present for the sake of the future, a loss of faith in old beliefs and no new vision to take their place. These are the danger signals, and they are flashing now.

There is an alternative: to become inner-directed again. This means recovering the moral dimension that links our welfare to the welfare of others, making us collectively responsible for the common good. It means recovering the spiritual dimension that helps us tell the difference between the value of things and their price. We are more than consumers and voters; our dignity transcends what we earn and own. It means remembering that what's important is not just satisfying our desires but also knowing which desires to satisfy. It means restraining ourselves in the present so that our children may have a viable future. It means reclaiming collective memory and identity so that society becomes less of a hotel and more of a home. In short, it means learning that there are some things we cannot or should not outsource, some responsibilities we cannot or should not delegate away.

We owe it to our children and grandchildren not to throw away what once made the West great, and not for the sake of some idealised past, but for the sake of a demanding and deeply challenging future. If we do simply let it go, if we continue to forget that a free society is a moral achievement that depends on habits of responsibility and restraint, then what will come next – be it Russia, China, ISIS or Iran – will be neither liberal nor democratic, and it will certainly not be free. We need to restate the moral and spiritual dimensions in the language of the twenty-first century, using the media of the twenty-first century, and in ways that are uniting rather than divisive.

The moral and spiritual dimensions of human flourishing are what the Templeton Prize and the Templeton Foundation have always been about, and it will be by developing these themes globally, together with others, over the coming years that I hope I can repay a little of the honour you have bestowed on me today.

The Mutating Virus

On 27 September 2017, Rabbi Sacks delivered an address in The European Parliament on the history and nature of antisemitism as part of 'The Future of the Jewish Communities in Europe' seminar.

The hate that begins with Jews never ends with Jews. That is what I want us to understand today. It wasn't Jews alone who suffered under Hitler. It wasn't Jews alone who suffered under Stalin. It isn't Jews alone who suffer under ISIS or al-Qaeda or Islamic Jihad. We make a great mistake if we think antisemitism is a threat only to Jews. It is a threat, first and foremost, to Europe and to the freedoms it took centuries to achieve.

Antisemitism is not about Jews. It is about antisemites. It is about people who cannot accept responsibility for their own failures and have instead to blame someone else. Historically, if you were a Christian at the time of the Crusades, or a German after the World War I, and saw that the world hadn't turned out the way you believed it would, you blamed the Jews. That is what is happening today. And I cannot begin to say how dangerous it is. Not just to Jews but to everyone who values freedom, compassion and humanity.

The appearance of antisemitism in a culture is the first symptom of a disease, the early warning sign of collective breakdown. If Europe allows antisemitism to flourish, that will be the beginning of the end of Europe. And what I want to do in these brief remarks is simply to analyse a phenomenon full of vagueness and ambiguity, because we need precision and understanding to know what antisemitism is, why it happens, and why antisemites are convinced that they are not antisemitic.

First let me define antisemitism. Not liking Jews is not antisemitism. We all have people we don't like. That's OK; that's human. It isn't dangerous. Second, criticising Israel is not antisemitism. I was recently talking to some schoolchildren, and they asked me: 'Is criticising Israel antisemitism?' I said 'no' and I explained the difference. I asked them: 'Do you believe you have a right to criticise the British Government?' They all put up their hands. Then I asked, 'Which of you believes that Britain has no right to exist?' No one put up their hands. 'Now you know the difference,' I said, and they all did.

Antisemitism means denying the right of Jews to exist collectively as Jews with the same rights as everyone else. It takes different forms in different ages. In the Middle Ages, Jews were hated because of their religion. In the nineteenth and early twentieth century they were hated because of their race. Today they are hated because of their nation state, the State of Israel. It takes different forms, but it remains the same thing: the view that Jews have no right to exist as free and equal human beings.

If there is one thing I and my contemporaries did not expect, it was that antisemitism would reappear in Europe within living memory of the Holocaust. The reason we did not expect it was that Europe had undertaken the greatest collective effort in all of history to ensure that the virus of antisemitism would never again infect the body politic. It was a magnificent effort of anti-racist legislation, Holocaust education and interfaith dialogue. Yet antisemitism has returned despite everything.

On 27 January 2000, representatives of forty-six governments from around the world gathered in Stockholm to issue a collective declaration of Holocaust remembrance and the continuing fight against antisemitism, racism and prejudice. Then came 9/11, and within days conspiracy theories were flooding the internet claiming it was the work of Israel and its secret service, the Mossad. In April 2002, on Passover, I was in Florence with a Jewish couple from Paris when they received a phone call from their son, saying, 'Mum, Dad, it's time to leave France. It's not safe for us here any more.'

In May 2007, in a private meeting here in Brussels, I told the three leaders of Europe at the time, Angela Merkel, President of the European Council, José Manuel Barroso, President of the European Commission, and Hans-Gert Pöttering, President of the European Parliament, that the Jews of Europe were beginning to ask whether there was a future for Jews in Europe.

That was more than nine years ago. Since then, things have become worse. Already in 2013, before some of the worst incidents, the European Union Agency for Fundamental Rights found that almost a third of Europe's Jews were considering emigrating because of antisemitism. In France the figure was 46 per cent; in Hungary 48 per cent.

Let me ask you this. Whether you are Jewish or Christian, Muslim: would you stay in a country where you need armed police to guard you while you prayed? Where your children need armed guards to protect them at school? Where, if you wear a sign of your faith in public, you risk being abused or attacked? Where, when your children go to university, they are insulted and intimidated because of what is happening in some other part of the world? Where, when they present their own view of the situation they are howled down and silenced?

This is happening to Jews throughout Europe. In every single country of Europe, without exception, Jews are fearful for their or their children's future. If this continues, Jews will continue to leave Europe, until, barring the frail and the elderly, Europe will finally have become *Judenrein*.

How did this happen? It happened the way viruses always defeat the human immune system, namely, by mutating. The new antisemitism is different from the old antisemitism, in three ways. I've already mentioned one. Once Jews were hated because of their religion. Then they were hated because of their race. Now they are hated because of their nation state. The second difference is that the epicentre of the old antisemitism was Europe. Today it's the Middle East and it is communicated globally by the new social media.

The third is particularly disturbing. Let me explain. It is easy to hate, but difficult publicly to justify hate. Throughout history, when people have sought to justify antisemitism, they have done so by recourse to the highest source of authority available within the culture. In the Middle Ages, it was religion. So we had religious anti-Judaism. In post-Enlightenment Europe it was science. So, we had the twin foundations of Nazi ideology, Social Darwinism and the so-called Scientific Study of Race. Today the highest source of authority worldwide is human rights. That is why Israel – the only fully functioning democracy in the Middle East with a free press and independent judiciary – is regularly accused of the five cardinal sins against human rights: racism, Apartheid, crimes against humanity, ethnic cleansing and attempted genocide.

The new antisemitism has mutated so that any practitioner of it can deny that he or she is an antisemite. After all, they'll say, 'I'm not a racist. I have no problem with Jews or Judaism. I only have a problem with the State of Israel.' But in a world of fifty-six Muslim nations and 103 Christian ones, there is only one Jewish state, Israel, which constitutes one quarter of 1 per cent of the land mass of the Middle East. Israel is the only one of the 193 member nations of the United Nations that has its right to exist regularly challenged, with one state, Iran, and many, many other groups, committed to its destruction.

Antisemitism means denying the right of Jews to exist as Jews with the same rights as everyone else. The form this takes today is anti-Zionism. Of course, there is a difference between Zionism and Judaism, and between Jews and Israelis, but this difference does not exist for the new antisemites themselves. It was Jews, not Israelis, who were murdered in terrorist attacks in Toulouse, Paris, Brussels and Copenhagen. Anti-Zionism is the antisemitism of our time.

In the Middle Ages Jews were accused of poisoning wells, spreading the plague, and killing Christian children to use their blood. In Nazi Germany they were accused of controlling both capitalist America and Communist Russia. Today they are accused of running ISIS as well as America. All the old myths have been recycled, from the Blood Libel to the Protocols of the Elders of Zion. The cartoons that flood the Middle East are clones of those published in *Der Stürmer*, one of the primary vehicles of Nazi propaganda between 1923 and 1945.

The ultimate weapon of the new antisemitism is dazzling in its simplicity. It goes like this. The Holocaust must never happen again. But Israelis are the new Nazis; the Palestinians are the new Jews; all Jews are Zionists. Therefore, the real antisemites of our time are none other than the Jews themselves. And these are not marginal views. They are widespread throughout the Muslim world, including communities in Europe, and they are slowly infecting the far left, the far right, academic circles, unions and even some churches. Having cured itself of the virus of antisemitism, Europe is being reinfected by parts of the world that never went through the self-reckoning that Europe undertook once the facts of the Holocaust became known.

How do such absurdities come to be believed? This is a vast and complex subject, and I have written a book about it [called *Future Tense**], but the simplest explanation is this. When bad things happen to a group, its members can ask one of two questions: 'What did we do wrong?' or 'Who did this to us?' The entire fate of the group will depend on which it chooses.

If it asks, 'What did we do wrong?', it has begun the self-criticism essential to a free society. If it asks, 'Who did this to us?' it has defined itself as a victim. It will then seek a scapegoat to blame for all its problems. Classically this has been the Jews.

Antisemitism is a form of cognitive failure, and it happens when groups feel that their world is spinning out of control. It began in the Middle Ages, when Christians saw that Islam had defeated them in places they regarded as their own, especially Jerusalem. That was when, in 1096, on their way to the Holy Land, the Crusaders stopped first to massacre Jewish communities in

* Jonathan Sacks, *Future Tense* (London, Hodder & Stoughton, 2009).

Northern Europe. It was born in the Middle East in the 1920s with the collapse of the Ottoman Empire. Antisemitism re-emerged in Europe in the 1870s during a period of economic recession and resurgent nationalism. And it is reappearing in Europe now for the same reasons: recession, nationalism and a backlash against immigrants and other minorities.

Antisemitism happens when the politics of hope gives way to the politics of fear, which quickly becomes the politics of hate. This then reduces complex problems to simplicities. It divides the world into black and white, seeing all the fault on one side and all the victimhood on the other. It singles out one group among a hundred offenders for the blame. The argument is always the same. We are innocent; they are guilty. It follows that if we are to be free, they, the Jews or the State of Israel, must be destroyed. That is how the great crimes begin.

Jews were hated because they were different. They were the most conspicuous non-Christian minority in a Christian Europe. Today they are the most conspicuous non-Muslim presence in an Islamic Middle East. Antisemitism has always been about the inability of a group to make space for difference. No group that adopts it will ever, can ever, create a free society.

So, I end where I began. The hate that begins with Jews never ends with Jews. Antisemitism is only secondarily about Jews. Primarily it is about the failure of groups to accept responsibility for their own failures, and to build their own future by their own endeavours. No society that has fostered antisemitism has ever sustained liberty or human rights or religious freedom. Every society driven by hate begins by seeking to destroy its enemies but ends by destroying itself.

Europe today is not fundamentally antisemitic. But it has allowed antisemitism to enter via the new electronic media. It has failed to recognise that the new antisemitism is different from the old. We are not today back in the 1930s. But we are coming close to 1879, when Wilhelm Marr founded the League of Anti-Semites in Germany; to 1886 when Édouard Drumont published

La France Juive; and 1897 when Karl Lueger became Mayor of Vienna. These were key moments in the spread of antisemitism, and all we have to do today is to remember that what was said then about Jews is being said today about the Jewish state.

The history of Jews in Europe has not always been a happy one. Europe's treatment of the Jews added certain words to the human vocabulary: disputation, forced conversion, inquisition, expulsion, auto-da-fé, ghetto, pogrom and Holocaust, words written in Jewish tears and Jewish blood. Yet for all that, Jews loved Europe and contributed to it some of its greatest scientists, writers, academics, musicians, shapers of the modern mind.

If Europe lets itself be dragged down that road again, this will be the story told in times to come. First they came for the Jews. Then for the Christians. Then for the gays. Then for the atheists. Until there was nothing left of Europe's soul but a distant, fading memory.

Today I have tried to give voice to those who have no voice. I have spoken on behalf of the murdered Roma, Sinti, gays, dissidents, the mentally and physically handicapped and a million and a half Jewish children murdered because of their grandparents' religion. In their name, I say to you: 'You know where the road ends. Don't go down there again.'

You are the leaders of Europe. Its future is in your hands. If you do nothing, Jews will leave, European liberty will die, and there will be a moral stain on Europe's name that all eternity will not erase.

Stop it now while there is still time.

Facing the Future Without Fear, Together

On 24 April 2017, Rabbi Sacks delivered his first TED Talk at the opening session of the 2017 TED Conference in Vancouver, Canada.

'These are the times', said Thomas Paine, 'that try men's souls,' and they're trying ours now. This is a fateful moment in the history of the West. We've seen divisive elections and divided societies. We've seen a growth of extremism in politics and religion, all of it fuelled by anxiety, uncertainty, and fear of a world that's changing almost faster than we can bear and the sure knowledge that it's going to change faster still. I have a friend in Washington. I asked him what it was like being in America during the recent presidential election. He said to me, 'Well, it was like the man sitting on the deck of the *Titanic* with a glass of whiskey in his hand and he's saying, "I know I asked for ice, but this is ridiculous."'

Is there something we can do, each of us, to be able to face the future without fear? I think there is. One way into it is to see that perhaps the simplest way into a culture and into an age is to ask, 'What do people worship?' People have worshipped so many different things, the sun, the stars, the storm. Some people worship many gods, some one, some none. In the nineteenth and twentieth centuries, people worshipped the nation, the Arian race, the Communist state. What do we worship? I think future anthropologists will take a look at the books we read on self-help, self-realisation, self-esteem. They'll look at the way we talk about morality as being true to oneself, the way we talk about politics as a matter of individual rights, and they'll look at this wonderful new religious ritual we have created, you know the one called 'the selfie'. I think they'll conclude that what we worship in our time is the self, the 'me', the 'I'.

This is great. It's liberating. It's empowering. It's wonderful. But don't forget that biologically we're social animals. We spent most of our evolutionary history in small groups. We need those face-to-face interactions where we learn the choreography of altruism and where we create those spiritual goods like friendship, and trust, and loyalty, and love that redeem our solitude. When we have too much of the 'I' and too little of the 'We', we can find ourselves vulnerable, fearful and alone. It was no accident that Sherry Turkle of MIT [Massachusetts Institute of Technology] called the book she wrote on the impact of social media *Alone Together*.*

I think the simplest way of safeguarding the future 'you', is to strengthen the future 'us' in three dimensions, the 'us' of relationship, the 'us' of identity and the 'us' of responsibility.

Let me first take the 'us' of relationship. Here, forgive me if I get personal. Once upon a time, a very long time ago, I was a twenty-year-old undergraduate studying philosophy. I was into Nietzsche, and Schopenhauer, and Sartre, and Camus. I was full of ontological uncertainty and existential angst. It was terrific. I was self-obsessed and thoroughly unpleasant to know until one day I saw across the courtyard a girl who was everything that I wasn't. She radiated sunshine. She emanated joy. I found out her name was Elaine. We met, we talked, we married, and forty-seven years, three children, and eight grandchildren later, I can safely say it was the best decision I ever took in my life because it's the people not like us that make us grow.

That is why I think we have to do just that. The trouble with Google filters, Facebook friends, and reading the news by narrowcasting rather than broadcasting means that we're surrounded almost entirely by people like us whose views, whose opinions,

* Sherry Turkle, *Alone Together: Why We Expect More from Technology and Less from Each Other* (New York: Basic Books, 2017).

whose prejudices even are just like ours. Cass Sunstein of Harvard has shown that if we surround ourselves with people with the same views as us, we get more extreme. I think we need to renew those face-to-face encounters with the people not like us. I think we need to do that in order to realise that we can disagree strongly and yet still stay friends. It's in those face-to-face encounters that we discover that the people not like us are just people like us. Actually, every time we hold out the hand of friendship to somebody not like us whose colour, or class, or creed are different from ours, we heal one of the fractures of our wounded world. That is the 'us' of relationship.

Second is the 'us' of identity. Let me give you a thought experiment. Have you been to Washington? Have you seen the memorials? Absolutely fascinating. There's the Lincoln Memorial, Gettysburg Address on one side, Second Inaugural on the other. You go to the Jefferson Memorial, screeds of text. Martin Luther King Jr. Memorial, more than a dozen quotes from his speeches. I didn't realise in America you read memorials. Now go to the equivalent in London in Parliament Square and you will see that the monument to David Lloyd George contains three words, 'David Lloyd George'. Nelson Mandela gets two, Churchill gets just one, 'Churchill'. Why the difference? I'll tell you why the difference, because America was from the outset a nation of wave after wave of immigrants, so it had to create an identity, which it did by telling a story which you learned at school, you read on memorials, and you heard repeated in presidential Inaugural Addresses. Britain, until recently, wasn't a nation of immigrants, so it could take identity for granted.

The trouble is, now the two things have happened which shouldn't have happened together. The first thing is in the West we've stopped telling the story of who we are and why, even in America. At the same time, immigration is higher than it's ever been before. When you tell the story and your identity is strong, you can welcome the stranger, but when you stop telling the story, your identity gets weak, and you feel threatened by the stranger.

That's bad. I tell you; Jews have been scattered, and dispersed and exiled for 2,000 years. We never lost our identity. Why? Because at least once a year on the festival of Passover we told our story, and we taught it to our children, and we ate the unleavened bread of affliction, and tasted the bitter herbs of slavery, so we never lost our identity. I think collectively we've got to get back to telling our story, who we are, where we came from, what ideals by which we live. If that happens, we'll become strong enough to welcome the stranger and say, 'Come and share our lives, share our stories, share our aspirations and dreams.' That is the 'us' of identity.

Finally, the 'us' of responsibility. Do you know something? My favourite phrase in all of politics, a very American phrase, is 'We the people'. Why 'We the people'? Because it says that we all share collective responsibility for our collective future. That's how things really are and should be. Have you noticed how magical thinking has taken over our politics? We say, 'All you've got to do is elect this strong leader, and he or she will solve all our problems for us.' Believe me, that is magical thinking.

Then we get the extremes: the far right, the far left, extreme religious, and the extreme anti-religious, the far right dreaming of a golden age that never was, the far left dreaming of a utopia that never will be, and the religious and anti-religious equally convinced that all it takes is God or the absence of God to save us from ourselves. That too is magical thinking, because the only people who will save us from ourselves is 'We the people', all of us together.

When we do that, and when we move from the politics of me to the politics of all of us together, we rediscover those beautiful counter-intuitive truths: that a nation is strong when it cares for the weak, that it becomes rich when it cares for the poor, that it becomes invulnerable when it cares about the vulnerable. That is what makes great nations.

Here is my simple suggestion. It might just change your life, and it might just help to begin to change the world. Do a search and replace operation on the text of your mind. Wherever you encounter the word 'self', substitute the word 'other'. Instead of 'self-help', 'other-help'. Instead of 'self-esteem', 'other-esteem'. If you do that, you will begin to feel the power of what for me is one of the most moving sentences in all of religious literature, 'Though I walk through the valley of the shadow of death, I will fear no evil for you are with me' (Psalm 23:4).

We can face any future without fear so long as we know we will not face it alone. For the sake of the future 'you', together, let us strengthen the future 'us'.

Thank you.

List of Published Works by Jonathan Sacks

Traditional Alternatives: Orthodoxy and the Future of the Jewish People (London: Jews' College Publications, 1989).

Tradition in an Untraditional Age (London: Vallentine Mitchell & Co Ltd, 1990).

Arguments for the Sake of Heaven (London: Jason Aronson Inc. Publishers, 1991).

The Persistence of Faith (London: Weidenfeld Paperbacks, 1991).

Crisis and Covenant: Jewish Thought after the Holocaust (Manchester: Manchester University Press, 1992).

One People? Tradition, Modernity and Jewish Unity (Oxford: The Littman Library of Jewish Civilization, 1993).

Will We Have Jewish Grandchildren? (Ilford: Vallentine Mitchell & Co Ltd, 1994).

Faith in the Future (London: Darton, Longman & Todd Ltd, 1995).

Community of Faith (London: Peter Halban Publishers Ltd, 1996).

The Politics of Hope (London: Vintage, 1997).

Celebrating Life: Finding Happiness in Unexpected Places (London: Fount, 2000).

A Letter in the Scroll (New York: The Free Press, 2000) (published as *Radical Then, Radical Now*, London: HarperCollins*Publishers*, 2001).

The Dignity of Difference: How to Avoid the Clash of Civilizations (London: Continuum, 2002).

The Jonathan Sacks Haggada (London: HarperCollins*Publishers*, 2003).

From Optimism to Hope: A Collection of BBC Thoughts for the Day (London: Continuum, 2004).

To Heal a Fractured World: The Ethics of Responsibility (London: Continuum, 2005).

The Authorised Daily Prayer Book (London: HarperCollins*Publishers*, 2006).

The Home We Build Together: Recreating Society (London: Continuum, 2007).

Covenant & Conversation: Genesis – The Book of the Beginnings (Jerusalem: Maggid Books, 2009).

Future Tense: A Vision for Jews and Judaism in the Global Culture (London: Hodder & Stoughton, 2009).

The Koren Sacks Siddur (Jerusalem: Koren Publishers, 2009).

Covenant & Conversation: Exodus – The Book of Redemption (Jerusalem: Maggid Books, 2010).
The Great Partnership: God, Science and the Search for Meaning (London: Hodder & Stoughton, 2011).
The Koren Sacks Rosh Hashana Mahzor (Jerusalem: Koren Publishers, 2011).
The Koren Sacks Yom Kippur Mahzor (Jerusalem: Koren Publishers, 2012).
The Koren Sacks Pesach Mahzor (Jerusalem: Koren Publishers, 2013).
Covenant & Conversation: Leviticus – The Book of Holiness (Jerusalem: Maggid Books, 2015).
Not in God's Name: Confronting Religious Violence (London: Hodder & Stoughton, 2015).
Lessons in Leadership: A Weekly Reading of the Jewish Bible (Jerusalem: Maggid Books, 2015).
The Koren Sacks Shavuot Mahzor (Jerusalem: Koren Publishers, 2016).
The Koren Sacks Sukkot Mahzor (Jerusalem: Koren Publishers, 2016).
Essays in Ethics: A Weekly Reading of the Jewish Bible (Jerusalem: Maggid Books, 2016).
Ceremony and Celebration: Introduction to the Holidays (Jerusalem: Maggid Books, 2017).
Covenant & Conversation: Numbers – The Wilderness Years (Jerusalem: Maggid Books, 2017).
Covenant & Conversation: Deuteronomy – Renewal of the Sinai Covenant (Jerusalem: Maggid Books, 2019).
Morality: Restoring the Common Good in Divided Times (London: Hodder & Stoughton, 2020).
Judaism's Life-Changing Ideas: A Weekly Reading of the Jewish Bible (Jerusalem: Maggid Books, 2020).
Studies in Spirituality: A Weekly Reading of the Jewish Bible (Jerusalem: Maggid Books, 2021).

Index